MIDLAND RAILWAY
CARRIAGES

Midland express passenger train comprised of Clayton bogie clerestory and bogie, 6-wheeled and 4-wheeled arc-roof carriages and hauled by Johnson '1400' class 2—4—0 locomotive carrying the express headcode in use up to 1897. (*Negative 1977/78 of P. C. Dewhurst Collection in Science Museum*)

MIDLAND RAILWAY CARRIAGES

VOLUME ONE

R. E. LACY BSc (Eng)

and

GEORGE DOW FRSA FCIT

WILD SWAN PUBLICATIONS LTD.

©Wild Swan Publications Ltd. and Joyce Lacy & George Dow 1984
ISBN: 0 906867 19 3

Designed by Paul Karau
Typesetting by Berkshire Publishing Services
Photo reproduction and offset plates by Oxford Litho Plates Ltd.
Printed in Oxford

Published by
WILD SWAN PUBLICATIONS LTD.,
Hopgoods Farm Cottage, Upper Bucklebury, Berks.

CONTENTS

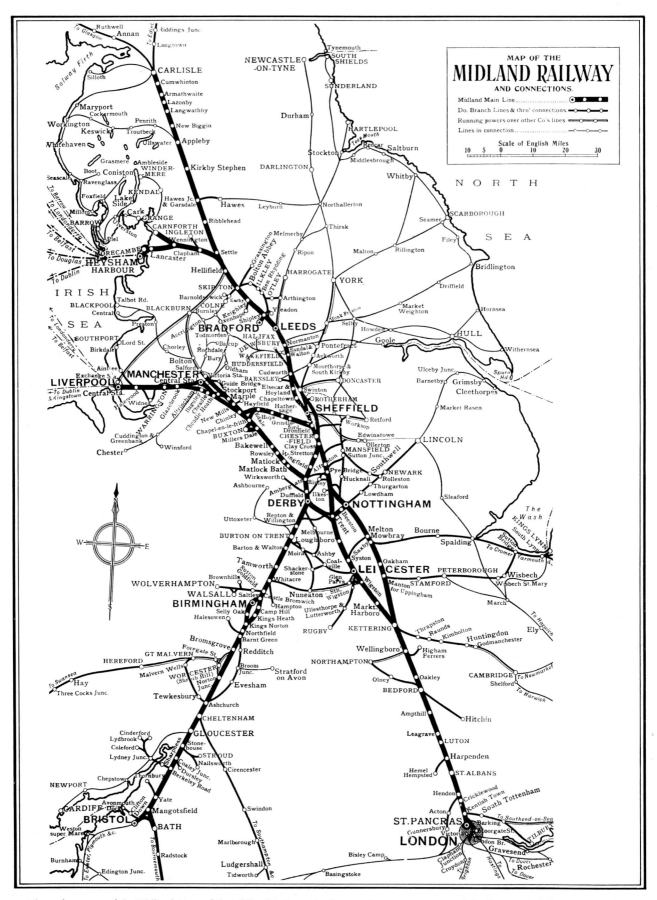

The main system of the Midland. Most of the Midland & Great Northern and Somerset & Dorset joint lines, and of the London, Tilbury & Southend are not shown, and the whole of the Swansea Vale and of the Irish lines are omitted.

Introduction and Acknowledgements

Notwithstanding the magnificence justly attributed to it by more than one writer, the Midland was the railway of the ordinary man. No other railway system did as much for the comfort of the third-class traveller. This was the outcome of a consistent policy, initiated by the sagacious and enterprising general manager, James Allport, in the 1870s, which was pursued until the end of the independent existence of the company at the close of 1922. Without in any way neglecting those who paid higher fares, it was Allport who first considered the well-being of the third-class traveller and, as has been said elsewhere, comforted him with cushions.

But it went far beyond that. To the third-class traveller was offered accommodation on *all* trains and a veritable cornucopia of through carriages. Away from his upholstered compartment he could enjoy the superb catering of dining cars, refreshment and dining rooms (with their luncheon and tea basket facility) and the all-round comfort of a group of splendidly appointed hotels. Taken as a whole, these well-knit, well-organised services have no equal anywhere today.

Their backbone was the Midland carriage which, over the years, earned an international reputation for excellence in design, materials, construction and finish. The well-groomed, crimson lake unity of the Midland passenger train, express or local, was a joy to behold and ride in and it provides me with youthful memories which I shall always treasure. Yet no work of reference concerning its development has hitherto existed, a deficiency which this book aims to make good.

The admiration and affection which the late Ralph Lacy and I had for the Midland since childhood was in no way diminished by the passing of the years. Indeed, with the short-sighted termination of its life by the Railways Act of 1921, the reverse was the case. Ralph Lacy's interest was chiefly directed towards the coaching stock, and his notes reveal that as long ago as 1933, when he was twenty years of age, he was measuring former Midland carriages at St. Pancras. As a professional railwayman, my own interest has been more comprehensive, and some of the most valuable information I have amassed about the Midland was taken from official sources during the latter years of my career as a senior officer of the London Midland region of British Railways.

In the mid-1950s, Ralph Lacy decided to put together a book outlining the development of the coaching stock of the Midland, much to the pleasure of the Historical Model Railway Society, of which he and I were active members since its foundation in 1950. He had made good progress, but much still remained to be done, when his untimely death occurred on 25th March 1980. Tragically, he died alone in a train taking him to Kew where it had been his intention to spend some hours in the Public Record Office upon research for his book. Thus it was that his widow Joyce invited me to complete the work he had started many years ago.

To a large extent the framework of the book follows that originally envisaged. Because of the dearth of information, due to fires, air raids, salvage campaigns and destruction of records through ignorance or by Philistines, Midland coaching stock up to 1873 is dealt with as a whole. From that year onwards, however, it is possible to categorise. In consequence, the development of the main line carriages is described chronologically in chapters 3-9 and 14, the Pullman cars meriting a chapter of their own; that of the suburban carriages in chapter 10; and that of the remaining types of vehicle in chapters 11-13. Reference to the coaching stock of the two prosperous railway companies absorbed by the Midland in 1903 and 1912, the Belfast & Northern Counties and London, Tilbury & Southend respectively, has not been overlooked.

In a work of this kind, useful data such as vehicle numbers and dates of withdrawal can, unless care is taken, easily dominate the text and make it indigestible to the reader. Such information, therefore, has been set out in tabular form in appendices wherever it is at all voluminous. For the same reason, sources of statements made, where they might be useful to the reader, are given in abbreviated form, thus:

Midland minutes		*Other sources*	
B	Board	MSWJ	Midland & South
CW	Carriage & Wagon		Western Joint
	Committee		Committee
GP	General Purposes	PRO	Public Record Office
	Committee	Post	Post Office records
L	Locomotive Committee		
T	Traffic Committee		

The vast majority of the illustrations in this work are of Midland Railway diagrams and photographs, collected by the authors over the years, and their official numbers have been denoted in every case where known. The National Railway Museum can provide many photographs of Midland Railway carriages, including those with DY negative numbers.

Chiefly by offering information, there are many who have helped to make this work as complete as possible. Regrettably, I cannot, for obvious reasons, record thanks to all those who assisted Ralph Lacy, and it is hoped that those who did so and whose names do not appear below, will forgive the omission:

W. G. Allen, D. J. Bartholomew, Duncan Burton, H. C. Casserley, R. M. Casserley, J. E. Cull, Andrew Ivor Dunbar, G. Y. Hemingway, A. Maclean, R. H. Offord, Edward Smith, J. T. Howard Turner, Alan Whitehead, K. C. Woodhead and the Postmaster General.

To them I would add the names of J. B. Radford, who was able to give me official information whenever it was sought, Dr. John Coiley and T. J. Edgington of the National Railway Museum, Peter Bunce, J. R. L. Currie,

Gregory Fox, J. H. Houston, R. G. Jarvis, Eric R. Mountford, F. W. Shuttleworth, W. H. Tate and Leicester Museums, Art Galleries & Record Service for help in various ways.

The typing of the manuscript and appendices was most competently carried out by Elizabeth Bradshaw and, as on previous occasions, I enjoyed the indispensable assistance of my wife in research and checking.

GEORGE DOW
Audlem, Cheshire
1983

Close-up of Clayton arc-roofed carriage of the Midland Railway, showing door handle and grab rail and, along the roof edge, the rings through which the communication cord passed when it was fitted externally.   *George Dow Collection*

CHAPTER I

CARRIAGES OF THE PREDECESSORS

THE Midland Railway was created by the first large amalgamation to take place in the railway world. In 1844, at the instigation of George Hudson, the first 'Railway King', the three lines radiating from Derby, the North Midland, of which Hudson was Chairman, the Midland Counties and the Birmingham & Derby Junction, all of them incorporated in 1836, were merged to form the Midland Railway. The two primary objectives of the amalgamation were to put an end to wasteful competition between the three companies and to reduce administrative and working expenses, both of which were duly attained in full measure.

Royal Assent to the authorising Act was given on 10th May 1844, to produce at once the then longest system and largest railway corporation in the United Kingdom. Its length was 181½ route miles and its capital more than £5 million, plus £1½ million raised on loan. George Hudson became the first Chairman, with John Ellis, of the Midland Counties as his deputy. Matthew Kirtley, of the Birmingham & Derby Junction, was appointed Locomotive Superintendent, with responsibility also for carriages and wagons.

Unfortunately, it is possible only to form a fragmentary picture of the coaching stock inherited by the Midland in 1844. There is scant information about that of the important North Midland, and what is available is largely confined to its Directors' Minutes (NOM 1/2 in PRO at Kew). The North Midland had been opened to the public between Derby and Masborough on 11th May 1840 and from Masborough to Leeds on 1st July of the same year. Consideration was first given to carriages on 7th February 1839, when it was resolved 'that 100 carriages of the first class and 100 of the second be ordered forthwith and circulars written to the following Coach Makers, restricting each maker to 25 carriages. Wagons, Trucks and Horse Boxes also.' The makers were not shown and there is no further record of these carriages in the North Midland minutes. On 20th August 1839 it was resolved 'that Mr. R. Stephenson be instructed to take the necessary steps for building Mail Carriages', and on 7th August 1841 it is recorded 'Mr. Hanson stated that it would be desirable to build 40 new Carriage Trucks, and likewise some more Composite Carriages, upon both subjects he was to report further to the Coaching Committee on Friday next'. This report does not appear in the minutes and there is now no trace of any Coaching Committee minutes.

The last complete year of the company, 1843, was far from prosperous and it could only manage to pay a dividend of 3½%. The anxiety of the Board to reduce expenditure in every direction induced it to resort to the extraordinary course of advertising for sale 60 new carriages, 30 second-class and 30 third-class. Clement E. Stretton, in his Midland history, mentions that the advertisement appeared on 11th March 1843, the North Midland stating that the reason for the sale was because it had too many coaches for current traffic needs, but he records nothing of the outcome.

According to the Board of Trade returns, the North Midland carried 59,983½ first-class passengers, 132,290½ second-class and 234,312 third-class, at fares of 3d, 2d and 1½d per mile respectively in the half-year ending 30th June 1844. These figures seem to indicate that there were roughly equal numbers of the three classes of carriage at this time.

As to their appearance, Herbert Rake in the *Railway Magazine* of December 1903 wrote that all were four-wheeled, the first class vehicles being of a similar design to those of the Grand Junction Railway; the second-class carriages had the compartments separated by close-boarding but remained open at the sides; whilst the third-class were literally open wagons with standing accommodation only! The same source stated that North Midland carriages were externally painted Spanish brown, picked out in black. This is the likely finish of second- and third-class vehicles. Those visible in Sam Russell's lovely engraving of the interior of Derby station, executed soon after the line was opened, were undoubtedly North Midland first-class carriages and it will seem from the reproduction of the oil painting in *Fig. 1* that all wore a two colour livery, probably dark brown and pale yellow. No other illustration of North Midland coaches has been traced.

The Midland Counties, like the North Midland, was opened to the public in instalments, the first being from Derby to Nottingham on 4th June 1839, followed by Trent to Leicester on 5th May 1840 and Leicester to a junction with the London & Birmingham at Rugby on 1st July of the same year. Data about its carriages is somewhat more comprehensive.

Long before these openings, on 12th August 1836 (B 8), it was ordered 'That the engineer (Mr. Vignoles) be directed forthwith to prepare models of the most approved kind of Waggon and that he report immediately to the Directors the number he would recommend to be ordered by the Company.' This report does not seem to have survived, indeed it may never have been prepared, for the next reference to rolling stock is in B 86, of Christmas Eve 1838, when it was resolved 'That Messrs Cropper, Rathbone and Garnett be appointed a sub-committee authorised to contract for the Machinery and tools requisite for the

Fig. 1. Derby station by C. Hamilton Ellis, based upon Sam Russell's lovely engraving of 1839. A North Midland carriage is being moved manually by turntable to another track, a popular contemporary means of shunting vehicles. The picture is one of 24 oil paintings the artist was commissioned by the present author to execute for London Midland carriage compartments, all now being in the safekeeping of the National Railway Museum.

repairs of the Locomotive Engines and also for such further supply of Engines, not exceeding Twenty-five, Tenders, Carriages, Horse Boxes, Carriage Trucks and Luggage Wagons as it may seem expedient to provide for the entire opening of the Railway.' The wording of this minute suggests that no carriages or wagons had yet been ordered and that the number required had not even been agreed.

There are no further references to rolling stock before the opening of the first part of the line in 1839. A contemporary press report then noted 'several elegantly painted carriages, with the Company's arms richly emblazoned on the panels.' A Michael Bishop water colour of a Midland Counties train, preserved in the Leicester Museum of Technology, shows first- and second-class carriages in a livery of black upper and green lower panels, the windows being lined red, and an open third-class carriage with red sides and black lining, frames and wheels.

Two line drawings of Midland Counties carriages were illustrated in the classic presidential address which S. W. Johnson, the Locomotive Superintendent of the Midland, delivered to the Institution of Mechanical Engineers on 27th April 1898 and are reproduced as *Figs. 2* and *3*. The second-class carriage was open from end to end and had no glass in the sides. Its body length was 15 ft 8 ins, wheelbase 8 ft and wheel diameter 3 ft. The third-class vehicle was also carried on 3 ft wheels with a wheelbase of 8 ft 3 ins, but had a body length of 17 ft 9 ins and width of 8 ft 5 ins. It was completely uncovered, with seats around the sides and ends and in the centre. In neither case was the seating capacity given.

The initial fares charged are not recorded, but they were soon revised. B 112 of 20th June 1839 stated that after

23rd June fares between Nottingham and Derby were to be: first-class 3s 6d, second-class 2s 0d and third-class 1s 0d, thus making it clear that there were third-class carriages in service by this time. The following B 113 seems to suggest that there were none, reading as it does 'Resolved that the Third Class Carriages shall be without Seats and that they run only Morning and Evening each

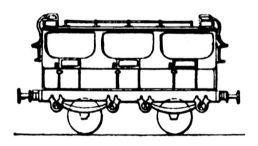

Fig. 2. Midland Counties Railway second-class carriage of 1844.

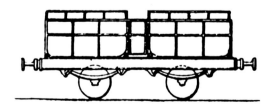

Fig. 3. Midland Counties Railway open third-class carriage of 1842.

way.' It may, perhaps, refer to some others that were to be built, or merely confirm the existing state of affairs.

B 137 of 5th September 1839 ordered that steel spring buffers were to be fitted to all carriages used for the conveyance of passengers. In the following month a further attempt to improve passenger comfort by enclosing the second-class carriages was discouraged. B 156 of 18th October recorded that the London & Birmingham Railway, having decided to charge first-class fares to all persons travelling on their line in closed carriages, made any alteration to Midland Counties second-class carriages unnecessary.

The following minute stated that an order given to Dunn & Wise for 12 horse boxes at £122 each and 20 carriage trucks at £126 each was to be countermanded, and the next, B 158, resolved that one horse box and one carriage truck to the improved plan of those belonging to the London & Birmingham were to be ordered as samples from Dagley & Smith.

Tenders for additional rolling stock are set out in B 207 of 18th February 1840, when that submitted by Dagley & Smith, with delivery by 1st June, was accepted. It was made up of 12 second-class carriages, the same in every respect as those used by the London & Birmingham on their night trains, with lockers additional, at £210 each; 12 second-class open carriages with spring buffers, mahogany panels and rails round the top, at £168 each and 4 third-class carriages at £143 each, both types to be similar in every respect to those of Midland Counties already in use between Derby and Nottingham; and 24 luggage vans, like those on the Birmingham & Derby Junction, at £78 each.

Assuming that the carriages were intended for the new lines to Leicester and Rugby, as well as on trains thence to London, it would seem that the second-class closed carriages would only be used on the night trains to London, unless passengers north of Rugby were to be favoured with the improved accommodation. The reference to rails round the top of the open seconds appears to indicate that they were not only open at the sides but roofless. In this case the main difference between them and the third-class carriages would be in the provision of seats.

The increase in rolling stock now justified an increase in staff and on 4th May 1840 a Mr. Hamer was engaged as superintendent of the building and repairing of carriages at a salary of £140 per annum. This did not, however, mean that the Midland Counties intended to build carriages itself.

A reminder of the inadequate signalling arrangements of the time is given by B 249, also of 4th May, which ruled that whenever a special train was despatched a red flag must be hung from the last carriage of the previous train, but that no train be allowed to start longer than 20 minutes after such train.

B 726 of 11th April 1843 made the first mention of fourth-class carriages. It is generally said that fourth-class carriages were not introduced until somewhat later, certainly not before Gladstone's Act of 1844, but this minute shows that they were already in existence. It is difficult to imagine any carriages more stark than the original seatless open vehicles of the Midland Counties, and perhaps by now they had been redesignated fourth-class and replaced by superior third-class carriages. The minute decreed that ten sets of wheels and axles of increased strength be ordered forthwith for the third- and fourth-class carriages to the following specifications:

'The arms of the wheel to be 8 in number, of the best rolled iron 3¼ in x ⅝ in and to have Low Moor tyres 5 in wide and finished 1½ in thick at the outer edge, the wheels to be 3 ft in diameter. The axles to be procured from the Patent Shaft & Axletree Company, to be 3½ in the middle, 4 ⅛ through the wheel, and the bearings to be 6 ft 3 in from centre to centre, and the wheels to be keyed on the axles with one square steel key ¾ ths x ⅝ ths.'

The order of a dozen short couplings for carriages was recorded in B 746 of 25th April 1843.

Towards the end of 1843, following a disastrous period of competition, the North Midland, Midland Counties and Birmingham & Derby Junction began to prepare for the joint working of their lines. The arrangements for this prelude to a merger are given in B 1022 of 4th October 1843 and include the following resolutions: 'That a Composite Carriage be run through between Nottingham and Birmingham with such trains as may be convenient; that the Carriages of the three Companies be worked in such manner as may be found most convenient to the Trade; that the three Companies be considered by the Clearing House as one Company in calculating the Mileage of Carriages, Trucks, Horse Boxes and Wagons.' In fact, the last resolution was reconsidered and not implemented, the returns remaining separate until after the amalgamation of the three railways had been consummated.

The reference to a composite carriage is the first to be made in the minutes of the Midland Counties. The carriages concerned may, of course, have belonged to one of the other companies. The second resolution evidently meant that any carriage could be used by any of the three companies as was convenient, whoever owned it, thus probably affording the first instance of common-user of rolling stock.

During January to June 1844 the Midland Counties carried 38,244 first-class passengers, 118,367½ second-class and 63,344 third-class, the fares being respectively 3d, 2d and 1d per mile.

Very little information is available about the carriages of the Birmingham & Derby Junction. Board and Traffic Committee Minutes from 1840 exist, but they are not indexed and an examination has produced no references to carriages. It is quite likely that some would be in the earliest minute books, but these are not in the possession of the Public Record Office.

The total passenger rolling stock was doubtless relatively small because the line was short, although one or two carriages were probably worked to London each day over the London & Birmingham via Hampton. The number of passengers carried in the first half of 1844 was 17,335½ first-class, 39,725½ second-class and 24,810½ third-class, the fares per mile being 2.91d, 2.18d and 1.50d respectively. The number of passengers using the line was considerably less than on either the North Midland or Midland Counties.

Two Birmingham & Derby Junction carriages were illustrated in S. W. Johnson's presidential address mentioned earlier, both built in 1839 and therefore part of the

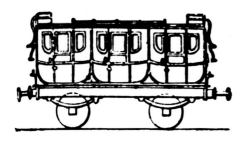

Fig. 4. Birmingham & Derby Junction Railway first-class carriage of 1839.

original rolling stock of the company. The first-class carriage, shown in *Fig. 4*, was 15 ft 6 in long, 6 ft 6 in wide and 5 ft 0¼ in high inside from floor to centre of roof, its 3 ft diameter wheels being set at 8 ft 6 in centres. It was said to seat 12 passengers in three 4 ft 11 in long compartments, but from the width 18 is more likely. In appearance it resembled the Liverpool & Manchester carriages, with a seat for the guard on the roof at each end. The second-class carriage, illustrated in *Fig. 5*, seated 24 passengers in three compartments each 4 ft 2 in long by 5 ft 4¼ in high, open from end to end above seat backs. The body width was 6 ft 5½ in, but only 13 ft long, yet despite its small size it was superior to many other contemporary second-class vehicles in that it was fully enclosed with glass windows. It, too, was carried on 3 ft diameter wheels.

According to C. R. Clinker's paper *The Birmingham & Derby Junction Railway*, published by The Dugdale Society in 1956, the external finishes adopted by the company for its carriages were: first-class seating 18, bright yellow; second-class seating 24, blue; third-class seating 40, dark brown. Each carried the company's coat of arms on the centre door panel.

One of the first fruits of the formation of the Midland Railway was a reduction in passenger rolling stock. It became possible to dispose of 53 carriages in September and October 1844, as shown in the following list taken from B 176, 177, 219 and 220:

Class and original owner		Number	Cost each £	Railway to which sold
First-class	MCR	8	170	Newcastle & Darlington Junction
First-class	MCR	2	175	Ballochney
		10		
Composite	NMR	4	150	Newcastle & Darlington Junction
Composite	Not known	6	150	Stockton & Hartlepool
		10		
Second-class	NMR	18	120	Newcastle & Darlington Junction
Second-class	MCR	2	120	Leicester & Swannington
Second-class	MCR	2	125	Ballochney
Second-class	B & DJ	2	125	Ballochney
Second-class	Not known	4	125	Stockton & Hartlepool
		28		
Third-class	NMR	1	90	Ballochney
Third-class	Not known	4	80	Stockton & Hartlepool
		5		

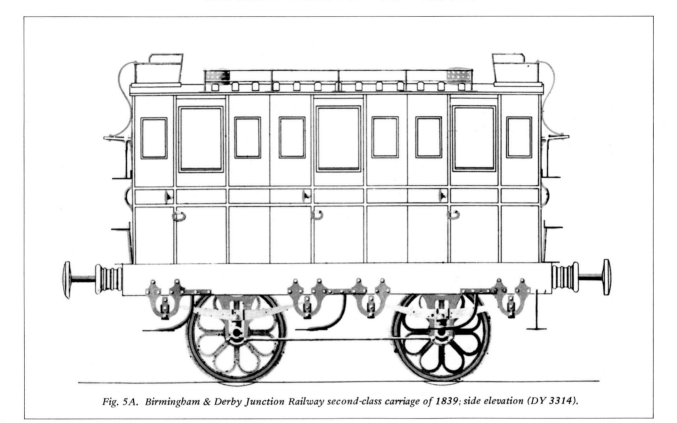

Fig. 5A. Birmingham & Derby Junction Railway second-class carriage of 1839; side elevation (DY 3314).

The eighteen North Midland second-class carriages shown above were referred to as 'unclosed' which, if not an error for 'enclosed', means carriages with roofs but without glass in the sides, like those of the Midland Counties in *Fig. 2*.

Reference can conveniently be made in this chapter to contemporary railways, known to possess coaching stock, which became part of the Midland during the years 1845-1873. The oldest of them, much older than the Midland, was the Mansfield & Pinxton, which had been incorporated on 16th June 1817 and opened for goods traffic by horse traction on 13th April 1819. It was vested in the Midland on 8th July 1847 and operated by steam traction with the completion of its reconstruction as part of the Kirkby-in-Ashfield-Mansfield line on 9th October two years later. Whether any Mansfield & Pinxton passenger vehicles were taken over by the Midland is not known, but a two compartment second- and third-class composite was certainly built at Derby for the line in 1848, the illustration of it in *Fig. 9* being taken from S. W. Johnson's presidential address. It is shown as carrying 26 passengers, the second-class compartment being 4 ft 3 in long and the third-class 6 ft 6 in, both having a height of 5 ft 8 in inside. The body length was given as 11 ft, the width as 6 ft 6 in, the diameter of the wheels being 2 ft 6 in and the wheelbase 4 ft 6 in.

This was not the only venture of the Midland into horse-drawn passenger rail vehicles. On 20th November

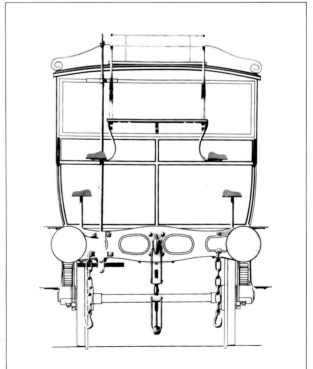

Fig. 5B. Birmingham & Derby Junction Railway second-class carriage of 1839; end elevation (DY 3315).

Fig. 6. Leicester & Swannington Railway open passenger carriage of 1832
(Leicester Museums, Art Galleries & Records Service).

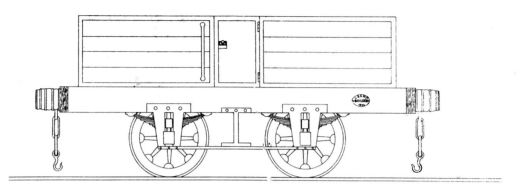

Fig. 7. Leicester & Swannington Railway first-class carriage of 1832
(Leicester Museums, Art Galleries & Records Service).

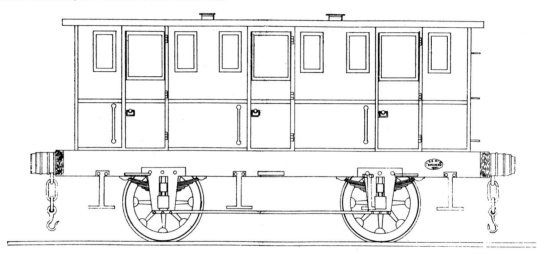

Fig. 8. Leicester & Swannington Railway first- and second-class composite of 1833
(Leicester Museums, Art Galleries & Records Service).

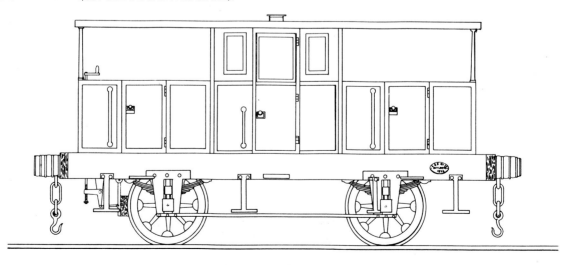

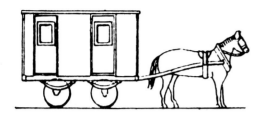

*Fig. 9. Mansfield & Pinxton Railway horse-drawn second-
and third-class composite of 1848.*

1849 the Traffic Committee agreed that the Tewkesbury branch should be worked by horse instead of steam traction and asked the Locomotive Committee to provide two light composite coaches for the purpose. The Midland also worked five trips daily between Southwell and Rolleston Junction with a horse-drawn two compartment carriage from 1st November 1848 until 31st July 1849.

Another absorbed line older than the Midland was the Leicester & Swannington, which was incorporated on 29th May 1830 and brought into use on 18th July 1832, but its passenger business represented only some 5% of the annual receipts and when it was vested in the Midland on 27th July 1846 it owned no more than six carriages, according to Clement E. Stretton in his history of the railway. Only three have been described, these having been constructed at the company's workshops at West Bridge. The oldest was a four-wheeled open vehicle built in 1832 on a frame 14 ft long with sides about 2 ft high; it was carried on 3 ft diameter wheels and weighed empty a mere 1 ton 12 cwt; it is shown in *Fig. 6*. Later in the same year a four-wheeled enclosed first-class carriage was completed. This embodied three compartments on a 17 ft frame carried on 3 ft diameter wheels, the tare weight being 2½ tons; it is illustrated in *Fig. 7*. The third was a composite carriage, completed in 1833 and similar to the vehicle just mentioned, but with a roofed, open-sided second-class compartment either side of an enclosed first-class compartment in the middle. *Fig. 8* depicts its appearance.

It is believed that these vehicles were given an unadorned external finish of middle blue, the shade of which is to be seen in the Leicester & Swannington picture of the series of carriage panels which the present author commissioned C. Hamilton Ellis to execute in oils for British Railways early in the 1950s, now in the National Railway Museum.

No details or drawings of the carriages of the Sheffield & Rotherham appear to have survived. The little line, which was granted its Act on 4th July 1836, began public services on 1st November 1838 and was taken over by the Midland on 21st July 1845. Not much more is known of

the carriages of the Leeds & Bradford, which was incorporated on 4th July 1844, opened to the public on 1st July two years later, leased to the Midland on 26th August 1846 and vested in it on 24th July 1851. Peter Baughan records, in his admirable *North of Leeds* (Roundhouse Books 1966), that in February 1846 the Leeds & Bradford ordered from W. Hamer of Leicester 4 first-class carriages at £350 each, 2 composites at £300 each, 10 second-class coaches, with brakes, at £280 each and 12 third-class at £165 each, but no illustrations of any of these can be traced.

The most important lines acquired were the Birmingham & Gloucester and Bristol & Gloucester, which had been worked as one from 14th January 1845 under the title of Bristol & Birmingham Railway, and which gave the Midland its main line to the south west when it took over their management on 7th May 1845. They were vested in the Midland on 3rd August of the following year.

Incorporated on 22nd April 1836, the Birmingham & Gloucester was the older of the two. It was opened for public traffic in five instalments in 1840, the final one taking place on 17th December. Fortunately for posterity, drawings of its first-class and second-class carriages were published in *Railway Practice* of 1847, of which *Figs. 10* and *11* are reproductions. These distinctive vehicles were rather low-slung, the floors being only 2 ft 8 in above rail level, and it will be seen that both types had brakes on each pair of 3 ft diameter Bramah & Fox patent loop form wheels, operated by an upright rod terminating in a handle alongside one of the roof seats. Both types had identical under-carriages 8 ft 6 in wide over the iron plate foot-steps, with spiral sprung drawbar and buffers, the latter being at 6 ft centres and 2 ft 2½ in above the rails. The first-class coach had a wheelbase of 10 ft and the third only 6 ft 6 in. Externally they were painted a dark buff picked-out in black, with the railway company's coat of arms emblazoned on the middle doors; no doubt the device was akin to the company's seal, which consisted primarily of the arms of Birmingham and Gloucester.

An unusual feature of the first-class coach was the inclusion of two coupé compartments. These each measured 3 ft 4 in long by 6 ft 10½ in wide and it seems that they were much sought after by invalids and ladies travelling alone; the two centre compartments were each 5 ft long and seated six. The seats were 1 ft 8 in wide, fixed 1 ft 6 in from the floor, and the doors were 1 ft 9 in wide and 4 ft 7 in high. Overall length of the body was 17 ft 4 in, its overall width 7 ft and its roof 7 ft 7 in above the rails. The second-class coach seated 24 passengers in its three compartments, which were open to each other above dwarf partitions, the roof being supported by iron standards in the centre of each partition. Body length was 15 ft 2 in, its width 7 ft 4 in and its roof 7 ft 7 in above the rails. The third-class vehicles were hardly worthy of illustration! They were both seatless and roofless, with a closed compartment for luggage in the centre.

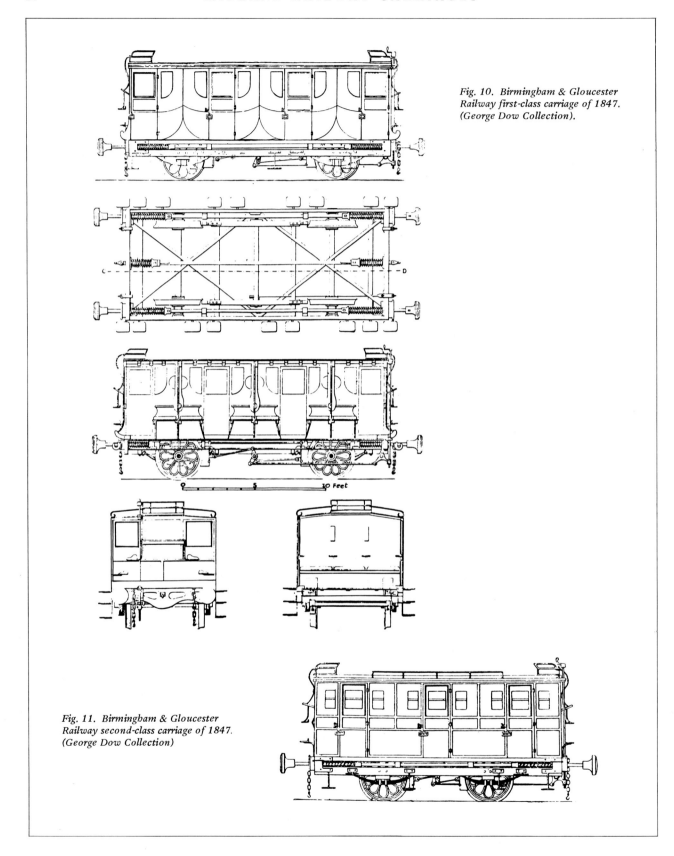

Fig. 10. Birmingham & Gloucester Railway first-class carriage of 1847. (George Dow Collection).

Fig. 11. Birmingham & Gloucester Railway second-class carriage of 1847. (George Dow Collection)

It is not known how many Birmingham & Gloucester carriages were taken over by the Midland.

Unlike the others, the Bristol & Gloucester was originally built to Brunel's preposterous 7 ft 0¼ in gauge. It was incorporated on 1st July 1839, when it acquired the Bristol & Gloucestershire Railway, a nine mile local coal carrier, and was opened throughout to the public on 8th July 1844. Carriages were hired from Stothert, Slaughter & Co. under a ten-year contract. Twenty were used at first and there are brief descriptions of some of them in the records of the Bristol & Exeter Railway, which bought thirteen from the Midland in 1856. The first-class carriages had three compartments each seating four passengers a side and the second-class four compartments seating six a side. Both types ran on six 4 ft diameter wheels. One carriage, which became No. 49 of the Bristol & Exeter, was described as having four second-class compartments, one for the guard and one for the luggage. The third-class vehicles were roofless four-wheelers and accommodated standing passengers only. All carriages were given a brown external finish.

Drawings have survived of the Bristol & Gloucester third-class carriage of 1845 used on Parliamentary trains and are reproduced in *Fig. 12*. Nothing more or less than a canvas-covered wagon, it had no night lamp and was provided with one narrow door on each side. There was no provision for the admission of air in bad weather, when doors and windows were closed. This badly-lit and badly-ventilated vehicle seated 54 passengers in a space 21 ft long by 8 ft 6 in wide overall.

After the Midland took over the management of the line in 1845 it purchased the carriage stock from Stothert, Slaughter & Co. According to Colin Maggs' *The Bristol & Gloucester Railway* (Oakwood Press, 1969), tenders for two more broad gauge composite coaches were obtained in August 1845 and in the following February the Board asked for the second-class carriages to be more effectively enclosed. The same source records that in March 1846 an extra door was provided in the third-class carriages and in April 1847 Kirtley was instructed to order 6 first-class and 8 second-class broad gauge carriages from J. Knight at £420 and £280 each respectively. To what extent these various developments were fulfilled is not known. But that some additions to the broad gauge stock were made by the Midland is confirmed by a drawing of a 27 ft long six-wheeled third-class coach built in 1848, which was reproduced in S. W. Johnson's presidential address. It is shown in *Fig. 13* and was open from end to end above

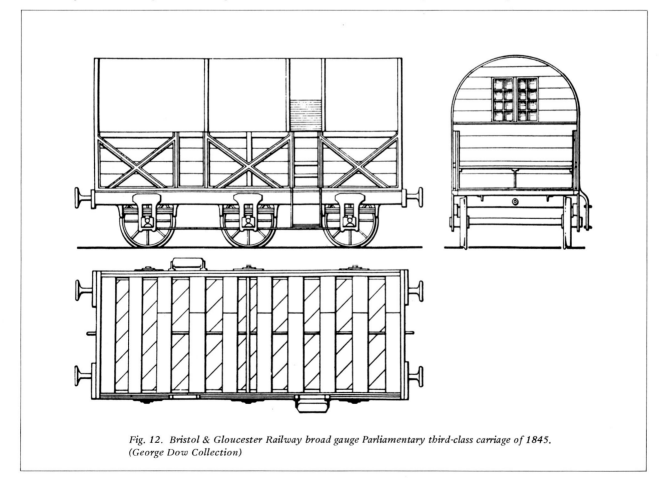

Fig. 12. Bristol & Gloucester Railway broad gauge Parliamentary third-class carriage of 1845.
(George Dow Collection)

the seat backs. The 3 ft 6 in diameter wheels were spaced at 9 ft centres.

By means of mixed gauge track between Bristol and Standish junction, Stonehouse, and its own metals thence to Gloucester, which were brought into use on 29th May 1854, the Midland finally shook off its broad gauge incubus. Kirtley's half-yearly report to the Locomotive Committee on 5th February 1857 (the only one, unfortunately, that has survived) showed that the greater part of the broad gauge carriage and wagon stock had been reconstructed for standard gauge use and that the remainder would be replaced by new standard gauge vehicles as fast as means permitted, the cost being charged to revenue.

An attempt was made in 1854 to sell much of the remaining Bristol & Gloucester broad gauge stock to the Bristol & Exeter Railway; the units included 6 first-class, 2 coupé, 1 mail, 2 second and 4 third-class carriages, together with 4 passenger 'break' vans (L 1762 6th June). It was unsuccessful because the potential buyer was more interested in hiring them. On 5th June 1855 (L 2006) it was reported that 6 tilt wagons, 12 low-sided goods wagons, 3 horse boxes and 3 carriage trucks had been sold to Brassey & Company. In the following month it was agreed (L 2041 31st July) to lend to Brassey an engine and 6 broad gauge carriages at Clearing House rates, namely 100 miles per carriage per day and '£2 10s. 0d. per day for engine and tender and he to keep stock in repair'. These 6 carriages, 4 composites and 2 second-class, were doubtless those which were sold to Brassey in November 1855 (L 2121), all fetching £150 each. The last broad

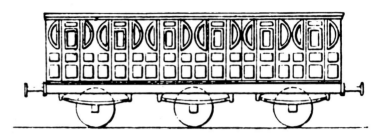

Fig. 13. Midland Railway broad gauge third-class carriage of 1848.

gauge vehicles to be sold to Brassey were 4 goods 'break' vans and 3 passenger vans at £110 and £40 each respectively, a rather surprising result (L 2136 15th January 1856). It seems very likely that the passenger vans were the three unsuccessfully offered to the Bristol & Exeter in 1854.

On 15th April 1856 (L 2189) it was ordered that the remaining broad gauge stock be advertised for auction at Gloucester early in May. The items consisted of a passenger engine, a goods engine, 7 first-class, 5 composite, 6 second-class and 6 third-class carriages, 3 horse boxes, 3 carriage trucks, a six-wheeled timber truck, 8 low-sided wagons and 29 high-sided wagons. At the auction no bids were received and, in consequence, it was decided that, as Brassey's interest in any of them could not be aroused, they should all be broken up (L 2720). Before this could be done, however, the Bristol & Exeter decided to buy 13 of the carriages for £1,300 (L 2740 1st July 1856). The types concerned were not recorded in the Midland minutes, but in Bristol & Exeter records the following information is given about them:

MR No.	MR class	B & E class	B & E No.	Subsequent alterations	Year condemned
124	first	first	26	To second-class No. 10 in 1866	1873
125	first	first	25	To fish van No. 29 in January 1865	10/75
126	first	second	54	—	9/71
127	first	first	24	—	1/70
128	first	second	55	To fish van No. 30 in February 1865	1874
129	first	first	27	—	4/68
73	compo	second	51	—	7/73
74	compo	second	49	—	1/67
75	compo	second	52	—	1870
not known	compo	second	not known	—	not known
147	second	second	11	—	1/67
246	third	second	50	—	1867
247	third	second	53	—	1864

The Midland numbers 124 to 129 for the first-class carriages are about what one would expect from the quantities of vehicles in stock in 1849-50. The numbers of others, however, are higher than expected, but this cannot be explained. There is some doubt as to whether No. 147 was second-class or third-class and the identity of one vehicle is not known. Otherwise the records are fairly clear and throw some light on a hitherto obscure phase of Midland carriage history.

Final takeover to be noted was that of the North Western, often referred to as the 'Little' North Western to avoid confusion with the London & North Western. Incorporated on 26th June 1846, its last section was opened on 1st June 1850, to complete a system extending from Skipton via Lancaster Green Ayre to Poulton (now Morecambe), with branches to Ingleton and Lancaster Castle. The Midland assumed responsibility for working the line, and for all the rolling stock, on 1st June 1852, including the section between Morecambe station and pier, over which horse-drawn goods wagons only were operated! The North Western was leased to the Midland on 1st January 1859 and was purchased as from 1st July 1871.

Midland Locomotive Committee minutes record that 41 North Western carriages were added to the company's stock in the half-year ending 30th June 1852. They consisted of 6 first-class, 13 second-class, 7 third-class and 10 composites, together with 5 'break' vans. Two were saloons, the only vehicles of which further information is known. L 2790 of 14th October 1856 states 'The General Manager suggested the desirability of a Saloon Carriage for the use of families and pleasure parties and it was Resolved that the Locomotive Committee be requested to alter the two Saloon Carriages taken of the North Western Company in time for next season. W. E. Hutchinson.'

It is likely that all North Western coaching stock was replaced by new vehicles during the 1860s.

Fig. 14. Matthew Kirtley, Midland Railway Locomotive Superintendent from 1844 to 1873. *(DY 8841)*

CHAPTER II

THE KIRTLEY ERA

1844–1873

FOR information about the carriage stock of the Midland Railway in its earliest years reliance has to be placed almost entirely upon the sparse notes in minute books and on some data and line drawings in S. W. Johnson's presidential address of 1898.

From the first days of the new company there was a separate Locomotive & Carriage Department, usually referred to simply as the Locomotive Department, and Matthew Kirtley was its Superintendent. Appointed on 13th June 1844 at £250 a year (B 25), he was given early advances and was enjoying a salary of £700 on 1st April 1846. There were then no separate committees of the directorate for the different departments. All business was dealt with by the full Board or its Committee of Management, and the signature of George Hudson is to be seen on many of the early minutes. Not until September 1849 were separate committees set up for the Locomotive & Carriage Department, the Traffic Department, the Stores Department and others. Unfortunately, no references to carriages appear in the Board Minutes after 12th July 1845, and from this time until October 1849 there is gap in the records.

The original passenger rolling stock of the Midland was made up of first-class, composite (having first- and second-class compartments), second-class and third-class carriages, with some ex-Midland Counties fourth-class vehicles as well. The Midland Counties had sponsored some of the earliest excursion trains ever to run in this country; B 519 of 12th July 1845 refers to the conversion of four second-class carriages to fourth-class, no doubt specifically for excursion trains, but there is no mention of fourth-class in the Board of Trade returns.

A contemporary by-law, No. 7, reads: 'Dogs will not be suffered to accompany Passengers in the Company's Carriages.' This suggests that some of the vehicles of 1844 embodied built-in dog boxes, as did passenger vans and horse boxes of the 1870s.

The earliest known list of Midland carriages is that given in L 432 of 14th June 1850, which sets out the composition of the carriage and wagon stock in 1849 and 1850, as in the adjoining column.

It will be observed that nearly a third of the third-class carriages were open, no doubt of a pattern resembling those of the Midland Counties. Apparently they continued in this state for some years, because not until 1859 is there a directive (L 3293 of 19th April) which orders ' . . . all the open Third Class Carriages to be enclosed

during the present year.' In the meantime, it was resolved (L 1459 of 31st March 1853) 'That Locks be forthwith put on the Doors of Open Carriages.'

The number of first-class carriages did not increase by more than 20 per cent in the next 25 years, while as far as can be determined the stock of second-class carriages remained virtually stationary until abolition of second-class travel on 1st January 1875. On the other hand, in the same period the number of composites increased nearly ten-fold and third-class carriages more than five times.

Early repair facilities on the company's premises must have been somewhat restricted; B 63 of 2nd July 1844 records 'Ordered that 6 First Class Carriages be sent to Mr. Wright to be thoroughly repaired.' This is no doubt the Mr. Wright of Saltley whose carriage-building business was the forerunner of the Metropolitan Railway Carriage & Wagon Company. In September of the same year it was ordered by B 159 'That 1 First and 2 Second Class Carriages be sent to Mr. Brown of Birmingham to be altered into 3 Composite Carriages.' Mr. Brown was presumably one of the partners, in later years, of Brown, Marshalls & Company.

There are no further references to first-class carriages in the Board minutes and the next one to be found is L 396 of 14th May 1850, in which it is ordered that '2 large first-class carriages be altered into compos, viz 1st and 3rd class, guard and compos, 2 2nd class to be made

Type of vehicle	Half year ending 31/12/1849	Half year ending 30/6/1850	Increase + or Decrease −
First-class	125	123	−2
Composite	55	58	+3
Second-class	182	175*	−7
Third-class enclosed	130	137*	+7
Third-class open	57	56	−1
Guards vans	145	143	−2
Post Office and Mails	11	11	
Horse boxes	111	111	
Carriage trucks	100	100	
	916	914	−2
Break Wagons	68	75	+7
Wagons	6,850	6,862	+12
	6,918	6,937	+19

* including 2 under construction

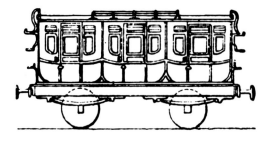

Fig. 15. First-class carriage of 1848.

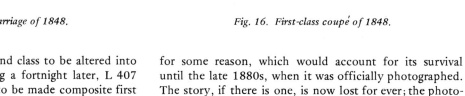

Fig. 16. First-class coupé of 1848.

into 1st class, six old 1st or 2nd class to be altered into 3rd class.' At the next meeting a fortnight later, L 407 directed that 2 carriages were to be made composite first and second class; the original class is not given, but it was almost certainly first. The stock of first-class carriages was increased by the conversion of 10 second-class to first-class ordered by L 554 of 5th November 1850, so raising the total to 133.

It is probable that the earliest Midland first-class carriages were generally similar to those of the Birmingham & Derby Junction of 1839 shown on page 6. These measured only 4 ft 11 in between partitions and 5 ft from floor to ceiling. To the modern traveller, accustomed to walking upright in a railway carriage, these dimensions will seem impossibly cramped, for it would have been necessary to bend double to enter, as one does today when getting into a motor car. Another decade was to elapse before carriages were high enough for the average passenger to stand upright in them. The 1848 vehicle illustrated in *Fig. 15* may have been the initial first-class carriage design of the Midland. Each compartment had seats for 6 passengers, as did first-class carriages for many years to come, though gradually increasing in space. These new carriages were a great improvement on the B & DJ vehicles, with body width increased from 4 ft 11 in to 5 ft 10 in and height from 5 ft to 5 ft 9 in; the 3 ft 6 in diameter wheels were set at 10 ft centres. Luggage was carried on the roof, a practice to stay for the next twenty years or more, but they may have been the last Midland carriages to be fitted with guard's seats on the roof.

First class coupé No. 5, illustrated in *Figs. 16* and *17*, was of similar construction, 15 ft 6 in long, but a mere 4 ft 9 in wide, so accommodating only two passengers a side. It was shown by S. W. Johnson to have been built in 1848, rather late for the construction of such a narrow-bodied vehicle, and perhaps the explanation is that an old body was put on a new underframe turned out in that year. It is not unlikely that the carriage was noteworthy

for some reason, which would account for its survival until the late 1880s, when it was officially photographed. The story, if there is one, is now lost for ever; the photograph index at Derby is unhelpful, simply calling it 'old carriage No. 5.'

As mentioned in Chapter I, 6 first-class carriages were taken over from the North Western in 1852 and they would have increased the Midland stock accordingly, but L 1914 of 23rd January 1855 shows that in that month there was a total of 130 first-class carriages at work (including 7 broad gauge). This suggests that the conversion of 10 second-class carriages to first-class was not carried out in 1850-51, unless about the same number of first-class vehicles was scrapped or altered to another type without record in the minutes.

In September 1856 it was decided to purchase foot-warmers for use in first-class carriages and L 2771 records that the Board 'be requested to decide tomorrow as to kind of footwarmers to be adopted.' The number acquired at this time is not given, but in November 1860 a further 250 were ordered and on 18th December 1870 the total number in hand was 1,033.

L 2790 of 14th October 1856 notes that two family saloons were to be provided by the conversion of two North Western saloons, but it is uncertain whether the latter were first-class vehicles or composites. If the altered carriages contained a servants' compartment they would probably be listed in the composite stock; the conversion may in this case have reduced the first-class stock by two.

In a minute concerning new Post Office vans (L 3087 of 18th May 1858) reference is made to 'the two Post Office vans originally constructed having been altered to First Class Carriages.' No other record of this alteration is known, nor is the date of conversion given. The wording suggests that the vans concerned may have been the two 'flying Post Offices' ordered from Mr. Wright in September 1844. Presumably this change brought the number of first-class carriages up to 132.

It was probably about this time that a special carriage was first provided for the company's directors to make their tours of inspection. The earliest known vehicle of this type is illustrated in *Fig. 18*, from which the drawing in *Fig. 19* has been prepared. According to a note by the late P. C. Dewhurst on the print of the photograph in his collection preserved in the Science Museum at South Kensington, the carriage was built in 1858. But it is thought that this date, if correct, is likely to be the year it appears to have been converted from a three-compartment first-class carriage, so it is not impossible that one under construction was adapted for the purpose. No record of its construction has been found in the minute books, which suggests that it might have been a replacement of an older vehicle, such as one inherited from a predecessor company. It was given the first number in the first-class series, a practice which was continued throughout the life of the Midland.

The dimensions shown in the drawing have been estimated from the photograph and should not be far wrong.

It appears that there were no internal partitions, and that there was a window in the far end. A handbrake was fitted, with wooden brake blocks on all four wheels, presumably actuated by a guard riding in the vehicle. The modern buffers and plain headstocks suggest a rebuilding of the underframe after about 1872. By the time the photograph was taken in the late 1880s the iron-spoked wheels had been fitted with Mansell retaining rings, probably in 1876. These may not have been the original wheels for it is likely that the vehicle would have been given teak-centred wheels in or before 1876, and these may have been taken off when the carriage was replaced in 1880, doubtless to be down-graded to service use. In the photograph it appears to be painted wagon grey, with lettering specially applied for the occasion.

On 31st July 1860 the Locomotive Committee agreed to ask for 50 new carriages, 10 of them to be first-class, and on 2nd July 1861 to request a further 30 first-class. The records of vehicles constructed at Derby show that from April 1860 to November 1861 twenty-six first-class

Fig. 17. First-class coupé of 1848, photographed in the late 1880s. (DY 3039)

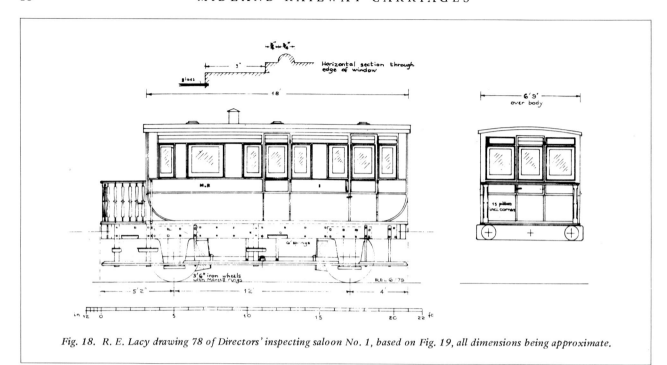

Fig. 18. R. E. Lacy drawing 78 of Directors' inspecting saloon No. 1, based on Fig. 19, all dimensions being approximate.

Fig. 19. Directors' inspecting saloon No. 1 of 1858.

R. E. Lacy Collection

Fig. 20. Midland train at Dursley photographed by F. A. Cook between 1865 and 1872. The leading carriage is a 23 ft first- and second-class composite, as altered to six-wheeler in 1865; the second carriage appears to be a four-wheeled brake-third, converted from first in 1864. The locomotive is 0—4—2WT No. 202, an ex-North Western 2—2—2WT rebuilt by Kirtley in January 1865.   *George Dow Collection*

carriages were built as additions to stock, as well as eleven replacements. About half these additional carriages were built before the first of the two proposals just mentioned, and it is doubtful, therefore, whether they can be those referred to in the minutes. However, no first-class carriages were ordered at this time from outside builders, so it is apparent that they were built in the company's shops at Derby. In November 1861 twenty composites were ordered; the first-class accommodation in these would be equivalent to that in about thirteen first-class carriages and it is likely that they were built in lieu of them.

These first-class carriages will have had an external appearance similar to that of the composite of 1861 shown in *Fig. 35*, embracing three compartments within an overall body length of about 19 ft. The body appears to have been designed as a unit and not as an assembly of three separate compartments. So at last there were signs of a break away from the stage-coach type of carriage which had lasted for over thirty years on railways. Only the curve of the bottom mouldings remained as a reminder of their ancestry.

By now there were some 158 first-class carriages in service, the largest number at any time until about 1876. Those just mentioned were needed to meet the increase in traffic. Midland dividends in 1860-1 were higher than at any time since 1847; they were rather lower in 1862-3 but

in 1864 reached the record value of £7 7s. 6d. In spite of this, the Traffic Committee requested 'that 50 old 1st class carriages be converted as quickly as possible into third class and be painted the same colour as the first class' (L 4675 of 17th May 1864). The vehicles concerned were probably of the very oldest three-compartment type taken over from the constituent companies in 1844.

There are few records before 1858 of the renewal of carriages, but during 1858-63 it is known that 38 first-class vehicles were renewed. It is likely that before this time there was little replacement of old stock, except for those built as renewals of the Bristol & Gloucester broad gauge carriages. By 1864 there may have been 50 or more carriages surviving from those taken over from the old companies in 1844, and these would be the ones converted to third-class. It is likely that the conversion was undertaken, not because of any decrease in demand for first-class accommodation, but because the old carriages were no longer suitable for the traffic. The rear carriage of the train shown in *Fig. 20* may well have been one of the converted firsts. If so, it is the only known photograph of a pre-Midland carriage.

During 1864-7 a further 56 first-class carriages were built at Derby as renewals, exemplified by *Fig. 21*, but it seems clear that they did not replace the 50 converted to third-class, unless in the following six years about 50 more

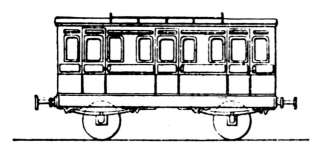

Fig. 21. First-class carriage of 1867.

old carriages were broken up without being replaced. It is most unlikely that this would happen without record in the minutes, and it is safe to assume that the 50 converted firsts were not replaced, so that the number of first-class carriages was reduced to about 108.

It is evident that this reduced accommodation proved to be insufficient, and on 17th April 1866 (L 5232) a request was made for more carriages, including 20 first-class and 50 composite first- and second-class. In June 1866 the tender of the Metropolitan Railway Carriage & Wagon Company for the supply of the first-class carriages at £269 each was accepted, the price not including wheels and springs. They were 20 ft long with three compartments and are illustrated in *Figs. 22* and *23*. For the first time complete information regarding the design and appearance of an early Midland carriage is available, because the original tracing is still in the possession of the builder's successors. In the photograph, which was probably taken in the late 1880s, the vehicle is in a dirty state, with no trace of lining; the lettering seems to have been done in white paint for photography. Bearing no maker's plate, No. 101 was likely to have been constructed at Derby *circa* 1866 and, with the absence of any form of brake, must have spent its last years on colliers' trains, or in departmental service.

The first-class carriages built as renewals at Derby during the years 1864-7 will have been similar in design to No. 101, but from 1863 most additional first-class accommodation was provided in composite carriages, largely in first-second twin-compos, but also in a good number of tri-compos.

In 1869 three more first-class carriages were renewed, followed by seven more in 1870-1 and 1873. As 91 had been renewed in the period 1860-7 and 50 of the oldest had been altered to third-class in 1864, it is evident that almost all the stock was of fairly recent construction by the end of 1867. No particulars of these carriages have survived except for the reference in L 7086 of 14th May 1872, which states that the four-compartment first-class carriage built at Derby cost £354 to make, including

general charges. Their length would have been about 27 ft. In 1872-3, following trials on the running of carriages in 1870-1, the 6 ft long springs on first-class vehicles were exchanged for 7 ft springs.

At 30th June 1873 the number of first-class carriages is calculated to be 149, but there is reason to believe that this should be 146, because Kirtley's successor, T. G. Clayton, numbered his new 29 ft carriages 147-246. Apparently three must have been scrapped or altered without record in the minutes. The changes since 1844 are summarised in Appendix 1. No attempt has been made to suggest numbers for any of the carriages, for it seems certain that there must have been some renumbering if the total stock of about 158 in 1861 was reduced to 146 by mid-1873. It is known that the first Clayton carriages were numbered from 147 upwards, so there were no gaps below this number.

The Midland inherited a considerable number of second-class carriages from the constituent companies. Taking into account the disposals and conversions mentioned in earlier pages and the influx of Birmingham & Gloucester and Bristol & Gloucester vehicles in 1845, the stock of second-class carriages stood at 182 at the close of 1849 and 175 at 30th June 1850 (L 432). On 19th November 1850 it was reported that Kirtley was to alter 10 second-class carriages into first-class, but it is believed that this conversion was, in fact, to composite first- and second-class.

There appeared to be some complaints about the standard of comfort provided for second-class passengers because on 20th July 1858 (L 3120) it was resolved 'That 6 second-class carriages be provided with cushions and be ready for inspection of Traffic Committee at next meeting as requested.' Evidently the committee was satisfied, although it was not until 19th April 1859 that L 3293 reported a Traffic Committee minute of 5th April, which reads 'Resolved that all the Second Class Carriages to be cushioned and padded, all the Open Third Class Carriages to be enclosed during the present year and that all Cattle Wagons as renewed to be made 18 feet long.' Obviously there was to be increased comfort all round! The way in which the padding was carried out is not revealed, but it is known that in 1874 the second-class compartments were lined with American cloth, while photographs taken around 1869 show the typical shiny surface of this material.

Two vehicles turned out of the Derby shops in December 1860 and January 1861 had the distinction of being the last second-class carriages built for the Midland as *additions* to the ordinary stock, but 155 were constructed over the years 1866-72 as renewals of old carriages broken up.

In 1870 further improvements in the furnishings of second-class carriages were taken in hand. L 6385 of 20th September 1870 records a request from the Traffic Committee for all second-class carriages to be fitted with racks,

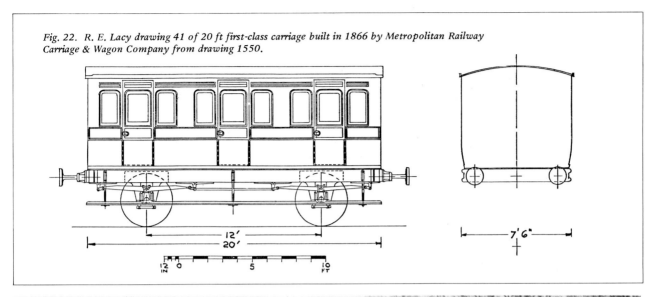

Fig. 22. R. E. Lacy drawing 41 of 20 ft first-class carriage built in 1866 by Metropolitan Railway Carriage & Wagon Company from drawing 1550.

Fig. 23. 20 ft first-class carriage No. 101 built at Derby c.1866 and photographed in the late 1880s. *(DY 6457)*

hat strings and blinds. Kirtley was asked for his opinion and reported that the cost would be about £10 per carriage. It was ordered that the work be carried out as the carriages came in for repairs. Second-class compartments in composites would have been similarly treated.

The standard second-class carriage of 1866-7 was 22 ft long with four compartments, carried on 3 ft 6 in diameter wheels at 13 ft centres; it is illustrated in *Fig. 26*. Those being made in 1872 also had four compartments, cost £213 each to construct at Derby (L 7086) and were probably 22 ft-23 ft long. No more were built before the abolition of second-class travel on 1st January 1875, when the second-class accommodation was redesignated third-class. The alteration was in name only, for although the original intention was to strip the cushions and linings, what in fact happened was that the third-class carriages were improved to bring them up to the level of the old second-class.

It would appear from the alterations to stock recorded in the minutes that after the last additional vehicle was completed in July 1872 there was a total of 201 second-class carriages in use, but lack of detailed records between 1850 and 1858 make the exact total uncertain. Other calculations recorded later in this chapter suggest a total of 194, but there is not enough evidence to resolve the difference between the two estimates. The changes over the years 1844-74 are given in Appendix 2.

In 1875 all the former second-class carriages were renumbered into the third-class series. They probably took new numbers in a series from 1182 to about 1380, following the series of brake-thirds then on order from the Swansea Wagon Company, and all were replaced by new Clayton third-class coaches before the end of 1887. Some appear to have been sold and not broken-up, for in a list of carriages sold to the Eastern & Midlands Railway in 1887 are shown Nos. 1271, 1245, 1188, 1306, and 1310 which, from their numbers, would appear to be among those altered from second-class.

No details can be traced of the third-class carriages acquired by the Midland from its three constituent companies beyond the Midland Counties open carriages of 1842, to which reference has already been made. Those of the North Midland and Birmingham & Derby Junction were doubtless equally primitive. But the Midland soon displayed an enlightened attitude. On 10th September 1844, B 158 'Ordered that the Secretary apply to the Board of Trade requesting to be informed the description of carriages their Lordships will require for the conveyance of Third Class Passengers.' This action on the part of the Midland Board arose out of the provisions of the Regulation of Railways Act of 1844, which was better known as the Cheap Trains Act from its sections about penny-a-mile Parliamentary trains. No reply to the approach is quoted; but it was considered necessary to order improved third-class carriages which would comply with the provisions of the Act. Tenders for the supply of six such

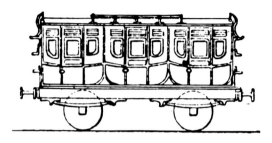

*Fig. 24. Second-class carriage of 1848.
10 ft wheelbase, 3 compartments.*

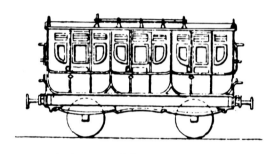

*Fig. 25. Second-class carriage of 1858.
10 ft wheelbase, 3 compartments.*

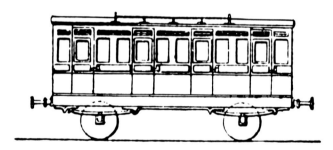

*Fig. 26. Second-class carriage of 1867.
13 ft wheelbase, 4 compartments.*

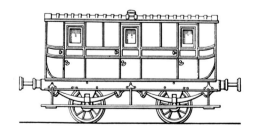

Fig. 27. Midland Railway third-class Parliamentary carriage of 1845 seating 30 passengers. The door windows could be opened or shut as desired, the framed glass window falling into a recess in the door when opened. Centrally in the roof was a half sphere of glass with Argand oil lamp.
　　　　　　　　　　　　　　　　　(George Dow Collection)

carriages were received on 20th January 1845 (B 341). The offer of Smith & Dagley was accepted, the price being £85 each, without springs and wheels; the other tenders were from Mr. Hamer (£88) and Mr. Thomas Brown (£157), the latter price including 'drawing bars and buffers'.

The drawing in *Fig. 27* shows the type of carriage ordered from Smith & Dagley. It is taken from a volume of lithographed plans entitled 'Railway carriages for conveying third class passengers at or under one penny per mile,' which is the Return to an Order of the House of Commons dated 26th February 1845 and ordered to be printed on 26th June 1845. The description states that the carriage held 30 passengers and that the internal dimensions are 15 ft 4 in by 6 ft 9 in by 5 ft 5 in high. The spaces for admitting air and light are given as 22 in by 11½ in, one in each door or six in each carriage; glass in all, size 15 in by 12 in. In fact, the width of the opening should have been shown as 1 ft 5 in or thereabouts, not 11½ in. The drawing includes a transverse section which shows that the three compartments were separated by dwarf partitions with central roof supports.

Following the dimensions a note states that 'The Regulations issued by the Lords of the Privy Council for Trade are that their Lordships cannot certify any carriage for these trains to be sufficiently protected from the weather, in the sense of the Act, unless it is capable of being entirely closed, with the provision for the admission of light and air. By order, D. O'Brien.'

A table was included setting out the services in which the Midland Parliamentary carriages ran. They were Rugby 1.30 p.m. to Derby 4.45 p.m. (50 miles); Derby 11.40 a.m. to Rugby 3.20 p.m.; Leeds 6.50 a.m. to Derby 11.30 a.m. (73 miles); Derby 5.0 p.m. to Leeds 9.40 p.m.; Birmingham 2.0 p.m. to Derby 4.45 p.m. (41 miles); Derby 12.5 p.m. to Birmingham 2.15 p.m.; Nottingham 3.30 p.m. to Derby 4.45 p.m. (16 miles); Derby 11.40 a.m. to Nottingham 12.40 p.m. In every case doors were locked on one side of the carriage. Thus there were 8 trips daily, to be worked by 6 carriages, so that at least one pair of carriages must have been used all the way from Leeds to Nottingham, Rugby or Birmingham, connecting with others at Derby in either direction. All the trips outward from Derby were faster than those inwards; the difference was possibly recovery time to make sure that connections were made at Derby.

L 396 mentioned earlier in this chapter refers to six old first- or second-class carriages which were to be converted to third-class. It is believed that second-class carriages were so altered, quite likely some of the unclosed ones with roofs but no glass in the side openings. These evidently account for the increase in the number of third-class carriages to 193 by 30th June 1850. By the same date the number of open carriages had fallen to 56, so

apparently one had been broken up and replaced by a closed carriage.

In November 1850 the Midland sought tenders for 100 third-class carriages, to seat 40 passengers each. Quotations were received from a dozen firms, the prices ranging from £87 to £130 each. The tender of Brown, Marshalls & Company for £90 per vehicle was accepted, their specification including India teak for bottom, sides, ends and top rails, and seasoned English oak for the remainder of the body framing. The wheels, axles, springs and brasses were to be supplied by the Midland at a cost of approximately £4,500, thus making the total cost of each carriage about £135. The order represented an increase of over 50 per cent in the third-class stock and suggests a heavy upsurge in traffic. Doubtless they were ordered in anticipation of the increased travel the Great Exhibition of 1851 would generate. In the event there was indeed an enormous increase in the number of people travelling to London to visit the Great Exhibition, encouraged by incentives such as a Leeds-London excursion fare of five shillings, but traffic elsewhere on the system more or less correspondingly decreased.

Two passenger carriages visible in the background of the earliest known photograph of Derby station and works (DY 13192), taken in about 1860, appear to be Brown, Marshalls thirds ordered in 1850. From a greatly enlarged section of this photograph it has been possible to prepare the outline drawings in *Fig. 28*, it having been assumed that the vehicles were 20 ft in length. Fine detail cannot be picked out from the enlargement, but it is likely that steps, door furniture and underframe details were generally similar to those on the carriages of the mid-1860s. Strikingly different are the external framing and straight sides and ends, representing a complete break with stage-coach design. This method of construction is exemplified in the photograph of the Dursley branch train in *Fig. 28*, the leading carriage of which is a brake-third, apparently converted from a Brown, Marshalls 1850 third. From its opening for passenger traffic in 1856 until 1861, when the Midland took over the Dursley & Midland Junction Railway, the carriages for the service between Dursley and Dursley Junction (which was renamed Coaley Junction on 1st October 1870) had always been lent by the Midland. Externally framed third-class vehicles lasted some 15-20 years and would have been given two oil lamps in place of one after about 1860.

In the latter part of 1852 two third-class and two composite carriages were hired from Brown, Marshalls & Company for a few months. In the same year North Western Railway carriages were taken into Midland stock, including seven third-class carriages. At this time the works at Derby were unable to cope with all the carriage repairs and on 2nd May 1853 the Locomotive Committee decided to send 40 third-class carriages to Mr. Wright for

Fig. 28. Dursley branch train consisting of Midland externally framed brake-third and an earlier composite which were lent to the Dursley & Midland Junction Railway until it was taken over in 1861. The locomotive was used in the construction of the D & MJ, which acquired it in 1857. Stroud Museum photograph said to have been taken on 18th September 1856, the day passenger services began.

George Dow Collection

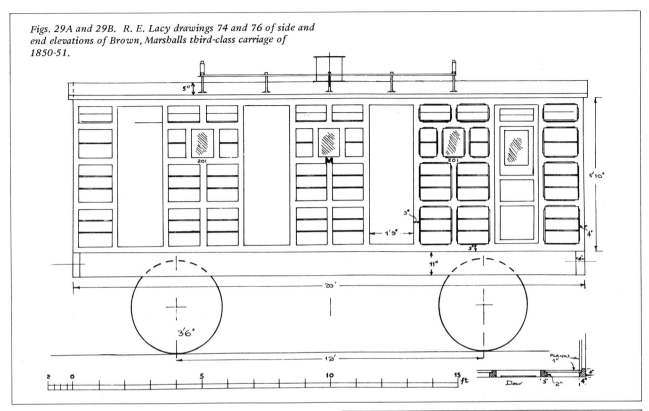

Figs. 29A and 29B. R. E. Lacy drawings 74 and 76 of side and end elevations of Brown, Marshalls third-class carriage of 1850-51.

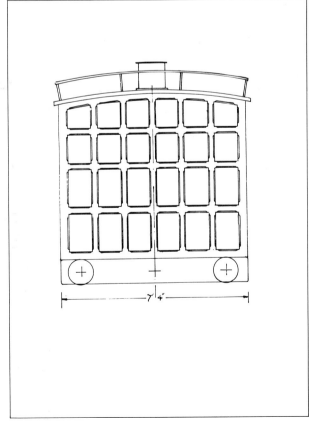

repair and painting. A little later, on 31st May 1853, L 1459 records that locks must forthwith be put on the doors of open carriages, these doubtless being third-class vehicles.

There are no further references to third-class carriages until 17th February 1858, when it was decided to get tenders for 40 of them. Wright & Sons' quotation of £120 each was accepted (L 3056-60) and on 16th March an order was given to Patent Shaft & Axletree Company for 3 ft 6 in wheels and axles at £32 12s. 6d. per set. Then on 19th April 1859 it was resolved by L 3293 that '. . . all the open Third Class Carriages to be enclosed during the present year . . .' Most of these would have been of the roofless kind and some may have been unclosed, with roof and open sides.

On 31st July 1860 it was decided to build 50 carriages, costing £10,000 in the company's shops, 30 of them to be third-class. They must be among the 54 third-class carriages which were added to stock in the period March 1860 to June 1861, but no reference can be found to the other 24. Another development in the same year related to lighting. On 23rd October 1860 L 3770 reports that additional lamps be provided in the third-class carriages 'in accordance with the minute of the Board of Trade'. As in 1866 only two lamps were fitted to new carriages it is evident that no more than one can have been provided before 1860.

From 1865 there was a more rapid increase in the number of third-class carriages, 604 being ordered from outside builders in 1865-72, as well as 66 constructed at

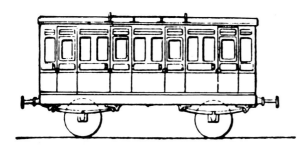

Fig. 30. 20 ft third-class carriage of 1865.

Derby. In this period additional lines opened enabled Midland trains to enter Manchester London Road station and its own new and magnificent London terminal at St. Pancras.

The first to be ordered were 100 on 15th February 1865, fifty being from the Oldbury Company at £128 10s. 0d. each and fifty from Gloucester Wagon Company at £129 18s. 6d. Although drawings of this particular carriage have not survived, it was illustrated in S. W. Johnson's presidential address, *Fig. 30*, and in the Gloucester Wagon Company's official photograph 36, reproduced as *Fig. 31*. The carriages were 20 ft long and 7 ft 8 in wide

outside, the inside height being 6 ft 6 in at the centre. Their wheels were 3 ft 6 in in diameter and the wheelbase was 12 ft. Although there were normally four compartments, the partitions did not reach above the level of the back-rest, as in all third-class carriages designed by Kirtley. Two oil lamps provided light for the whole carriage and there was a luggage rack on the roof. The seating capacity was 40.

A little over a year later 100 more third-class carriages were requested. On 1st May 1866 it was reported that Kirtley submitted plans for them, which implies fresh designs, but it is quite certain that they were similar to the previous batches. This time they were all ordered from Gloucester Wagon Company at a price of £136 each and probably carried the numbers 562-661.

Four more of the same type by the same builder were acquired in September 1866, when the stock of Spalding & Bourne Railway was purchased, and were in all likelihood numbered 662-5 by the Midland. The Spalding & Bourne was opened for traffic in 1866, all the rolling stock having been built by the Gloucester Wagon Company to Midland drawings. On 23rd July of the same year it became a constituent company of the newly formed Midland & Eastern Railway. The latter decided to sell the almost new Spalding & Bourne vehicles and the Midland bought them (L 5331 of 4th September 1866) at cost

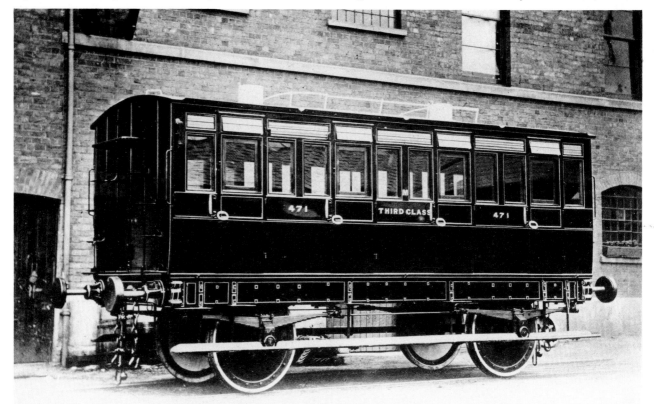

Fig. 31. No. 471, one of fifty 20 ft third-class carriages built by Gloucester Wagon Company for the Midland Railway in 1866. *(Gloucester Railway Carriage & Wagon Co. photo 36)*

Fig. 32. Spalding & Bourne Railway 24 ft first- and second-class composite No. 1 designed by Kirtley and built in 1866. (Gloucester Railway Carriage & Wagon Co. photo 42)

price less 7½%. The deal embraced 6 covered and 20 open goods wagons, 6 cattle wagons and 2 goods brakes, and the following passenger carriages:

Number of vehicles	Type	Cost each £	S & B Nos.	Estimated Midland Nos.
6	24 ft Composite carriages	310	1-6	312-7
4	20 ft Third-class carriages	203	1-4	662-5
2	18 ft Passenger vans	186	1-2	230-1

The composite and third-class carriages are illustrated in *Figs. 32* and *33* and the passenger van in *Fig. 44*. In all cases their Midland design was emphasised by the presence of the letter 'M' on the axleboxes.

There was a lull in construction until 1869. On 19th October of that year L 6061 records Chairman's Committee minute 1123 asking for the supply of a large number of vehicles, including '200 third-class carriages, 20 third-class compo break carriages'. An order for 100 third-class carriages at £122 17s. 6d. each from Brown, Marshalls and for a like number at £107 10s. 0d. each from the Railway Carriage Company is recorded in L 6172 of 1st March 1870. There is no further mention of the 'third-class compo break carriages', which it is assumed were brake-thirds, but L 6431 of 18th October 1870 notes rolling stock construction costs in the company's shop, including 5 'third-class breaks' at £1000. The 20 brake-thirds must have been among the 53 additional third-class carriages

built in the shops in 1869-70, some of which were recorded as 'breaks'. The carriages built by Brown, Marshalls were all delivered by 31st August and those by the Railway Carriage Company by 17th September 1870.

Contemporary accident reports and photographs show that branch line trains now quite commonly included one or two brake-third carriages, because there was usually not enough passengers' luggage to warrant the use of full brake vans. The brake-thirds had sufficient luggage accommodation and saved a good deal of weight. An old photograph taken at Barton station, Hereford, in about 1869 has permitted the production of a drawing of one of these vehicles, shown in *Fig. 34*. The passenger section seems to have been identical with that of third-class carriage No. 471, except that the doors were hung in the more usual way, with hinges on the left when viewed from outside. The guard's compartment had double doors, each with a drop-light, but no lookout. No luggage racks were fitted on the roof and it may be that by 1869 the Midland practice of providing them on carriage roofs had ceased. The brake gear would have resembled that on the brake van depicted in *Fig. 44*. The number 671 shown is an estimation.

Another type of brake-third appears in a photograph of St. Pancras station taken in 1868. Although generally similar to the 20 ft vehicle, it is clearly shorter, perhaps 18 ft or even a little less. The passenger accommodation seems to be the same, but the guard's compartment is only some 8 ft long, with double doors about 1 ft 6 in from the end. There is no mention in the records of the construction of brake-thirds in 1868, so the 18 ft type was perhaps a replacement of old stock. A drawing of it, based upon photographic evidence, is reproduced in *Fig. 47*.

During the period February 1871 to May 1872, 13 additional third-class carriages were built at Derby, these including 2 third-class and 5 brake-thirds for the London suburban service to and from Moorgate Street. Before the opening of St. Pancras on 1st October 1868 a Midland passenger service had been started between Bedford and Moorgate Street on 13th July of that year. The trains travelled to Kentish Town, whence their new 2—4—0T condensing locomotives took them forward via St. Paul's Road junction, King's Cross junction (underground) and over Metropolitan Railway metals to Moorgate Street. Ordinary carriages, gas-lit, with short buffers and couplings, were employed, so affording the first Midland example of close-coupled sets in suburban train operation.

Neither the number of trains originally provided for this service, nor their usual formation, is recorded. But the composition of the 10.48 a.m. train from Moorgate Street on 3rd August 1868, when it was involved in an accident near Hendon, is given in the Board of Trade accident report. It consisted of brake-third, third, second, 2 first, second, first, 2 second, brake-third, ten carriages in all and probably typical of the make-up of these set trains.

Further trains were provided in 1871, including four-compartment first-class and three-compartment second- and third-class carriages. When these new trains were completed there were probably 9 altogether in service. On 2nd January 1872 the Traffic Committee asked for a couple of additional trains of 10 carriages each for the Moorgate Street services. These appear to have been constructed at Derby between February and August 1872, for among the carriages turned out in this period were 12 first-class, 11 second-class, 2 third-class and 5 brake-thirds, enough for 2 trains with some spares.

These set trains were unusual in that they were gas-lit from their first appearance, although the majority of main line carriages continued to be lit by oil until the middle 1890s. At first the gas was carried in a bag enclosed in an iron box on the roof of the carriage. In 1871 two lamps were being fitted to each compartment (it is not known whether the first carriages had one or two lamps), an arrangement which became a permanent feature of these trains.

Further additional stock, amounting to over 500 vehicles and including 150 third-class carriages and 50 brake-thirds, was requested by the Traffic Committee on 2nd January 1872. Tenders accepted on 6th February were: 20 third-class at £160 each from Lancaster Carriage & Wagon Company; 35 third-class at £176 each from Metropolitan Railway Carriage & Wagon Company; 65 third-class at £174 15s. 0d. each, 30 third-class with

Fig. 33. Spalding & Bourne Railway 20 ft third-class carriage No. 1 built by Gloucester Wagon Company in 1866 to Midland drawings. *(Gloucester Railway Carriage & Wagon Co. photo 43)*

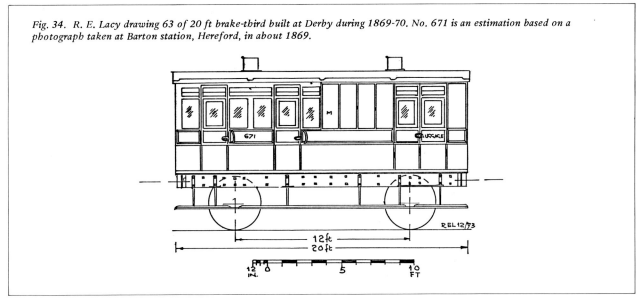

Fig. 34. R. E. Lacy drawing 63 of 20 ft brake-third built at Derby during 1869-70. No. 671 is an estimation based on a photograph taken at Barton station, Hereford, in about 1869.

luggage compartment at £175 each and 50 brake-thirds at £184 each from the Oldbury Company.

These orders were closely followed by the initiation of a policy of general improvement of standards of passenger comfort for which the Midland was to become world-famous. On 19th March 1872 the company announced that from 1st April next third-class passengers would be carried by all Midland trains. The outcome of this courageous and far-sighted move, inspired largely by the sagacious James Allport, the General Manager, is described in the next chapter.

Third-class carriages now being built had five compartments. They cost £224 to make in the company's shops and £233 from private firms, these figures including wheels and springs, which did not form part of the estimates previously given. Photographs of trains show that these new third-class carriages resembled the composite shown in *Fig. 41*, the overall length being about 25 ft and the wheelbase 19 ft. The brake-thirds will have been similar in length, with three passenger compartments and a brake compartment.

The known changes in third class stock since 1844 are given in Appendix 3. It is believed that the very first of the third-class carriages built by Clayton in 1876 as an addition to the capital stock was numbered 1132. Thus on 30th June 1873 there would have been 1131 third-class carriages in the capital stock. The list in Appendix 3 shows 193 third-class carriages in stock on 30th June 1850, with 921 additions after this, giving a total of 1114, leaving 17 carriages unaccounted for. These may have been built at Derby in the period 1850-58, before regular reports of renewals and additions to stock built in the works were included in the minutes, although the absorption of the stock of one or more of the smaller railways mentioned in the previous chapter may account for the difference.

Some composite carriages came into the possession of the Midland in 1844 and, as recorded on an earlier page, 10 of them were sold in September and October of that year. At the time this took place it was ordered that a first-class and a couple of second-class carriages were to be altered to 3 composites (B 159 of 10th September 1844). More composites were acquired when the Birmingham & Gloucester and Bristol & Gloucester Railways were taken over, the broad gauge vehicles of the latter being sold or replaced by standard gauge carriages by the end of 1857. L 432 shows that on 31st December 1849 the carriage stock included 55 composites, almost exactly 10% of the passenger carrying stock.

The earliest mention of a first- and third-class composite occurs in L 396 of 14th May 1850, when Kirtley was directed to convert 2 large first-class carriages into composites made up of first- and third-class and guard's compartments. A fortnight later it was ordered that a couple of carriages were to be altered to composites each seating 8 first- and 20 second-class passengers. On 6th April 1858 it was decided that a composite should be built at Derby 'to replace No. 6, which has not been in the company's possession since September 1852, and the Clearing House not being able to furnish any tidings respecting it' (L 3067). This is by no means the only report of missing vehicles in the minutes; it seems to have been quite easy for carriages to go astray in those days!

On 1st October 1861 tenders were sought for 20 composites, each 23 ft long and on 5th November Brown, Marshalls' tender for them at £245 each, with delivery in four months, was accepted. They consisted of 2 first- and 2 second-class compartments and are shown in *Fig. 35*, taken from S. W. Johnson's presidential address. They were larger than the previous standard gauge carriage on the Midland, with 15 ft wheelbase and compartments 6 ft 2 in and 4 ft 11½ in long by 7 ft 0 in wide. The inside

height was 6 ft 6 in, some 1 ft 6 in greater than the
B & DJ carriage of 1839, so at last it was safe to stand up
in a carriage! They were provided with three oil lamps
mounted so that each first-class compartment saw half of
each of two lamps and the second-class half of one.

From this time onwards there was an increasing use of
composite carriages, until by 1873 they numbered nearly
ten times as many as in 1850. In three accidents in 1867-9
the trains involved were composed entirely of composites
and guard's vans.

The *Bedfordshire Mercury* of 26th May 1862 contained
the following report: 'During the past week many persons
have visited the Midland station at Wellingborough to see
the express train pass which leaves London at 5.35 p.m.
and passes Wellingborough at about 7.01 p.m. A carriage
for Wellingborough passengers is attached to the train and
when it nears this station the guard, by a string attached
to the coupling irons, unfastens them and this carriage is
left behind to find its way to the station . . . .' which is a
rather quaint contemporary description of the first venture
of the Midland into the use of slip-carriages, initially introduced by the London, Brighton & South Coast Railway in
February 1858.

Midland slip-carriages were always composites, but
although the company's working timetable for December
1872 lists 13 slip-carriage services, no illustration of a
Kirtley-built vehicle can be traced. The services operated
in 1872 involved 11 trains, two of them from St. Pancras
having successive slips, Luton and Market Harborough
from one train and St. Albans and Kettering from the
other. In only one case is the return of the slip-carriage
mentioned: the 8.45 p.m. train from Leicester to Derby
departed from Kegworth at 9.29 p.m., and there is the
ambiguous note 'Three minutes allowed after leaving
Kegworth station to attach Slip Carriage.'

The probable stock of slip-carriages at the end of
Kirtley's régime was a minimum of 15 vehicles, allowing
for one or two to be in the shops for overhaul at any one
time. From 1874 onwards better documentation is available and the story of their development is continued in
Volume Two.

Certain types of saloons, such as the family saloon and
the invalid saloon, were rightly regarded as composite
vehicles in that they embodied a compartment for servants
travelling second- or third-class. Two of the earliest
appearing in Midland minutes were the former North
Western saloons mentioned in the previous chapter; they
were altered to family carriages in 1856 and thus probably
became composites. Two family saloons built in August
and September 1866 may have replaced them.

The earliest known reference to an invalid saloon is
contained in a notice dated 23rd January 1858. It reads:
'Invalid Carriages. A Carriage, with Couch, upon which an
invalid can recline, is kept at Derby Station, and can
(unless previously bespoken) be had, upon due notice

being given to the Station Master here, for the use of any
Passenger requiring such accommodation. Double the
usual First Class Fare of the Train travelled by is to be
charged for the Invalid using the same, and Single Fares
for other Passengers travelling therein.' It is not known
whether first-class and third-class accommodation, a
feature of later invalid carriages, was available.

In 1862 the Traffic Committee asked for a new family
saloon carriage and this was proceeded with under L 4190.
It is likely that it embodied a first-class section for the
family and a separate compartment for servants. It was
turned out of Derby works in December 1862, probably
carrying the number 107. The records show that two
other family carriages had been completed as additions to
stock in January 1862, doubtless similar to No. 107 and
in all likelihood numbered 105-6.

The next large order was for 60 twin-composite
carriages. This was the first use of the description 'twin-
composite', meaning a carriage of four compartments,
two first-class in the middle and a second- or third-class
compartment at each end. From about 1871 most twin-
composites had a luggage-box in the middle, between the
first-class compartments. The order went to Metropolitan
Railway Carriage & Wagon Company (L 4365 of 5th May
1863) who quoted £226 per vehicle, with delivery in July
to December. At the same time a tender was accepted for
the supply of 60 sets of 3 ft 6 in wrought iron wheels with
teak centres and Mansell's patent fasteners at £40 a set.
This was probably the first lot of carriages to be ordered
with wooden Mansell wheels, for the first trial batch of
these wheels had been ordered as recently as 1861. The
twin-composites were 23 ft or 24 ft in length.

Only four months later a further order was placed with
the same builder for 90 composites at £235 each, with
delivery by April 1864. No details are given, but they are
believed to be 24 ft long twin-composites, and all 150
would be generally similar to the Brown, Marshalls composites of 1862. It is, however, possible that the last 90 were
tri-composites with one third-class compartment. First-
and second-class composites now had a lamp to each
compartment.

Up to now almost all standard gauge carriages had been
carried on four wheels, but at the Locomotive Committee
meeting held on 17th January 1865 it was agreed that the
tender of the Metropolitan Company for altering twin-
composite carriages from 4 to 6 wheels be accepted. The
number of carriages to be dealt with is not recorded.

Records of vehicles built in the Derby shops show that
4 more family carriages were completed in August and
September 1865 as additions to stock. No more details
are given and the estimated numbers of them are 258-61;
it is known that Nos. 258 and 261 were Kirtley family
carriages, fitted with the Westinghouse brake in 1877.

The construction of more composites was authorised
on 5th June 1866, when an order was given to the Metro-

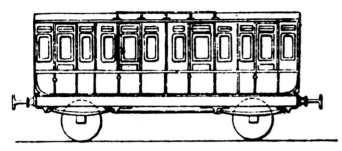

Fig. 35. First- and second-class composite of 1861.

politan Company for 50 at £258 each, springs and wood-centre wheels being ordered separately. They were 24 ft long and identical with those taken over from the Spalding & Bourne Railway, having 2 first- and 2 second-class compartments; they are illustrated in Fig. 36. At the same Locomotive Committee meeting it was agreed that 4 saloon carriages needed should be built in the company's shops. On the face of it this seems to indicate that they were to be additions to stock, but in fact they must have been the 2 first-class family saloons and the 2 family carriages built as renewals in August and September 1866.

It was still not possible to repair all carriages at Derby and on 5th May 1868 tenders of Brown, Marshalls and Metropolitan Railway Carriage & Wagon Company were accepted for repairing, repainting and retrimming 50 twin-composites. On the following 15th December it was decided to have 50 more twin-composites dealt with similarly. The Metropolitan Company was given the order at £62 per carriage, mahogany panels at 2s. 6d. each and whitewood castings at 1s. 6d. per sq ft being supplied by the firm. The Metropolitan Company was also successful

in getting a contract for 60 more 24 ft composite carriages at £230 each, awarded on 16th June 1868.

On 1st March 1870 a batch of three different types of carriage was ordered from the Metropolitan Company. It consisted of 30 twin-composites at £233 10s. 0d. each, 20 with 1 first-class, 2 second-class and 1 luggage compartment at £197 10s. 0d. each, and 10 with 1 compartment each for first-, second-, third-class and luggage. The last named tri-composites were the first to be recorded, but others were built subsequently. Their likely appearance would be similar to the carriage shown in Fig. 42, but in the older square-light style.

It was mentioned earlier that some composites were altered to six-wheelers in 1865. In 1870-1 experiments with the running of carriages were carried out, but precise details of the tests and conclusions reached therefrom have not survived. It is known, however, that four-wheeled carriages gave the best results, and that improved riding was afforded by 7 ft long bearing springs in comparison with the 6 ft type presently in use. The experiments are referred to somewhat obliquely in L 6665 (18th April 1871) in which is mentioned the resolution 'that 100 carriages of the length of No. 351, namely 24 feet, be altered to the pattern of No. 351 in accordance with the recommendation . . . . . report of experiments of 20 October and that experiment be continued . . . . . and especially as to Carriages of the length of 20 feet.' The latter would be the first-class vehicles, but No. 351 must have been one of the composites built in 1868, and had been altered and made the subject of the experiment. Some 7 ft springs must already have been purchased and L 6750 of 18th July 1871 refers to a decision to buy 100 more sets for composites.

On 20th June 1871 Kirtley reported that in accordance with instructions received from Mr. Price (the then Midland

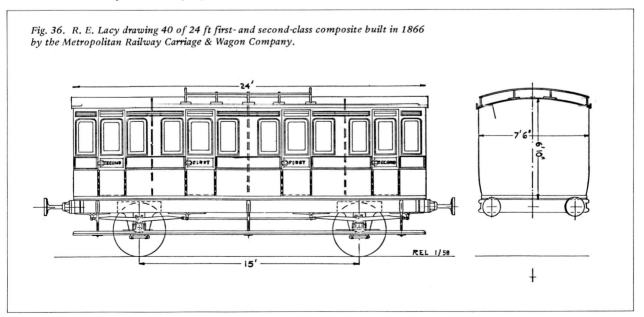

Fig. 36. R. E. Lacy drawing 40 of 24 ft first- and second-class composite built in 1866 by the Metropolitan Railway Carriage & Wagon Company.

Chairman), he had accepted a tender from Klett & Company of Nuremburg to supply a composite carriage, similar to those on the Hesse-Ludwig Railway, for the sum of £450 delivered at Nuremburg. The reason for the purchase is not known; perhaps it was the outcome of a Continental peregrination by a member of the Board! The drawing of the vehicle in *Fig. 37* was prepared from an illustration on page 266 of *Railway & Travel Monthly* of 1914. The body was 24 ft long by 8 ft 6 in wide overall, nearly a foot wider than Kirtley carriages, and 6 ft 6 in high inside. It seated 9 first-class passengers (3 in the coupé, which had observation windows and ledge table) and 16 second-class. The roof lamps, double handles to the doors, side handles, Roman numerals on the doors and other fittings were all of contemporary German pattern and the exterior was painted dark green. Because of the Franco-Prussian war it could not be delivered until November 1872. Numbered 146, it was put to work in the Leeds and Bradford district, where it was not appreciated by passengers. The Midland, sensitive to the views of its users, withdrew the carriage around 1880 and broke it up in May 1886.

There is no record of an officers' inspecting carriage before 1871 but on 18th July of that year the Traffic Committee asked for one to be provided. It was reported on 5th December that it had been completed and, in contrast to the directors' inspection carriages, which were numbered in the first-class series, it became No. 439 in the composite series. It is illustrated in *Figs. 38* and *39*, the former having been based on the photograph and a drawing in the Metropolitan-Cammell collection of a 27 ft 6 in carriage of the same generation, with round-cornered mouldings. The leading dimensions are estimated, but the internal arrangements are unknown, apart from the two partitions indicated. The device on the roof of the main saloon appears to be a siren for use when the vehicle was being propelled and as a means of communication with the engine driver. Apart from the facts that it was re-numbered 0439 when its replacement was built in 1887 and again 4390 not long before it was broken up *circa* 1905, nothing is known of its history.

On 2nd January 1872 a further request for more carriages was made (L 6938) and tenders for them were accepted on 6th February. The Oldbury Company was to build 15 twin-composites at £307 10s. 0d. each and the Metropolitan Company 60 twin-composites at £309 8s. 0d. each, 6 family carriages at £419 each and 4 invalid carriages at £269 15s. 0d. each. All were believed to be in the style adopted for the officers' inspection carriage, with round-cornered mouldings. The invalid carriages were numbered 446-9 and lasted until 1887, when they were replaced by new vehicles of Clayton's design; one of them, No. 448, was sold in July 1887 to the Eastern & Midlands Railway, being then described merely as a saloon. They included a third-class compartment for servants, but no illustration has survived, the drawing in *Fig. 40* having

Fig. 37. Composite No. 146 built 1872 by Klett & Co. of Nuremburg. Drawn by Gregory Fox from an illustration in 'Railway & Travel Monthly' of 1914.

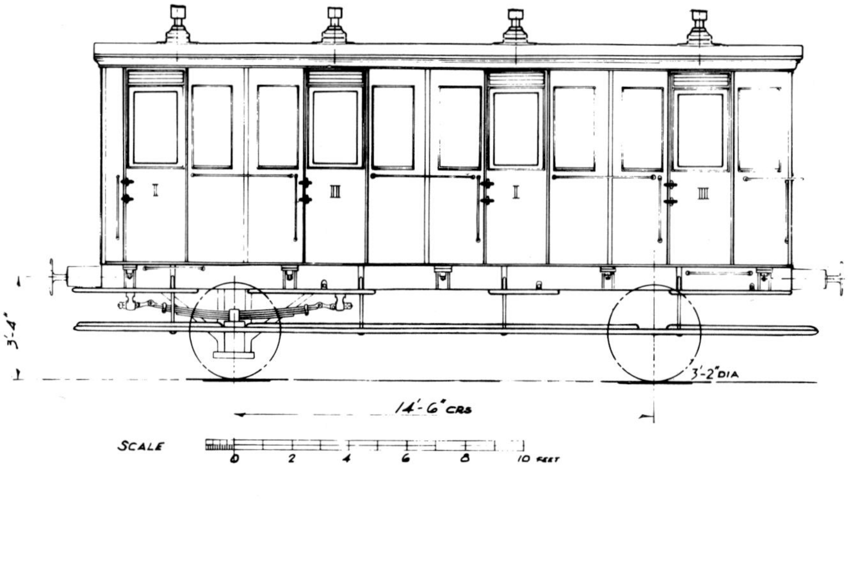

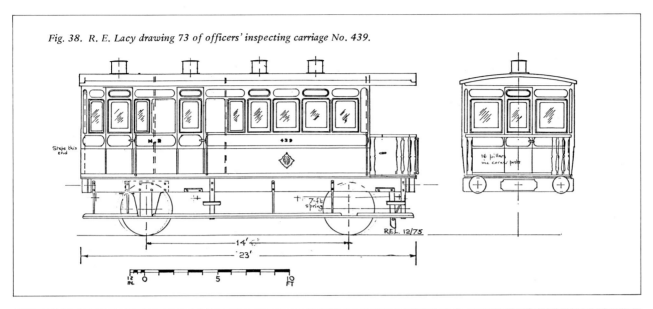

Fig. 38. R. E. Lacy drawing 73 of officers' inspecting carriage No. 439.

Fig. 39. Officers' inspecting carriage No. 439 built at Derby in 1871. *(DY 6569)*

Fig. 40. R. E. Lacy drawing 72 of 22 ft invalid carriage No. 447 built 1872
by Metropolitan Railway Carriage & Wagon Company.

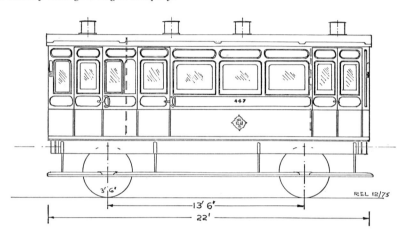

Fig. 41. R. E. Lacy drawing 42 of 27 ft 6 in 1st/2nd class composite with luggage compartment,
built 1872. Originally Nos. 228-287, renumbered 450-509 in 1874.

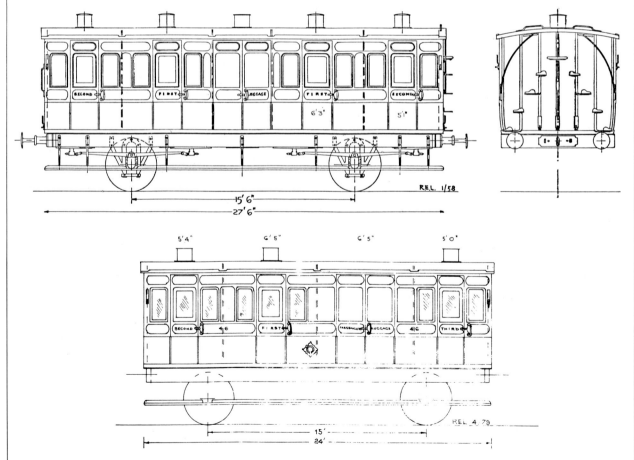

Fig. 42. R. E. Lacy drawing 58 of 24 ft tri-composite with luggage compartment built 1872-3.

Fig. 43. Interior of St. Pancras station in June 1876, photographed from the Midland Grand Hotel. *(George Dow Collection)*

been prepared from photographs of a grounded body near Derby. The six family carriages Nos. 440-5, also lasted until 1887 in the capital stock, No. 442 being sold in 1890 to the contractors Logan & Hemingway for £130. The twin-composites are illustrated in *Fig. 41*, which was copied from a tracing lent by the Metropolitan-Cammell Company. The original tracing shows droplights in the luggage doors, but the windows are crossed out, indicating that plain doors without windows were actually used.

These were the last additional composites built while Kirtley was in office, although others were constructed as renewals of old stock. L 7231 records, on 20th August 1872, the Traffic Committee's desire that for one year, as an experiment, no alteration was to be made in second- and third-class stock needing renewal, but composites renewed were to consist of 2 first-, 1 second- and 1 third-class compartments. This was agreed and doubtless the 10 composites built as renewals from November 1872 to September 1873 were of this type. No illustration of them has survived, but the first-class compartments were almost certainly in the middle, with a second-class at one end and a third-class at the other.

Fig. 42 has been drawn from what appears to be one version of these vehicles which can be seen in a photograph of St. Pancras station taken in June 1876, reproduced in *Fig. 43*. It seems to have had a luggage compart-

ment and a first-class compartment in the centre, with a third-class compartment at each end. T 19575 of 16th February 1875 refers to these carriages as follows: 'Alterations to carriages. It was explained that there were 32 carriages having one first-class, two third-class and a luggage compartment, which could be utilised with greater advantage if the luggage compartments were converted into first-class compartments. It was Resolved that the Carriage & Wagon Department be requested to alter them.' By this time all tri-composites would have been converted into first-third composites, and these 32 vehicles were presumably in part built as tri-composites and in part as first-second composites. Most will have been of the 1869 variety of carriage, with a few of the 1873 pattern. The example in the photograph still has a luggage compartment, for there are only three lamps on the roof.

Alterations to the stock of composite carriages during the years 1844-1873 are summarized in Appendix 4. The 14 carriages, Nos. 69-82, not accounted for were probably added between 1850 and 1858.

Remaining passenger-carrying vehicles calling for mention are the saloon carriages for pleasure parties, sometimes called picnic saloons. They contained one or more long compartments, usually with seats along the sides and tables down the middle. They were designed for only one class of passenger (mostly for first-class passen-

Fig. 44. Spalding & Bourne Railway 18 ft passenger brake van No. 1 built 1866. (*Gloucester Railway Carriage & Wagon Co. photo 44*)

gers during the Kirtley era) and did not accommodate servants, like the family and invalid saloons.

Two first-class saloons were ordered on 5th June 1866 and built at Derby. They are recorded as replacements, and it is not known whether they replaced old saloons or ordinary carriages, but it is likely that they were eventually altered to third-class vehicles. In 1870 a further first-class saloon was built as an addition to stock; it is mentioned in L 6431 of 18th October 1870 as then under construction in the company's shops at a cost of £350. The last saloons of Kirtley design were 6 ordered from the Metropolitan Company on 6th February 1872 and it is thought that they were generally similar to the invalid saloons built in the same year. They and the saloon of 1870 were probably numbered 1615-20 and 1614 respectively when they were all altered to third-class in 1884, only to be replaced two years later by new vehicles.

Before the introduction of continuous brakes the passenger brake vans, often called 'break' vans or simply passenger vans, were an essential part of every passenger train. They were, in fact, the only braked vehicles, except in the very earliest days when it was not uncommon to have a brakesman riding on carriages. Often there were two or more brake vans, depending on the length of the train, each with a guard who applied his handbrake when the driver whistled for brakes. According to Midland Appendix No. 13 to the Working Timetables of 1st February 1880, trains with more than 10 vehicles carried two guards, one in the front brake van and one in the rear. Trains with more than 20 vehicles had a third guard in a van near the middle. Pullman or bogie carriages counted as two vehicles. When the train ran over a foreign line it

seems to have been usual to provide a guard from this line in addition. Indeed, in one accident report there is a reference to three in a Midland van, one each from the Midland, S & DJR and LSWR.

There is no reference to passenger brake vans in the minutes of the old constituent companies, but F. S. Williams in his classic *The Midland Railway: its rise and progress* gives the following stock figures on page 120 of the 1878 edition: 'Breaks and parcels vans' 56 in 1845, 104 in 1846 and 167 in 1847, on 31st December each year. According to L 432, there were 145 'break vans' at the end of 1849, this number being reduced to 143 by 30th June 1850. It is not clear whether 'breaks and parcels vans' were brake vans which carried luggage, or whether reference was being made to two separate classes of vehicles.

Nothing is known of the first passenger brake vans, no drawing having been traced. The earliest built to Midland design, of which a full photograph exists, is one of the two Spalding & Bourne Railway vehicles constructed by the Gloucester Wagon Company in 1866, mentioned on page 27. It is illustrated in *Fig. 44*, which shows the unusual single lookout.

An older type of Midland brake van, of about 1860, is partly visible in a photograph of Temple Meads station at Bristol, taken before 1875 and in the collection of the Historical Model Railway Society. The picture is not clear, but in *Fig. 45* an attempt has been made to depict the general appearance of the vehicle. Its length is estimated to be 16 ft and its height the same as that of contemporary third-class carriages. From the photograph it seems to be narrower than the carriage to which it is coupled, so a width of 6 ft 7 in is not unlikely; the height from floor to roof centre is almost certainly the same, namely 6 ft 6 in. The late author thought that it may have had the single lookout embodied in the drawing, but the present author is of the opinion that whilst this might have been acceptable to a minor line such as the Spalding & Bourne, such an operational oddity is unlikely to have suited the Midland.

Changes in the stock of passenger brake vans over the years 1844-74 are set in Appendix 5. Renewals are shown in monthly returns given in the minute books, while in L 4331 of 17th March 1863 it is recorded that the Traffic Committee had asked for 20 extra vans, these to be built in the company's shops to capital account. Minutes indicated that 18 were constructed during May to September 1863 and maybe the other 2 were recorded erroneously as renewals.

The Oldbury vehicles of 1864 and 1866 cost £94 7s. 6d. and £112 10s. 0d. each respectively and the Spalding & Bourne vans £186 the two. The Railway Carriage Company vehicles of 1869 and 1870 cost £105 7s. 6d. and £107 each respectively and the 50 from the Oldbury Company in 1872 £140 each.

From these prices it may be surmised that there was little or no change in size and, possibly appearance, over the years 1863 to 1870, but the vehicles ordered in 1872 were appreciably more expensive and therefore probably bigger. In appearance they resembled the later Kirtley carriages. *Fig. 46* is a tentative drawing of one of the 1872 20 ft passenger brake vans. An accident report of 1875 notes their weight as 6 tons 12 cwts.

The records show that 178 passenger brake vans were renewed in 1859-73, which is about 40 more than the stock in 1852. It seems therefore that the vans built in

Fig. 45. R. E. Lacy drawing 77 of 16 ft passenger brake van of circa 1860, based on negative 17627 of the Historical Model Railway Society.

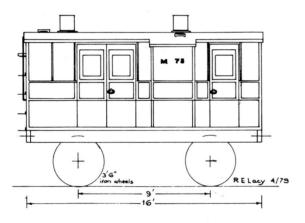
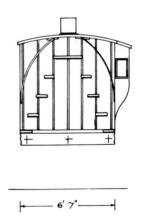

Fig. 46. R. E. Lacy drawing 59 of 20 ft passenger brake van of 1872, based on available photographic evidence.

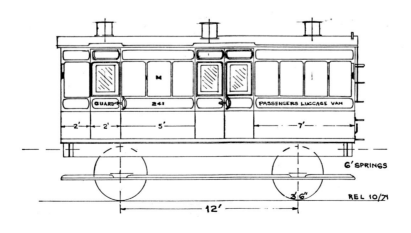

1859-61 must have been renewed by 40 new ones built at Derby in 1870-73, no doubt because the old ones were too light for the heavier trains which had come on the scene. If, as it is believed, there were 331 passenger brake vans at the end of 1873, the stock was probably made up of: 50 of the latest type built by the Oldbury Company in 1872; 20 similar built at Derby in 1872-73; 142 of the smaller vans made by firms in 1863-70; and about 120 of the same type turned out of Derby in 1862-71. CW 975 records that 9 of the newest Oldbury vehicles, Nos. 285/94/95, 304/8/15/21/23/26 were fitted with the Westinghouse automatic brake in 1875.

Before turning to the other non-passenger carrying vehicles some further information gleaned from the minute books should be mentioned.

Wheels on the earliest carriages were generally 3 ft in diameter, but by 1848 had been increased to 3 ft 6 in. L 2167 of 4th March 1856 records an instruction to Kirtley that wrought iron wheels were to be used henceforth exclusively for the renewal of carriages and wagons. The first reference to the use of Mansell-type wheels is given in L 4001 of 1st October 1861, when it was decided to order 10 sets of wheels with wood centres and iron tyres from the Patent Shaft & Axletree Company at a cost of £42 per set.

From this time onwards all additional passenger carrying vehicles were provided with teak-centred wheels with Mansell patent fasteners, but other vehicles continued to have spoked wrought iron wheels, while it seems that older carriages were not altered, because a report dated 5th October 1875 shows that there were still 2,020 four-wheeled carriages fitted with wrought iron wheels. There had been several accidents in the preceding few years as a result of carriage and locomotive tyres breaking. In most cases the break occurred through one of the screwed holes by which the tyres were attached to the rim of the wheel. The Board of Trade Inspectors of Accidents had frequently called attention to the dangers of this method of fixing, but the Midland had taken no action to replace them.

By the 1850s some railways were already fitting brakes to all their stock and in L 2180 of 1st April 1856 there is a reference to the requirements of the East Lancashire Railway with regard to the fitting of Midland carriages with Newall's brakes, but no subsequent action can be traced. Not until 1864 is there any further mention of Midland carriages being fitted with brakes and, presumably, a guard's compartment, when it was agreed that 50 old first-class vehicles were to be altered to third-class with brakes. These would have had one compartment for the use of the guard and so merit the description of brake-third.

The increasing number of fatal train accidents demanded the development of satisfactory automatic continuous brakes, which the Board of Trade had frequently advocated in the early 1860s. The Midland, well to the fore with block signalling, had not given continuous brakes the attention they deserved. However, in the autumn of 1869, as E. G. Barnes records in *The Midland Main Line* (1969), the Midland Board initiated trials with the Wilkin & Clarke chain brake. Spread over nine months, these were carried out successively between Leeds and Bradford and between London and Bedford in the winter of that year, on the Birmingham-Bristol line, including the Lickey incline, during April 1870 and between London and Leicester three months later. Thereafter Kirtley reported that this form of brake was unsuitable 'being subject to mechanical and maintenance difficulties'. Another five years were to elapse before further brake trials took place.

On 5th August 1851 L 786 directed that side chains were forthwith to be fitted to all carriages. This was amplified on 4th November, with the order to fix side chains to all passenger carriages, horse boxes, carriage trucks and goods wagons as quickly as possible. So began a practice which, on passenger train stock, was to last until 1896.

Communication between guard and engine driver became more difficult when the former left the carriage roof for a brake van at the rear of a train, and a somewhat drastic method of achieving direct contact is noted in L 961 of 14th October 1851, wherein it was resolved 'That the side steps of the carriages, Horse Boxes and Carriage Trucks used on Passenger Trains be lengthened so as to enable the Guard to communicate with the Driver in case of need. This practice having been recommended by Capt. Wynn and approved by the London & North Western Railway Company' One doubts whether the gallant captain ever attempted such a dangerous feat! There is no evidence that these alterations were ever carried out, and L 1601 of 27th December 1853 reads 'In accordance with the proceedings of the Clearing House delegates at their meeting on 14th December, Mr. Kirtley was instructed to apply the Communication between Guards and Drivers to the through Passenger Trains between Leeds and Rugby and Mr. Kirtley's own plan between Syston and Peterboro'. ' Information as to the system adopted is not given in the minutes and no details can be traced of Kirtley's arrangement. But an earlier minute, L 1440 of 2nd May 1853, had referred to a Railway Clearing House meeting on passenger communication cords and mentioned there was to be a bell on the engine. It took some time to fit all the necessary apparatus, and L 2098 of 6th November notes a report from Kirtley that by the end of the year he should be prepared to effect the communications between the guard and the driver of all passenger trains. This system was used for some years, but on 16th March 1869 the following Board minute of 3rd March was reproduced in L 5931: 'Resolved that the Locomotive Department be requested to fit up with all possible despatch the Company's Passenger Carriages and Vans in accordance with the principle of the cord communication between Passengers and Guard as approved by the Board of Trade.' The way in which this differed from the earlier system is not given.

In the photograph of third-class carriage No. 471 on page 26 three rings on the bottom moulding to carry a cord between guard and driver may be discerned. By 1870, however, the cord was strung along the edge of the roof, on pulleys fastened to the guttering, so that the cord could be reached through the droplight by a passenger. Some ten years later there was a reversion to rings, doubtless because they were cheaper and less liable to jam.

The normal illuminant for carriages was oil. The earliest reference to it in Midland minute books is in L 247 of 1st January 1850, which mentions the supply of oil for the travelling post office between Rugby and Normanton. There is no record of the kind of lamps used, but on 21st April 1857 it was resolved to adopt the London & North Western pattern, if endorsed by Allport and Kirtley. As mentioned earlier, the lighting of the older carriages was very meagre. The 23 ft composites built in 1861-3 had only 3 lamps, fitted above the partitions, so that each second-class compartment saw only half a lamp and the first-class 2 half lamps. The 24 ft composites of 1864 were more generously provided, having a lamp over the middle of each compartment. The outer casing of these lamps appears to have been a fixture, only the lamps proper being lifted out in the daytime for attention.

Oil lighting was continued for most Midland carriages for many more years, but with the opening of the London extension in 1868 gas lighting was provided in the suburban trains running over the Metropolitan Railway to and from Moorgate Street. L 5742 of 16th June 1868 reports the acceptance of the tender of W. Dalziel to fit up the carriages on these trains. This embraced gas apparatus and fittings for 3 lamps per carriage at £25 per carriage, with extra charge of £2 for each additional set of lamps required over 3 sets, and the supply of a steam engine and boiler for charging the carriages with gas at £300. Evidently at this time only one lamp per compartment was fitted, but in later installations there were two. This is made clear by L 6736 of 4th July 1871, which records acceptance of tenders from the Railway Carriage & Steam Boat Gas Lighting Company of Bury, to equip four-compartment first-class carriages with 8 lights at £48 10s. 0d. and three-compartment second-class and third-class carriages with 6 lights at £45 each. Bags were £3 5s. 0d. each and galvanised iron covers £4 10s. 0d., the former being conveyed inside the latter on carriage roofs.

When the Midland came into being its by-laws forbade smoking in carriages. In time some relaxation took place and L 5689 of 17th March 1868 reads 'Smoking Carriages. Upon consideration of Traffic Committee Minute No. 14813 requesting that all first and second class Passenger Compartments should be made available for smoking it was suggested that as a great part (perhaps the majority) of our Passengers feel objections to the smell of Tobacco,

which adheres to Carriages which have been used for smoking, it would appear to give better accommodation to our Passengers as a *whole* if the fittings for the purpose of smoking be attached only to one first and one second class compartment in each twin Composite Carriage, and to one compartment in each First Class Carriage of three compartments.'

The members of the Traffic Committee must have been heavy smokers to countenance such a recommendation as *all* first- and second-class compartments and the restraint of the Locomotive Committee is most commendable. Indeed, this restraint had been tightened by the late 1870s. The Midland Appendix to the Working Time Table dated 18th April 1878 laid it down that station masters must be guided by the circumstances of each case as to the number of compartments to be reserved for smokers, but considered that as a rule 2 first-class and 3 third-class compartments per train would be sufficient. The Appendix gave further instructions as to the use of the boards, which were lettered 'Smoking Compartment' and placed in slots fixed to receive them over the compartment doors on both sides. They were kept at each of the principal terminal stations and the station masters held personally responsible for their proper fixing and storage.

Destination boards antedated smoking boards. L 3046 of 2nd March 1858 ordered the supply of 200 'notice' boards and brackets for fixing on the carriages of through trains, similar to the pattern approved. The Appendix just mentioned directed that the labelling of carriages with destination boards should be carried out with great care and at least fifteen minutes before the train concerned is due to depart; that boards on incoming trains at terminal stations are to be removed immediately on arrival of the trains and before the carriages are shunted; and that station masters must appoint one or more of their staff to attend to the fixing and removal of the boards.

Special roof boards with the legend 'Midland. To and from Moorgate Street' were carried by the diminutive brake-thirds of the suburban trains operated over the Metropolitan Railway, as exemplified in *Fig. 47*. These were fixed permanently, not slotted in brackets. Their finish is not recorded, but it is almost certain to have consisted of gilt lettering on a crimson lake background to match that of the carriages.

Of the remaining non-passenger carrying vehicles the earliest, so far as coaching stock is concerned, were carriage trucks and horseboxes, the former to transport the road carriages of the gentry, the latter their horses. F. S. Williams' Midland history records 95 carriage trucks and horse-boxes in use at the end of 1845, 151 a year later and 225 at the end of 1847. Stocks of each type of vehicle were kept at the principal stations, so that passengers could drive up in their own horse and carriage (at least a quarter of an hour before time of departure, requested a Grand Junction Railway timetable of 1837), these then being put aboard the train so that they would be ready on

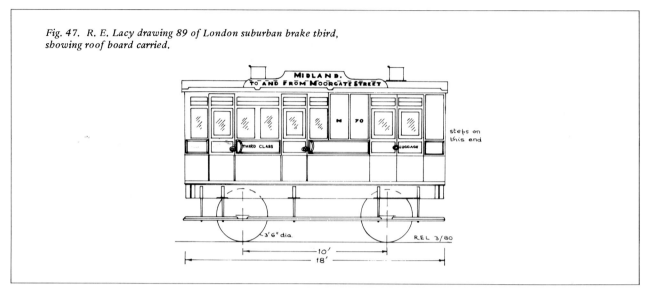

Fig. 47. R. E. Lacy drawing 89 of London suburban brake third, showing roof board carried.

arrival at destination, which demonstrates that there is nothing new about Motorail of the present day! Old engravings show passengers riding in their own carriages conveyed on a carriage truck, but it is not known whether this was permitted on the Midland and if so, how long the practice lasted. By the time that photographs began to be taken of trains it was usual for horse-boxes to be marshalled at the head of passenger trains and open carriage trucks at the rear.

On 31st December 1849 the Midland stock of horse-boxes totalled 111. The oldest known type consisted of a short central compartment holding up to 3 horses side by side, flanked fore and aft by shallow harness or dog-boxes with sloping lean-to roofs. One of these vehicles is shown in an engraving of a passenger train near Leicester, illustrated on page 386 of F. S. Williams' Midland history; another may be seen in *Fig. 43* of St. Pancras. The sketch of it in *Fig. 48* is based on the drawing of a similar Great Northern Railway horse-box reproduced by D. K. Clark and modified to agree with the vehicle in St. Pancras.

L 4172 of 5th August 1862 mentions the alteration of horse-boxes as they require renewal, but gives no details. But it undoubtedly heralded the appearance of a new style of vehicle embodying a compartment in which an attendant groom could travel. L 4331 of 17th March 1863 directed that a dozen of these improved horse-boxes were to be constructed in the company's shops to capital account, but in the event they were ordered from the Gloucester Wagon Company on 5th May 1863 at a price of £95 10s. 0d. each, to be delivered in July and August. It is believed that the batch was numbered 133-144. The internal fittings were so arranged that up to three horses could be accommodated, with their heads nearest the groom's compartment, which was simply furnished and oil-lit. The drawing in *Fig. 49* is based on known dimensions of Kirtley carriages, with proportions adjusted to agree with *Fig. 50*. In construction horse-boxes were

usually intermediate between a goods van and a passenger vehicle, often having a planked outer skin, made of tongued-and-grooved planks with a bevelled edge, but in later years the passenger compartment often had a coach-built finish.

About 125 horse-boxes were built in the Derby shops during the years 1858-73, all as renewals of old vehicles. Thus the great majority of these in service in 1858 must have been renewed during the following 15 years although the 1876 view of St. Pancras shows one of the pre-1862 vehicles.

L 6059 of 5th October 1869 reported that horse-boxes Nos. 18, 108 and 140 were missing. No. 18 was never found and was replaced by a new one with the same number in 1870. Alterations to the stock of horse-boxes during 1844-1873 are given in Appendix 6.

The Gloucester Wagon Company horse-boxes of 1863 and 1866 cost £95 10s. 0d. and £98 each respectively, those built by Brown, Marshalls £78 and those by Claye £92 17s. 6d., approximations which suggest little difference between them.

Two hound vans were built to Kirtley's design in March 1873 and a third at some unspecified date, all three being broken up in 1893. They may have been given numbers in the horse-box series.

Several different types of vehicles were numbered amongst the carriage trucks, and the minute books do not always make it clear whether the term carriage truck is being used as a collective description of the vehicles or means in fact carriage trucks proper. With this reservation the first to be dealt with are the carriage trucks proper, namely flat open vehicles designed to carry horse-drawn carriages, these being loaded from one end over suitable ramps. On 31st December 1849 there were 100 in stock and in the second half of 1855 16 were renewed. L 3736 of 4th September 1860 ordered an additional carriage truck to be built for the use of Holmes & Company, the

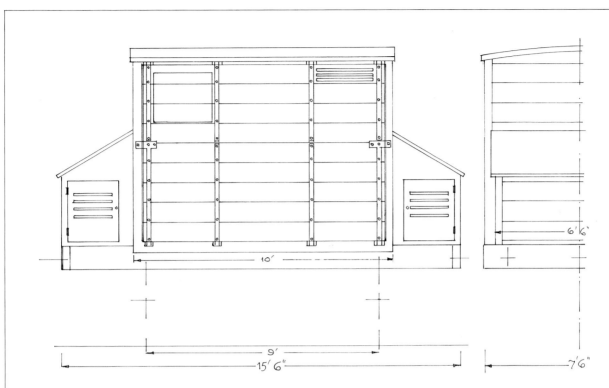

Fig. 48. R. E. Lacy drawing 64 of early pattern Midland horse box.

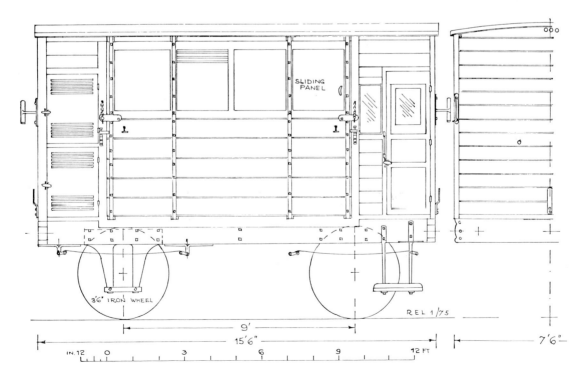

Fig. 49. R. E. Lacy drawing 65 of horse box built during the years 1863-73.

firm to be charged the cost less that of the wheels and framing. This vehicle was doubtless for the delivery of horse carriages newly built by Holmes and was one of six additional carriage trucks built at Derby in 1861. On 18th February 1862 approval was given to a request from James Allport, the General Manager, for a corpse van to be built in place of a carriage truck when broken up.

Although there were renewals each year there were no alterations to the stock until 1868, when the Traffic Committee asked for 20 open carriage trucks to be converted into covered carriage trucks. This was agreed and the cost charged to revenue (L 5811 of 5th September 1868). This seems to be the earliest reference to the covered type.

On 16th March 1869 there was a request for a further corpse van, but there is no reference to it replacing another vehicle and it is not known whether it was allotted to the carriage truck series or Post Office van series. On 1st February of the following year tenders were invited for more carriage trucks which, in fact, were built at Derby. There is a record of 21 being constructed in 1870, including a couple of the covered type.

A further large batch of stock included 50 carriage trucks, 6 milk vans and 10 open poultry trucks. The first named were ordered from the Lancaster Carriage & Wagon Company on 6th February 1872 and the others were taken in hand by the Derby shops. The milk vans cost £171 each and the poultry trucks £100, all being turned out during February-September 1872. A further 8 milk vans built early in 1873 were likely replacements of a similar number of carriage trucks, reducing the latter stock to 157, of which 22 were covered.

Appendix 7 summarises the carriage truck series during 1844-1873.

The final series of non-passenger carrying vehicles to be considered was one which, in addition to Post Office carriages, embraced a miscellany of vans for the conveyance of bullion, stores, parcels, newspapers and corpses.

It appears that there must have been a bullion van from early days, because one was renewed in 1862, but no details have survived either of the old one or its successor. Stores vans were used by the Stores Department and usually had a single compartment with various fittings for securing loads. Records indicate that an additional stores van was built in March 1864, 3 were renewed in 1865-66 and 2 more additional built in 1870, thought to be Nos. 45 and 46. Parcels vans very likely contained three compartments with special locks on the doors. It is known

Fig. 50. Horse box No. 144, one of twelve built in 1863 by Gloucester Wagon Company. *(Gloucester Railway Carriage & Wagon Co. photo 50)*

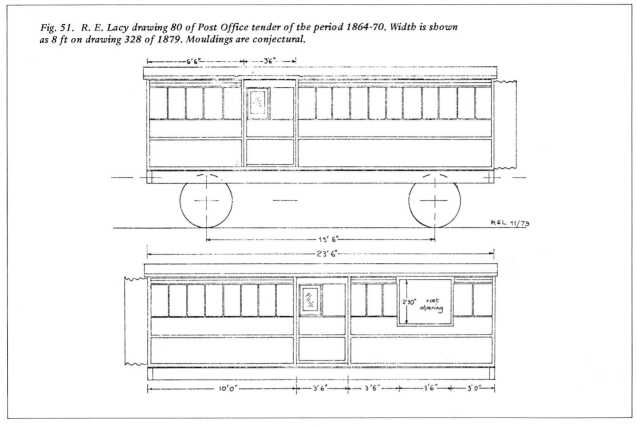

Fig. 51. R. E. Lacy drawing 80 of Post Office tender of the period 1864-70. Width is shown as 8 ft on drawing 328 of 1879. Mouldings are conjectural.

that 5 were renewed in 1868-69 and 9, believed to be Nos. 35-44, built in 1869-70 (L 6285). A newspaper train was certainly in use before 1873, but it is not known whether special vans were used. At least 2 of the newspaper vans built as renewals in 1880 took the numbers, 37 and 41, of parcel vans constructed in 1870. In 1888 4 corpse vans were renewed, 2 numbered in the carriage truck series and 2 in the Post Office carriage series, but only 2 are recorded before 1873; 1 was a renewal of a carriage truck, the attribution of the other being unknown. No photographs or drawings of any of these vehicles have been traced.

After successful experiments on the Grand Junction Railway, 4 travelling Post Office carriages were put into service by the London & Birmingham Railway between Euston and Denbigh Hall in 1838. Very soon the run was extended to Birmingham and then to Preston, and by 1848 had reached Carlisle, Glasgow and Aberdeen. In the meantime, the second travelling Post Office was established in May 1845 between Rugby and Newcastle-upon-Tyne, running via Derby, Normanton and York. It was operated by the Midland Railway as far as Normanton and thence by the York & North Midland and York, Newcastle & Berwick Railways. To work the service the Midland ordered two carriages. B 160 of 10th September 1844 states that it was 'resolved that Mr. Wright's tender to build two flying Post Offices in every respect the same as

the one he is building for the London and Birmingham Co. to be completed with all possible dispatch for the sum of £460 each be accepted.'

A Post Office record of 8th October 1847 states that 'between Rugby and Newcastle a TPO is maintained in connection with the night mail only, and for this service no additional charge is made by the Rly Cos.' However, on 14th June 1850 B 436 records that enquiry was to be made as to the mode of charging the TPO between the Midland, Y & NM, YN & B and North British companies.

The Trent Valley line between Rugby and Stafford was opened in 1847, but it was not until 1852 that the TPO between Rugby and Derby was discontinued, to be replaced by one between Tamworth and Derby, giving a direct link with the Gloucester and Tamworth TPO (which began on 1st July 1850), and thus between Gloucester and Newcastle. In April 1852 this train left Gloucester at 9.00 p.m. and arrived at Newcastle at 9.00 a.m., the return times being 4.00 p.m. and 4.10 a.m. Three years later, sorting began between Bristol and Gloucester, as a result of the accelerated timing introduced on 1st March 1853 following the installation of many more sets of mail exchange apparatus.

There was also a day mail running between Derby and Newcastle, but little is known of it. C. W. Ward, whose *English TPOs, their history and postmarks,* published in 1949, provides most of the TPO services information given in this chapter, stated that this day mail was certainly in operation in the years 1862-70 and was involved in accidents in 1864 at Darlington and Staveley. At least two carriages must have been in use and records (Post 30/179) indicate that two were built for the service in 1867.

According to Ward, a Rugby and Leeds day mail began to run in October 1852 and L 1284 of 17th November of that year records 'The Postmaster General is to require a TPO for Day Mail between Rugby and Leeds. The Midland Company to offer to take the present Rugby to Edinburgh carriages at a fair valuation, the present ones being too small. The Company is willing to join in, with the Y & NMR, YN & BR and NBR, the mileage cost of new ones to same size as those now on L & NWR between London and the North.' No information about the carriages built for this service appears to have survived. This day mail ran until after May 1854, but it is not known when it ceased and no postmarks have been found.

A Post Office carriage between Derby and Lincoln is believed to have been introduced in 1859. A bag tender was in operation between Tamworth and Lincoln by 1865 and by 1867 a sorting carriage was in use, connecting with the London & North Western TPO at Tamworth so that Irish mail need not go via London. The commencing date is in doubt but is generally supposed to be 20th May 1867, when sorting carriages had been prepared for the service. However, correspondence between the Post Office and the Midland suggests that two old Post Office carriages Nos. 13 and 17 may have been altered in October or November 1866 as a temporary measure to enable the service to begin as soon as possible.

In 1864 a night mail train was established between King's Cross and Leicester, via the Hitchin-Bedford line, but it is not known whether it was a TPO. It was succeeded sometime before 1875 by a St. Pancras-Derby service which connected with the Bristol-Newcastle TPO at Derby. References have also been found to two carriages used by the Post Office in 1867 on the 2.50 p.m. train from Derby to King's Cross (L 5448); to a St. Pancras-Masborough night sorting carriage of 1868; and to a St. Pancras-Leeds TPO service. But no further information about any of them can be traced and this brief and incomplete review of Midland postal services up to 1873 must now give way to the postal vehicles themselves.

The first two 'flying Post Offices' built by J. Wright of Birmingham in 1844 and mentioned earlier were 16 ft long, 7 ft high and 7 ft 6 in wide, which were the dimensions of the London & Birmingham vehicle. A replica of one of the latter was built by the LMS in 1938 for the L & BR centenary celebrations and is illustrated on page 22 of *Nineteenth Century Railway Carriages* by C. Hamilton Ellis (1949). L 432 of 14th June 1850 shows that on 31st December 1849 Midland postal coaching stock had grown to 11 Post Office and mail carriages, but the distinc-

tion between the two types is not apparent; perhaps mail carriages indicated storage vans only, with no facilities for sorting. There must have been sufficient spares to work the Gloucester-Tamworth TPO from mid-1850, for it was not until 28th August of that year that two Post Office sorting carriages were ordered for that service by L 481. Nothing is known of the type of vehicle and one must have been a spare since the trip was such a short one.

In 1852 new carriages were built for the Rugby-Leeds day mail. L 1284 is not too clear and can be interpreted to mean that the 'present Rugby to Edinburgh carriages' would be taken over by the Midland for use between Rugby and Leeds and replaced by new and larger vehicles for the Edinburgh service, being paid for jointly by the Midland, Y & NM, YN & B and North British Railways. There is no record of their construction nor which company nominally owned them.

L 2967 of 5th October 1857 refers to a letter from Allport, the General Manager, regarding new Post Office tenders but gives no details. A fortnight later, L 2978 notes a resolution that the shares of the North Eastern (formed in 1854 by the fusion of the Y & NM, YN & B and Leeds Northern Railways) in Post Office carriages Nos. 1, 2 and 3 amounting as per valuation to £363 2s. 3d. be charged to capital account. The implication is that Nos. 1, 2 and 3 might be the new tenders mentioned by Allport, replacing 3 old carriages bearing the same numbers. The previous ones were jointly owned with the North Eastern, but the new vehicles were to be wholly owned by the Midland.

It seems that two further Post Office vans were built soon afterwards, because L 3087 of 18th May 1858 orders that the cost of two new six-wheeled Post Office vans was to be charged to capital and notes that two vans originally constructed as Post Office vehicles had been altered to first-class carriages. The six-wheeled vehicles were the first to be recorded on the Midland. They were evidently replacements of 2 old vans, but regarded as capital additions because the old vans were altered to first-class carriages in the capital list. Both transactions occurred just before the minutes began giving monthly returns of stock built, so the details must remain obscure.

L 3709 of 17th July 1860 recorded a request for 3 additional Post Office carriages at a cost of £1,500. They were built at Derby in December 1860. There is no note of their intended use and their likely numbers were 15-16. In October 1861 one TPO tender was renewed and during the period April to August 1864 four of the old Post Office vans were replaced by new vehicles turned out of Derby.

Page 87 of Hendy's manuscript in the GPO Record Room indicates that gangways between vehicles were introduced on Post Office carriages in 1866, but it is not known whether all existing carriages were so fitted,

Fig. 52. Typical Kirtley train of c.1869. 2—4—0 No. 55 and 4 four-wheelers arrive at Barton station, Hereford, from Brecon. *(Hereford Library photo 5773A)*

Midland records being silent on the point. It is presumed that they were 2 ft wide, like those on the Clayton carriages of 1879.

Correspondence on the establishment of the Lincoln and Tamworth sorting carriages survives in GPO archives (Post 30/179) and the following extracts are of interest as showing the degree of control exercised by the Post Office over the design of carriages. The Inspector General of Mails had asked whether the Midland had any spare carriages suitable for the new duty; William Slade, of the Post Office, wrote him on 20th September 1866:

'I have been in communication with the Midland Railway Company's Carriage Builder, carefully compared the Mail Office and the Company's record of Mail Carriages. I have also examined the spare Railway Post Offices and Tenders, and I consider that there are no Sorting Carriages of any description belonging to the Company available for the proposed Lincoln and Tamworth duty. The two carriages used for the present Lincoln and Tamworth service are Nos. 13 and 17, they are rather too low in the roof, but they are good serviceable carriages and might, I think, easily be made suitable for a sorting duty for one clerk. Their dimensions are as follows: Length 15 ft 4 in, width 6 ft 1 in, height 5 ft 10 in (2 in higher between the roof timbers).'

In a further letter of 24th September, Slade thinks that there would be no difficulty in raising the roofs 'as has been done with other mail carriages, but seeing that the making of new doors and windows and adapting the carriage in other respects would involve a good deal of work, I think it doubtful whether it would not be better to build new shells entirely rather than raise the roofs if you think this really necessary.'

At this time consideration was being given to the design of the carriages used on the Derby-Newcastle day mail, following complaints on 22nd August and 23rd September 1866 by one of the staff that they had only one door, and that on the nearside, although the night mail tenders had a door both sides. Consequently it was necessary at some North Eastern stations to pass heavy mail-bags through a window on the offside, while at Newcastle the staff had to leave the carriage by climbing down to the track and thence on to the platform. This was not only dangerous, but contrary to railway regulations. The latter point seemed to decide the issue and it was agreed to build 2 new carriages for the Derby-Newcastle day mail modelled upon those in use between Bristol and Newcastle. A couple of the day mail TPOs were to be altered for the Lincoln and Tamworth duty. Harland, chief foreman of the Midland carriage shops, referred to as the 'carriage builder' in Post Office records, assented, saying it would take nearly three months to build two new carriages and that he could adapt the old ones temporarily for immediate use. On 12th October 1866 it was agreed: the Lincoln and Tamworth carriages Nos. 13 and 17 were not to be altered, but 2 new ones were to be built to the same design as 'No. 2 Railway Post Office'; new vehicles were to be built for the Derby and Newcastle day mail; the present day mail carriages were to be adapted for Lincoln and Tamworth duty; and temporary fittings were to be provided in Nos. 13 and 17.

L 5372 of 6th November 1866 records that 2 new Post Office vans for the Derby and Newcastle day mail were to be additions to stock and built in the company's shops at a cost of £1,000. One was completed in February 1867 and the other in the following April, their numbers believed to be 7 and 8.

A summary of Midland Post Office carriages during the period 1844-73 is given in Appendix 8.

During the first few years of the Midland it was customary to send carriages away to private builders for all but minor repairs. An 1844 map of Derby station and works reproduced in C. R. Clinker's Dugdale Society paper *The Birmingham & Derby Junction Railway* indicates that only a very modest area was allotted to carriage shops, originally erected by the North Midland. That some work was undertaken is confirmed by the list of painting contract prices for labour agreed to in L 197 of 6th December 1849 and reproduced below; indeed, there is a reference to new work in the list:

Coupé with 4 compartments	each	£12
First class	,,	11
Composite	,,	11
Second class	,,	9 10s.
Enclosed third class	,,	9
Open	,,	7
Van	,,	9
Carriage truck	,,	2 12s.
,,　　,,　　if new	,,	3
Horse box	,,	2
,,　　,,　　if new	,,	4

On 14th May 1850 L 396 ordered Kirtley to build 2 second-class carriages to replace those broken up and this is the first minuted reference to new construction in the Derby carriage shops. It is believed that from this time onwards the building of all carriages needed for the renewal of old ones broken up was carried out in the company's shops, although most additional stock continued to be constructed by outside contractors. In addition, batches of vehicles were from time to time repaired by contractors.

L 1543 of 11th October 1853 notes that 423 men were employed repairing carriages, that is, 50 per 1,000 vehicles, which represents the development of a substantial establishment. In L 1914 of 23rd January 1855 it is stated that in 1852, 1853 and 1854 respectively 9, 21 and 36 first-class carriages had been repaired and repainted at Derby; 7 were in hand, leaving 38 to be done, not counting 7 broad gauge vehicles; and 14 were to be repaired by the end of June. Towards the end of 1858 the practice of painting and making carriages by piecework was discontinued. This is no doubt connected with the fact that from November of that year a regular report is presented to the Locomotive Committee of the number of carriages and wagons built each month in the Derby shops. Usually those built as renewals are distinguished from those which were capital additions to stock. These monthly reports enable a close estimate at least to be made of carriages built and renewed at Derby over the years 1858-73. The total runs out at 1,404, of which 1,140 were renewals of old stock and 264 were additions to capital stock. In the same period, outside firms constructed 1,454 vehicles, all additions to stock. The actual stock figure at 30th June 1873, taken from CW 374, was 2,829 coaching vehicles.

After a prolonged illness, Matthew Kirtley died at his home on 24th May 1873, at the age of 60. He had worked under George and Robert Stephenson, driven locomotives of the London & Birmingham, had been locomotive foreman and Locomotive Superintendent of the Birmingham & Derby Junction before serving the Midland for 29 years as one of its chief officers. In his rise from the ranks he never lost his kindly manner, yet he was always firm and decisive when necessary, and in consequence enjoyed the esteem and respect of all those under his control.

Some of his locomotives, rebuilt by his successors, were to be at work for the best part of a century. His carriages, however, were of no more than average quality in comfort, convenience, technical features and appearance. There was no hint that in a few years the Midland was to stand for all that was best in carriage design.

CHAPTER III

EARLY CLAYTON

1873-1876

THE separation of responsibility for carriages and wagons from that for locomotives was debated in 1870. At the Locomotive Committee meeting of 18th October, after consideration had been given to the appointment of a competent carriage superintendent, Kirtley was asked to make enquiries as to the salaries paid such officers on other railways. At the next meeting, on 1st November, Kirtley produced the following list, recorded in L 6466:

L & NW carriage dept.	£600
″ wagon ″	500
South Eastern	550
Great Northern	450
Great Western	365
Great Eastern	250
North Eastern	200

which unexpectedly reveals a very lowly paid North Eastern man and well paid counterpart on the South Eastern, the smallest company shown. The fact that the latter officer was the able R. C. Mansell, inventor of the effective wood-centred disc wheel bearing his name, may have had something to do with the good salary paid by the South Eastern.

Fig. 53. Thomas Gething Clayton, Carriage & Wagon Superintendent of the Midland Railway from 1873 to 1901.

Nothing further happened, however, for the time being. The contemplated change was postponed in January 1871 and it was not until early 1873 that it was again considered because of Kirtley's illness, which led to his death later that year. With Kirtley's concurrence, L 7485 of 4th March recommended that the carriage and wagon responsibilities be placed under a separate superintendent and sought authority to advertise for a suitable person to fill the office. The Board agreed and L 7527 of 1st April noted that 41 applications had been received. A list of those who applied does not appear to have survived, but it will probably have included the carriage and wagon superintendents of several of the leading British railways!

Thomas Gething Clayton of the Great Western was selected by the Locomotive Committee on 6th May 1873 and his appointment at a salary of £700 per annum was recommended, subject to the approval of the Board (L 7542). Clayton had intimated that he was free to take up his duties on 1st July and on that day attended a meeting of the Locomotive Committee, when he expressed his desire to have a chief clerk and a draughtsman. It was decided that a Mr. Camall be appointed chief clerk at £150 a year and that press advertisements should be placed for a draughtsman. It was also agreed that future meetings of the newly constituted Carriage & Wagon Committee should be held at 11.30 a.m., the first taking place on 15th July, the initial minute of which (CW 1) requested Clayton to look over the applications for a draughtsman. H. N. Pitt of Birmingham was duly appointed, but it was subsequently discovered that he had destroyed many specifications and other documents belonging to his previous employer, the Midland Wagon Company, and he was dismissed (CW 22 of 2nd September). Peter Ellis of Manchester was appointed in his place at £200 per annum. This was a successful selection; Ellis remained with the Midland, latterly as Chief Draughtsman, until his retirement in June 1911 at the age of 66.

At this juncture it is appropriate to take a short look at the way the various Board Committees were organised. The Board of Directors itself, consisting of 15 important shareholders, was the main body dealing with general policy matters. Its decisions are recorded in the company's Board minutes and it reported to the shareholders at the latter's meetings held twice a year. The whole directorate also constituted the General Purposes Committee, which dealt with matters such as authorising expenditure recommended by the various working committees. All minutes had to be read twice, the second reading usually taking place at a subsequent meeting of the committee. The remaining committees were made up of 3 or 4 directors dealing with specialised matters. Those most concerned with the subjects covered by this book are the Carriage & Wagon Committee, the Locomotive Committee, which dealt with locomotives only from 1st July 1873, and the Traffic Committee, which concerned itself with traffic arrangements and requests for additional rolling stock. The remaining permanent committees were for Way & Works, Finance, Stores and Construction matters, with a Parliamentary Committee sitting when there was parliamentary business afoot. From time to time there were other committees, set up as required, such as the Carriage Warming Committee, which came into being when experiments in carriage heating were carried out.

The detailed design of the carriages was now the responsibility of the new Carriage & Wagon Committee, advised by the Carriage & Wagon Superintendent and, in the case of some details, by the Locomotive Superintendent. In practice, however, the committee responsibility must have been in the main formal, with the General Manager, the Traffic Superintendent and the Carriage & Wagon Superintendent between them deciding what was required, with the committees concerned making the necessary motions for agreement. It could not be expected that the committee members, elected as prominent shareholders, would be experts in carriage design; they must always have leaned heavily on their professional advisers.

On the day that Clayton took office, Samuel Waite Johnson from the Great Eastern began his term as the Midland's second Locomotive Superintendent. Another important change had already occurred. Edward Shipley Ellis, son of a former distinguished chairman of the company, took over that position on 20th May 1873 upon the retirement of W. P. Price. Ellis has been described as a man of great determination and cautious in his judgement, with a confidence which could not easily be shaken once his mind had become fixed on what he conceived to be adequate foundations. He worked closely with James Allport, who was destined to become one of the greatest of all railway general managers.

This strong quadrumvirate came into being just when it was needed, when the Midland was on the threshold of a vital period which established it as the most enterprising railway in this country. The harbinger had been the introduction of third-class accommodation on all trains from 1st April 1872. During the years embraced by this chapter the Midland introduced Pullman cars, abolished second-class, took a prominent part in the Newark brake trials, opened its epic Settle and Carlisle line and built new and adequate carriage and wagon works at Derby. Clayton was directly involved in all these notable developments.

Before 1877 the carriage and wagon workshops available at Derby were too small to undertake a great deal more than normal general overhauls. In Kirtley's time about three carriages a week were constructed in them, mostly as renewals. Clayton, who had to carry out a fairly extensive alteration of the running gear of the existing carriages, could not build more than about 80 carriages in 1873-6, all but one being renewals. The fitting of experimental braking systems which occupied one-third of the smiths and carriage builders at Derby for nearly three months and the abolition of second-class at the end of 1874 put a great strain on his resources. So it was necessary to order many carriages from private builders, some contracts for which had either to be cancelled or changed because of the disappearance of second-class.

In 1864 the old North Midland carriage shops adjoining the locomotive roundhouse at Derby had been supplemented at Etches Park by a new two-track carriage repair shed 300 feet long and a more commodious painting shed with some 2100 feet of track. The best that Clayton could ever get out of this plant was 46 vehicles repaired a month.

But with his arrival at Derby, fresh from his success in the design and construction of new carriage and wagon shops at Swindon, the Midland quickly grappled with its own lack of facilities. On 4th November 1873 it was resolved (CW 47) that newly-purchased land to the south west of London Road should be reserved for a new carriage and wagon works. Clayton's block plan was approved on 2nd December and he was asked to prepare details so that the Way & Works Department could get out estimates for approval in January of the General Purposes Committee. The latter duly signified its agreement and on 31st March 1874 the Way & Works Committee was requested to proceed at once with the erection of a saw mill, machine and fitting shop, smithy, stores and foundry. On 30th June the plan of new offices in the works was approved and on 16th March 1875 instructions were issued for the erection of a new wagon shop, carriage shop and carriage painting shop.

Before the new works were completed, the Works Manager, Robert Harland, died on 24th June 1876. He had joined the North Midland in 1840 as chief foreman on the carriage and wagon side, continuing in the same position on the Midland. He was succeeded by Thomas Peter Osborne.

On 6th February 1877 Clayton reported that machines were being moved from the old works to the new and that carriage repairs had begun in one of the shops. A month later he was able to say that all workmen had vacated the old shops, some had also moved from Etches Park, and nearly all the machinery had been transferred. In June he expressed a wish to retain the old painting shops at Etches Park so that freshly painted carriages could be stored there until the paint and varnish had properly hardened. It is presumed that this was approved, and carriage sheds have stood on the site until the present day.

With a report on 31st July 1877 that work had started on an order for 150 bogie carriages, it may be fairly concluded that the new works were by then in commission.

Apart from the 20 composite slip coaches ordered early in 1874 and dealt with in Volume II, Clayton's carriages were unlike any previously built for the Midland. There was a superficial resemblance to Great Western designs, especially in the case of the clerestory vehicles, although the bogies differed considerably; Clayton would have nothing to do with the Dean bogie. It is probably fair to say that in some measure he continued design practice with which he was familiar but followed Midland methods as necessary. For example, the general layout of the carriages would be determined by the Traffic Committee and would tend to follow existing patterns.

His first design was a four-wheeled four-compartment composite carriage which, with slight variations, set a standard style for some twenty years. The body was 28 ft long over panels and 8 ft wide outside, the compartment widths being 7 ft 6 in and height 7 ft 1 in in the centre. Compartment lengths had not yet settled down to a standard dimension and were 7 ft 3 in and 6 ft 4 in in first

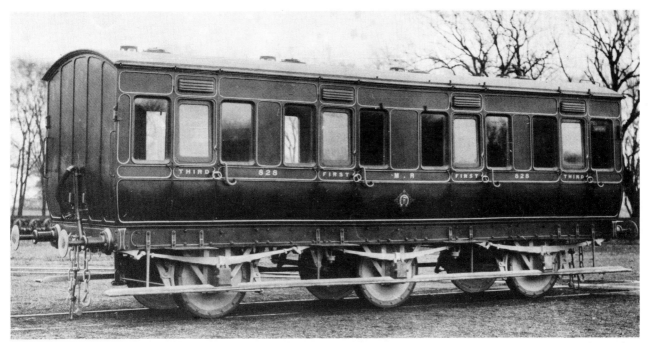

Fig. 54. 28 ft composite No. 828 ordered from Brown, Marshalls as a four-wheeler in 1874. Designed as first-second, altered to all first before completion. Altered to first-third composite in 1878-9 and converted to six-wheeler at about the same time. *(DY 5775)*

and second-class respectively. The roof section was a plain arc of 10 ft radius outside, struck from a centre 1 ft 6 in above rail level. The Midland drawing was No. 25 of February 1874, although the drawing register records a composite with a luggage compartment.

Externally the main difference between these vehicles and those designed a year later was the height of the waists. In the first of Clayton's designs the height of the lowest panel was only 1 ft 8 $\frac{1}{8}$ in, but by about mid-1875 this dimension was increased, for all subsequent designs, to 1 ft 10 $\frac{1}{8}$ in, the heights of the two upper panels being reduced by one inch each. A practice followed on Kirtley's carriages, and on Clayton's for a short while, was the placing of two sets of roof steps, leading to a centrally located uppermost step, at one end only. When this arrangement was abandoned in favour of a single set of steps at each end it was, however, continued on passenger vans and short-buffered carriages.

An initial order for 50 of the Clayton-designed composite carriages was placed with Brown, Marshalls by CW 97 of 31st March 1874, but before any had been delivered the Midland, on 7th October, announced its decision to abolish second-class as from 1st January 1875. This called for the alteration of all second-class compartments in service or on order to first- or third-class and the 50 composites were accordingly converted to first-class only at an extra cost of £48 per second-class compartment. But the change was not long-lived. On 14th May 1878 it was decided (CW 849) that the former second-class compartments were to become third-class 'as they do not make good firsts and there are too many firsts and not enough thirds'. When so altered in 1878-9 they were renumbered

into the composite series, probably as Nos. 817 to 866, keeping these numbers until being replaced by new carriages around 1899, except for No. 829. This vehicle was broken-up in a derailment at Manchester Central station on 2nd September 1880, when the accident report shows that it had become a six-wheeled composite weighing 11 tons 2 cwt. It was never replaced, the number remaining vacant until it was allotted to a new bogie composite built as an addition to stock in 1897. No. 828 is illustrated in *Fig. 54.*

Next to be ordered were 30 more composites and 100 third-class carriages (CW 126-7 of 30th June 1874), all to be 29 ft in length and generally similar to the 28 ft vehicles, including low waists, as depicted in *Figs. 55 and 56.* Metropolitan Railway Carriage & Wagon Company constructed 20 of the first-named at £464 each and Midland Wagon Company the remaining 10 at £435 each. The Metropolitan-built vehicles contained two first-class, one second-class and one third-class compartments, with a luggage compartment centrally; as designed the lengths of the three classes of compartment were respectively 6 ft 9 in, 5 ft 6 in and 5 ft 0 in, the last being so short that the quarter lights had to be made narrower than those of the other compartments. The 10 built by the Midland Wagon Company had two second-class but no third-class compartments.

As in the case of 28 ft composites, the second-class compartments were all made third-class before delivery. The minute CW 197 which ordered this does not mention any variation in the cost and it may be assumed that savings in furnishings were absorbed by the extra work in altering the sizes of compartments, at any rate in the tri-composites, for in these both third-class compartments

Fig. 55. 29 ft composite No. 571 with central luggage compartment built by Metropolitan Company in 1875. It was ordered as a tri-composite, but altered to first-third before completion. Converted to six-wheeler about 1880. *(DY 5768)*

Fig. 56. 29 ft composite No. 565 with central luggage compartment built by Midland Wagon Co. 1875. Ordered as first-second but completed as first-third. Converted to six-wheeler about 1880.

were made 5 ft 3 in long. Before the extinction of second-class, the third-class had bare wooden seats and backs but, as recounted later, they were subsequently given cushions and rather sparsely trimmed backs. All 30 composites were converted later to six-wheelers and all were gradually broken-up and replaced during 1898-9.

The 100 third-class carriages were to be to drawing No. 35 of 8th April 1874, 29 ft long with five compartments, and 50 were ordered from the Metropolitan Company at £318 each and 50 from Ashburys at £309 each. But none had been delivered by 18th November, and on that date it was minuted that because both contracts were in such an advanced state neither could be cancelled without payment of several thousand pounds compensation. It was therefore agreed to alter the carriages to first-class, involving an increase of some £26,000 in the contract

price, in accordance with drawing No. 86 of 2nd November. *Fig. 57* is based upon this drawing, which shows the low waist, but as an amended dimension 1 ft 10 $^1/_8$ in is also indicated it is likely that the later vehicles in each batch were given the high waist. The four compartments were each 7 ft 0½ in long, compared with 7 ft 3 in and 6 ft 9 in in the different composites already on order.

All these 29 ft first-class carriages became six-wheelers, as shown in *Fig. 59*. They were fitted with long buffers and were used on main line trains for most of their life. It is assumed that they were additions to capital stock, but they were not renewed in 1898-1900 like their composite and third-class contemporaries. As far as can be determined, they were renumbered in 1902 into the new capital list, becoming Nos. 2561-2660. A few were replaced in the next year or two, including Nos. 2591-2 by dining

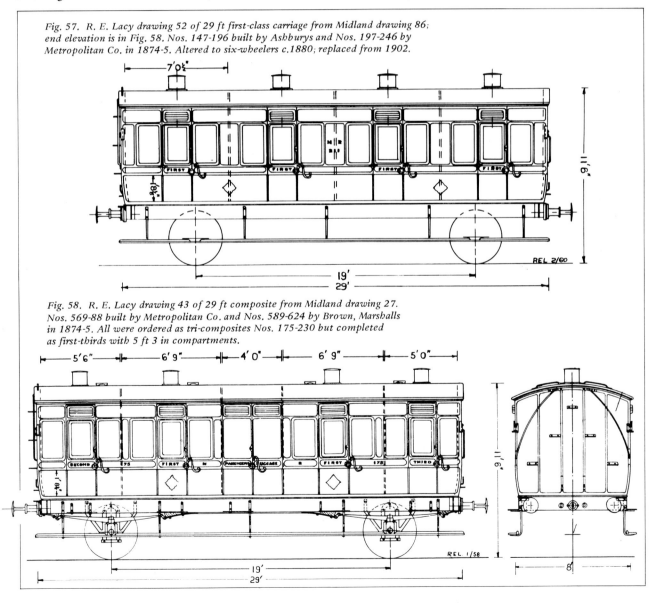

Fig. 57. R. E. Lacy drawing 52 of 29 ft first-class carriage from Midland drawing 86; end elevation is in Fig. 58. Nos. 147-196 built by Ashburys and Nos. 197-246 by Metropolitan Co. in 1874-5. Altered to six-wheelers c.1880; replaced from 1902.

Fig. 58. R. E. Lacy drawing 43 of 29 ft composite from Midland drawing 27. Nos. 569-88 built by Metropolitan Co. and Nos. 589-624 by Brown, Marshalls in 1874-5. All were ordered as tri-composites Nos. 175-230 but completed as first-thirds with 5 ft 3 in compartments.

Fig. 59. 29 ft first-class carriage No. 211 built by Metropolitan Co. 1875. Ordered as 5-compartment third-class but altered to 4-compartment first-class during construction. In about 1880 converted to six-wheeler. *(DY5817)*

carriages of lot 395 when these were altered from composites in 1902; Nos. 2593-8 by dining carriages of lot 555 in 1904; and Nos. 2643-6 by corridor brake-firsts of lot 570. A good many were scrapped without being replaced and by 1912 there were at least 39 vacant numbers in the series, Nos. 2602-22, 2630-42, 2649-51 and 2653-4, which were assigned in that year to former London, Tilbury & Southend carriages.

Orders for no less than 225 new carriages were authorised on 6th October 1874. Of these, 14 first- and second-class composites from Midland Wagon Company at £435 each and 36 tri-composites from Brown, Marshalls at £424 each, were repeats of previous orders and were completed as four-wheeled first- and third-class composites, later altered to six-wheeled. One of the Brown, Marshalls vehicles, No. 610, was involved in an accident on 22nd November 1876 whilst still four-wheeled; its weight was given in the report as 9 tons 1 cwt and the date of its construction as September 1875. A drawing of one of the Metropolitan tri-composites is shown in *Fig. 58.*

The remainder of the order was for 150 third-class and 25 brake-third carriages, 75 of the first-named to be built by S. J. Claye at £194 each and the remainder by Swansea Wagon Company at £248 each, the latter firm also being awarded the 25 brake-thirds at £264 each. Claye subsequently withdrew and on 20th October the Carriage & Wagon Committee decided to forego 50 of the thirds and amend the Swansea contract to 50 brake-thirds and 50 thirds, but even the last-named were cancelled on 1st

December 1874. In October of the following year Clayton complained of the slow delivery and poor workmanship of the Swansea vehicles, of which only 10 had been delivered. After discussion with the firm's manager it was finally resolved to accept only a total of 40 and this, in fact, was the number actually built. They are illustrated in *Figs. 60 and 61.* It will be seen that there were only three passenger compartments, with a relatively long guard's compartment. As was usual with Clayton's earlier brake carriages, a window was provided in each of the double doors.

Most of these brake-thirds were replaced by new 48 ft brake-thirds in 1902, although Nos. 1137-8, 1143-4, 1147-9 and 1161-3 were among the first 40 replacements in 1898-9. Despite Clayton's criticism about workmanship, one of them seems to have been the last of the carriages built in 1874-5 to survive on its own wheels. After withdrawal from passenger service it became No. 27528 in the Midland freight vehicle series and was transferred to departmental use. For some time in LMS days it was based on Speke Junction, but in January 1960 was noted in the breakdown train at Aston locomotive shed, when it still carried one of the Swansea Wagon Company builder's plates. It was removed and broken-up in the following June, in too bad a state for preservation.

The alterations, cancellations and subsequent extra expense arising in the case of new carriages ordered from private builders in the years 1874-5, summarised in Appendix 9, were trivial when set against the tremendous benefits of getting rid of second-class. The action of the

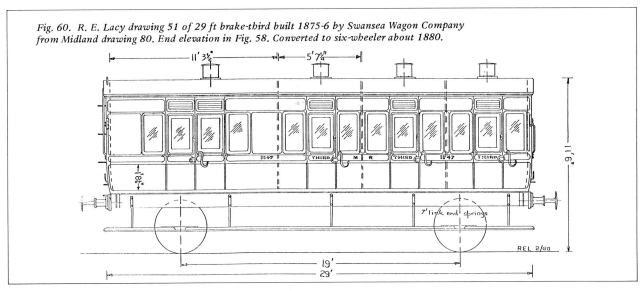

Fig. 60. R. E. Lacy drawing 51 of 29 ft brake-third built 1875-6 by Swansea Wagon Company from Midland drawing 80. End elevation in Fig. 58. Converted to six-wheeler about 1880.

Midland in introducing third-class on all trains in 1872 pointed the way. This enterprising move had produced a saving of some half a million train miles from the cessation of third-class only trains, representing £37,000, in the first year; yet in the same twelve months additional passengers conveyed totalled no less than 4 million, producing £220,000 more revenue!

Williams, in his Midland history, remarks that, of the increase of 113 million passengers using our railways in the years 1870 to 1873, no less than 111 million travelled third-class. On the Midland the returns for 1873 were:

First-class passengers	1,136,405	who paid	£228,739
Second-class passengers	2,487,590	” ”	208,395
Third-class passengers	18,370,053	” ”	961,312
	21,994,048		£1,398,446

which shows a strong preference for third-class travel and, with less than 15% of passengers travelling second-class, indicates an undue proportion of dead weight hauled in the form of poorly patronised second-class carriages. Would it not be better, pondered the Midland Board, not for the first time, to abolish the second-class carriage

Fig. 61. 29 ft brake third No. 1157 built by Swansea Wagon Company. (DY 5794)

altogether? The directors believed that if second-class was abandoned the passenger receipts would rise; in the first year that third-class passengers had been admitted to all trains receipts had jumped from 3/6d. to 4/8½d. per train mile, the highest since 1850. It was calculated that if all but third-class passengers were charged 1½d. per mile (the then second-class rate) and accommodated in first-class carriages, the maximum annual loss, in the unlikely absence of an increase in the number of passengers, would not exceed £25,000 a year. Yet the advantages derivable, marshalled by Allport, were considerable: a reduction in the number of new passenger vehicles needed for extensions, such as the Settle-Carlisle line, soon to be opened; a saving in coal through the use of shorter trains; a reduction in wear and tear of carriages and permanent way; and less labour in the ticket and audit department.

On 7th October 1874, taking these and other encouraging factors into account, the Board announced to the world at large that as from 1st January 1875 only two classes of passenger would be carried on the Midland Railway, first and third; that first-class fares would be reduced to 1½d. a mile and third-class fares continued as at present, and that return tickets at reduced fares would be discontinued.

The reaction of the Midland's competitors hardly concealed their chagrin and fears at the prospect of any loss of their first-class receipts. Ruinous retaliatory measures were threatened. One railway director declared to a member of the Midland Board, 'If you put your hand in our bread basket we'll put our hands in your coal scuttle'. A Lancashire & Yorkshire director even indulged in a coarse personal attack on Allport. The chief rivals of the Midland entered into a conclave of desperation at Euston. They sought to persuade Derby to hold its hand at least until the next half-yearly meetings were over and expressed their willingness to consider, with the Midland, what change, if any, should be made in the conduct of the passenger traffic of the country. They enjoyed some support from certain sections of the press which, 'instead of estimating the enormous value of the boon about to be conferred upon the public', wrote Williams, 'were critical, irresolute or adverse'.

But the Midland Board stood firm whilst the storm blew. On 5th November, Ellis, the Chairman, addressed a spirited circular to the shareholders, in which he answered the unfair criticisms and clearly explained the reasons which dictated the change. Twelve days later, at a special meeting of the shareholders held at Derby, he declared 'the question now to be determined by the shareholders is really whether your directors are to be allowed to manage their own affairs, or whether they are to submit to a policy to be determined by our rivals.' That clinched for him a reward of 44,305 votes as against 6,177, which immediately put an end to the threatened interference of other railways.

A more enlightened attitude soon became evident in the critical reactions of the press as the working out of the

Midland policy came to be seen . . . . . cushioned thirds with separate compartments, more space and, in winter, the blessing of footwarmers . . . . . second- and first-class standards of comfort for third- and second-class fares!

The earliest minute implementing the Board's new policy was CW 195 of 17th November 1874, which ordered the removal forthwith of the lining in second-class compartments. This refers to the rather meagre stuffed cushions and padding of the backs; the third-class had only bare wooden seats. Allport reversed the decision in a letter he wrote to Clayton on 21st November and reproduced in CW 201, '. . . . I shall be glad if you will not interfere with the accommodation in the second-class, but commence to put cushions on the third-class seats and in those cases where the third-class are open throughout the divisions of each compartment will have to be carried to the top'. The Carriage & Wagon Committee soon afterwards confirmed that the partitions in the thirds were to be continued to the roof, the lamps remaining in their present position, and that woollen repp was to be used for the padding of the seats in future instead of American leather cloth. The cost of these alterations was put at about £12,511 but the work evidently took some time to do, because in July 1875 Clayton reported that many carriages still needed final alteration. This was not surprising in view of all the other current demands on his resources.

One of them was the introduction of the bogie carriage. Clayton's first design for the Midland was for a 47 ft vehicle (drawing 53, 19th June 1874) with bogies of the very short wheelbase of 5 ft 6 in (drawing 56). The latter was apparently not favoured and a further one, with a wheelbase of 7 ft 8 in (drawing 60, 24th July 1874) was designed. Drawing 53 shows that it was intended to build the carriages with plain arc roofs, but although the two completed at Etches Park in 1876 were to this general design, they emerged with the tall clerestory roof depicted in *Fig. 62*. The underframe drawing is 99 of 2nd December 1874. They were composite carriages, with an end luggage compartment, unusual in that it had three windows in the side; it was customary for Midland luggage compartments to be windowless. The drawing shows a brake handle in the luggage compartment, one door of which was labelled 'GUARD', with brake shoes on both axles of the bogie beneath the compartment; this gear is crossed out on the drawing. Construction of the carriages must have started fairly early in 1875 since they were given the lower waistline used up to about March of that year. It is not known with which bogies they were fitted when built; but by about 1890 they had 8 ft bogies.

There is no record of their construction being authorised by the Carriage & Wagon Committee. They were probably regarded as renewals of old carriages, but even so it is surprising that they could be built without some special authorisation. The first mention of bogie carriages is in CW 203 of 1st December 1874, in which Clayton explained 'that it was necessary, in order to try out the action of the

Fig. 62. No. 35, one of the two 47 ft composites built at the old Derby works in 1876. *(DY 5748)*

Bogie Carriages that are about to be constructed, that a sharp reverse curve be temporarily put down at Etches Park'.

It is clear from the records that these two vehicles were the only two eight-wheeled carriages to be built at the old Derby works. It has been stated, on the basis of a contemporary article in *Engineering*, that 32 eight-wheeled carriages were built in 1874-5, but there is no doubt from the committee minutes that these two carriages were the first bogie carriages to be built by the Midland. Confirmation is given in the company's Photograph Album index, compiled in about 1890.

At the next meeting, on 15th December 1874, Clayton submitted ideas for 60 ft carriages carried on four-wheeled bogies, with estimates of their cost alongside the cost of ordinary four-wheeled carriages. These are given in tabular form below:

No. of carriages	Length ft	Compartments in each carriage	Capacity passengers	Luggage	Cost £
1	60	7 firsts and 1 luggage	42	yes	1,419
2	29	4 firsts	48	no	1,302
1	60	first class with through passage	36	no	1,357
1	60	9 thirds and 1 luggage	90	yes	884
2	29	5 thirds	100	no	768
1	60	third class with through passage	72	no	827

In all likelihood diagrams showing the layout and appearance of the bogie carriages contemplated were put forward at the same time, but they have not survived. Nor is there any apparent reason why in the minutes they are referred to as 60 ft carriages, whereas drawings show the bodies to be 58 ft long over panels, 60 ft being the length over buffers. The design was very different from that finally built; the through passages were doubtless modelled on the style of the Pullman cars, which are dealt with later in the next chapter.

Although the cost per seat of the bogie carriages was the greater, it was decided to go ahead with them. Drawings were prepared of the two designs adopted, No. 117 of the first-class carriage (*Fig. 63*), and No. 118 of the third-class, both dated 6th February 1875. Besides the original coloured drawings at Derby, there still exists a tracing of drawing No. 117 in the archives of the Metropolitan-Cammell Company. The first-class carriage was to have seven passenger compartments and a luggage compartment at one end, all the same size, the third-class nine passenger compartments and one for luggage. The solebars shown were to be made from two pieces of timber held together by a scarf-joint, and the iron sole-plates are shown in three pieces joined with fishplates; a similar arrangement was adopted for the 54 ft carriages built subsequently. The buffers and couplings were to be arranged so that connection could be made with the Pullman cars then under construction. Yet another bogie, with a wheel base of six feet, was designed for them. Tenders for their construction

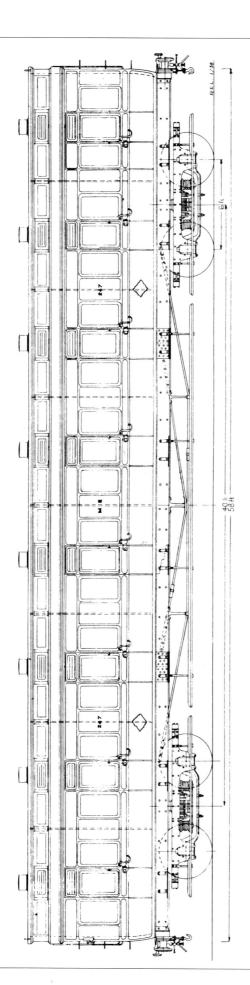
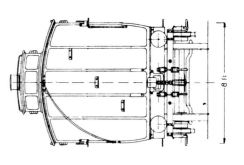

Fig. 63. R. E. Lacy drawing 44 of 58 ft first-class carriage, 12 of which were ordered in 1875 from the Metropolitan Company to Midland drawing 117, but not built.

were accepted on 2nd March 1875 (CW 240), 12 first-class vehicles at £1,242 each being ordered from the Metropolitan Railway Carriage & Wagon Company and 12 third-class at £820 each from the Ashbury Company. On 6th July, however, six-wheeled bogies were substituted for the four-wheeled ones at an estimated extra cost of £116 per carriage, Clayton having reported that observations had confirmed that the Pullman cars, on four-wheeled bogies, were not running as cool as they should.

At about this time the Traffic Committee was considering requirements for the Settle and Carlisle line, which was due to be opened for passenger traffic in the following year. It was agreed on 20th July (T 19861) that the class of stock needed for the Scotch traffic called for 20 bogie composites 54 ft long, 40 ordinary six-wheeled 30 ft composites and 24 brake-vans. This is the first mention of 54 ft bogie composites in any of the committee minutes. Their design was put in hand at once, and the drawing of them, No. 174, is dated 3rd August 1875.

Soon after this, somebody began to have second thoughts about the so-called 60 ft carriages which had been ordered in March, because on 3rd August the Traffic Committee suggested that they should all be composites. The Carriage & Wagon Committee assented and directed also that they should be 54 ft in length and carried on six-wheeled bogies, Clayton being asked to make the best arrangement he could with the contractors. The minute (CW 327) does not give the reason for the reduction in length, nor does it state who requested it. At the next

meeting a tender from the Metropolitan Company for the 20 bogie composites needed for the Scotch traffic at £979 each, including six-wheeled bogies, was accepted. All 44 composites now on order were of the same design, confirmation of which is to be found in the index to the Midland Railway Photograph Album.

Clayton arrived at a satisfactory understanding with the two contractors and CW 423 records that material prepared by them for the firsts and thirds originally ordered was to be used as far as possible for the construction of new ordinary carriages, which are referred to on page 62. So in the end none of the so-called 60 ft carriages was built, but one can see what they would have looked like. There is a fine 7mm to 1 ft scale model of one in the Derby Museum, made by W. G. Allen from the original tracing, before it was established that none of the prototypes had ever been constructed. The series of numbers allocated to the first-class carriages is likely to have been 247-58 (the drawing shows No. 247) and the third-class 1182-93.

The dating of the foregoing events gives rise to some difficulty over the numbering of those carriages which *were* built. The first British 12-wheelers, the Ashbury and Metropolitan batches of bogie composites, were numbered 625-36 and 637-48 respectively, and are represented in *Figs. 64* and *65*; the invalid and family carriages ordered from Metropolitan in July were numbered 649-58. Possibly the latter were originally intended to bear Nos. 625-34, but these were later allocated to the bogie carriages so

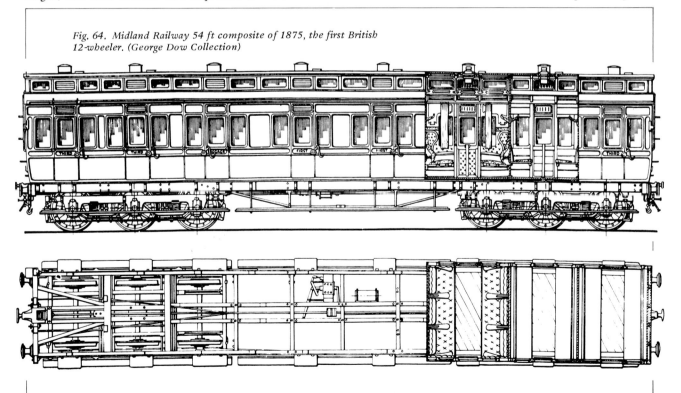

Fig. 64. Midland Railway 54 ft composite of 1875, the first British 12-wheeler. (George Dow Collection)

Fig. 65.   54 ft composite No. 632 built 1876 by Ashbury Company. *(DY 255)*

that they would all be numbered in accordance with the date of the original ordering. As none of the vehicles had yet been built this only involved a book-keeping change.

On May Day 1876 the Settle-Carlisle line was opened for passenger traffic, having been brought into use for goods traffic on 2nd August of the previous year. Yet none of the 20 bogie composites ordered from the Metropolitan Company had been delivered. At this time the railway carriage builders were having great difficulty in fulfilling all the orders placed with them. And on 1st August 1876, when the builders concerned with the Midland carriage contracts, save the Gloucester Wagon Company, attended a meeting summoned by the Carriage & Wagon Committee, the position was summarised as follows:

Before all the bogie carriages had been long in service, in fact before all had been delivered, the Traffic Department was asking for more illumination in them. So on 22nd August 1876 the Carriage & Wagon Committee approved a recommendation by Clayton that one of the carriages should be experimentally fitted up with the Pintsch patent appliance for lighting with gas. The estimate for 7 compartments containing 14 lights was £30 and it appears that the improved lighting was to be fitted in the lower decks of the roof, but no further information about the installation has been traced. Photographs of the later eight-wheeled clerestory carriages built in 1877-8 show that they were fitted with a single oil lamp to each compartment, on the clerestory top. At this time there were no facilities for recharging gas-cylinders on the Midland,

Date of order	Builder	Number and quantity of carriages	Number delivered	Number awaited
May 1875	Metropolitan Co.	12 bogie	10	2
May 1875	Ashbury Co.	12 bogie	6	6
July 1875	Brown, Marshalls & Co.	50 composite (4-wheeled)	21	29
July 1875	Metropolitan Co.	4 invalid	—	4
July 1875	Metropolitan Co.	6 family	3	3
August 1875	Metropolitan Co.	20 bogie	—	20
August 1875	Gloucester Wagon Co.	40 composite (6-wheeled)	4	36
August 1875	Gloucester Wagon Co.	24 passenger vans	3	21
November 1875	Midland Wagon Co.	50 passenger vans	21	29
November 1875	Birmingham Co.	20 passenger vans	8	12
		238	76	162

except those in London for the Moorgate Street services, and no doubt it was considered that the extra capital expenditure to provide them was not justified. Later on, in the early 1890s, almost the whole of the Midland coaching stock was equipped with oil-gas lighting, and photographs of trains taken around 1900 seem to show that these early clerestory carriages were fitted with gas lamps in the clerestory roof.

The original drawings of the 54ft composite of 1875 show the seats in the third-class compartments with padding, but with backs of bare wood. It has been thought, on the evidence of photographs assumed to show the carriages when newly built, that they had in fact been provided with stuffed backs when new. A minute of 19th March 1878 (CW 819) makes it clear that this was not so. In it is quoted T 21094 of a fortnight earlier requesting the Carriage & Wagon Committee to have the third-class carriages working on the Scotch trains fitted with cushions and stuffed backs and made as comfortable as those carriages working on the competing routes. This is a revealing statement, because it illustrates what is frequently noted in the minute books, that is, the close watch kept on the practice of other railways. It also shows that Midland standards were not yet as far ahead of those of other railways as is generally supposed.

All the bogie carriages built before the opening of the new Derby works have now been dealt with, but in 1875 a further design was prepared. This was for another 47 ft composite (drawing No. 196 of 14th October 1875), with clerestory roof and compartments arranged in a similar manner to those in the 54 ft counterparts, namely 2 thirds, 3 first, luggage, 1 third. There is no record of it in the minutes and the drawing is endorsed 'not built'. It is not known for what service it was designed and the drawing may have been prepared to show what Clayton had in mind when, as noted on a later page, he said he recommended the use of bogie carriages rather than six-wheeled ones.

In October 1876 four spare bogies were ordered from the Metropolitan Company for the 54 ft carriages at a cost of £62 10s. 0d. each. This enabled carriages to be kept in traffic whilst their own bogies were being repaired. The numbers of 24 of them are given in CW 975 (18th March 1879) in the returns of vehicles fitted with brakes: Nos 625-30, 637-45, 672-4 were equipped with the Westinghouse automatic brake in 1876-7 and Nos. 659, 660, 667-9 and 678 with the Westinghouse air pressure brake in 1878.

All the bogie composite carriages built in 1876-7 were replaced by new carriages in 1898-9, but most continued to run for some years more as duplicate stock. The minute books record that 2 were broken up in 1902 and 26 more in 1905-7. Another was sold for £125 to the Isle of Wight Central Railway in October 1907; it survived long enough to become No. 6988 of the Southern, having been put on four-wheeled bogies which the Midland sold its owner in

1920, the clerestory being removed at the same time. As far as is known, none were running on the Midland after about 1910, although for some reason unknown a ¼ in to 1 ft diagram, D 1104, was prepared of them in 1919.

In the old Memoranda Book of the Derby Drawing Office there is a record of one of them, No. 0648, being weighed in 1903. Its weight then was 24 tons 15¾ cwt, although, according to accident reports, the average weight of these carriages in 1876, fitted with the Westinghouse automatic brake, was 22 tons 17 cwt. Gas lighting and steam heating apparatus probably accounted for the heavier weight of 1903.

The Midland Board took a direct interest in the type of tyres used on passenger carriages. This had its genesis in an accident at Kilnhurst on 24th August 1875, when the bolted-on tyre of an iron wheel under composite No. 68 broke (CW 374). The Board of Trade Inspector who reported on the accident was much against this type of wheel, because if the tyre broke some of it would come away and cause a derailment; indeed, there had been several such accidents at about this time. Clayton reported that all new passenger vehicles built since 30th June 1873 had been given wooden Mansell wheels, with continuously fastened tyres. Under the 2,829 vehicles which were in stock at that date there were now (October 1875) 1,618 pairs of wooden wheels, but still 4,040 pairs of iron ones. Incidentally, these figures confirm that all carriages running at this time had four wheels only. Six weeks later, CW 395 contained a direction from the Board calling for the adoption of continuously-fastened tyres on wheels under the company's passenger carriages as soon as possible. The change was taken vigorously in hand and on 3rd October 1876 Clayton was able to report completion of the change, except in the case of 83 very old vehicles, some of which were to be broken-up, the others being in use in workmen's trains. The net cost of the conversion was £29,328 14s. 11d.

It is believed that from 1862 onwards Midland passenger-carrying vehicles built as additions to stock were fitted with Mansell wheels, but carriages built at Derby as renewals of old ones continued to be fitted with spoked wheels, the tyres of which were secured by screws through the rim into the tyre. Tax regulations were responsible for the difference in practice. Nevertheless, it is remarkable that the Midland used iron wheels under passenger carriages for so long.

Another aspect of coaching stock design, the continued use of the four-wheeled carriage or its replacement by the six-wheeler, was now in the melting-pot. With but one lapse in 1865, when some six-wheeled composites had been built by the Metropolitan Company, the Midland had remained faithful to the four-wheeled carriage and had even altered the six-wheeled composites to four-wheelers within five or six years of their appearance. Now Clayton had come to the conclusion that carriages exceeding 27 ft 6 ins in length or 9 tons in weight should be carried on six wheels. He said so in a letter to the Carriage

& Wagon Committee (CW 330 of 3rd August 1875) and added '. . . . we are now carrying about the same weight on four wheels as several other large Companies are carrying on six wheels; if six wheels were adopted we should not run so heavy on the tyres, axles and springs and I think the risk of breakages would be thereby lessened. On six wheel carriages the springs could be made more pliable and there would be less bumping when running . . . . ' The General Purposes Committee endorsed these arguments (CW 337) but Clayton, whose attention had been drawn to the carriage running trials of 1870-1, submitted a further discourse on the subject. It was undoubtedly motivated by his preference for bogie vehicles and, because of its importance, part of it is worth quoting in full.

He began by reiterating the conclusions and recommendations of the officers in charge of the trials. First, that the proper adjustment of the strength of the springs to the weight they have to carry is the most important element in the easy running of carriages; secondly, that the length of the wheelbase is the next most important point and that 13 ft 6 in is the proper wheelbase for a vehicle 24 ft long; thirdly, that springs 7 ft long give an easier motion than shorter springs; and, finally, that carriages running on lines where curves are numerous and sharp should not be too long, that they should not, under any circumstances, have more than four wheels and that 24 ft is quite long enough for carriages running on lines like that between Ambergate and Manchester.

Clayton agreed with the foregoing 'as far as it goes' and said it was for the Passenger Department to decide what room and accommodation should be afforded to passengers and whether 'carriages should be built with a special view of their being for the numerous and sharp curves between Ambergate and New Mills, or for the General Traffic on the other portions of the Railway. Will the Passenger Department', he asked, 'be satisfied with the 24 ft carriages on four wheels, the same as they experimented with in 1870 and 1871?' He then quoted current practice on the Great Northern, London & North Western, North Eastern and Great Western, demonstrating that composites and ordinary carriages then in use were from 30 ft to 32 ft in length, embodying four compartments and a luggage compartment, all being carried on six wheels with wheelbases varying from 19 ft to 23 ft. He pointed out that the Midland was putting on four wheels the same weight as the others carried on six and asserted that carriages 28 ft long and upwards and over 9 tons in weight have not been found to work satisfactorily on four wheels on any of the other principal railways. He went on to say:

'With regard to wheelbase, it has been found that the nearer the wheels are to the ends of the carriage the steadier they will run on the straight or slightly curved portions of the line, but a long fixed wheelbase is undesirable on quick curves (the wheels of the Pullman cars being so near the end being one of the principal reasons of their running so steady), but 6 wheel carriages may be constructed to go through the curves nearly as easily as 4 wheeled ones by giving sufficient external swing motion and by not shackling up the springs and axleboxes in the rigid way that has usually been done hitherto.

'I do not recommend six-wheeled carriages as I do not prefer them, but I find them necessary on account of the increased size throwing more weight on the axles, tyres, springs and other working parts, and the practice of the other leading Companies is (right or wrong) against us on the idea of safety.

'For my own part I recommend Bogie Carriages, that is carriages from 45 to 48 ft long on two four-wheeled bogies as they will suit both curves and straight roads, ride steadier and will not require more tractive power than two ordinary carriages. After all the carriages which are now ordered are delivered, it will be a question worth considering whether or not we have enough of the ordinary or old sort of carriages.'

This was sufficient for the Board to make a decision on future policy as regards carriages, and its minute 955 of 1st December 1875 approved a report dated 27th November, submitted by Clayton and E. M. Needham, the Passenger Traffic Superintendent. In it the five following recommendations were made: that the stock should consist of four-wheeled and bogie carriages only; that the four-wheeled carriages should be made as large as was consistent with the safety and efficiency of such a type up to 26 ft in length: that anything over this length was to run on bogies; that the bogie principle should be adopted to a much greater extent than hitherto; and that in renewing the old stock, one bogie carriage should be provided for every two four-wheeled carriages broken up.

Despite this Board decision, the only four-wheeled carriages subsequently to be built were the 27 ft vehicles for the Moorgate Street services and one batch of 26 ft brake-thirds constructed to use up old material! Large numbers of six-wheeled carriages appeared from 1882 onwards, yet nowhere is there to be found evidence of a decision modifying or countermanding Board Minute 955!

The 50 four-wheeled composites ordered from Brown, Marshalls in July 1875 and appearing in Appendix 9 were renewals of old carriages (CW 300). They were 30 ft long and their 7 ft long carrying springs were suspended on short J-hangers to give extra flexibility. They were built to drawing No. 148, the copy of it in the Brown, Marshalls archives being dated 10th July 1875 and signed by both Clayton and his draughtsman Ellis. Within a short time it had been decided to provide the carriages with six wheels, and alterations to the underframe are marked on the drawing in red ink and annotated 'The alterations in red are correct, see tracings of centre wheel arrangement in bundles Aug 14/75.' No brakes are shown on the drawing, although the copy at Derby has had the brake gear added in ink. Apart from these differences in the undercarriage, the vehicles were generally similar to the four-wheeled composites built previously. The extra length gave space for roomier compartments, the first-class being 7 ft 3 in long and the third-class 5 ft 6 in. The thirds were not at first given padded backs to the seats. *Fig. 66* illustrates the

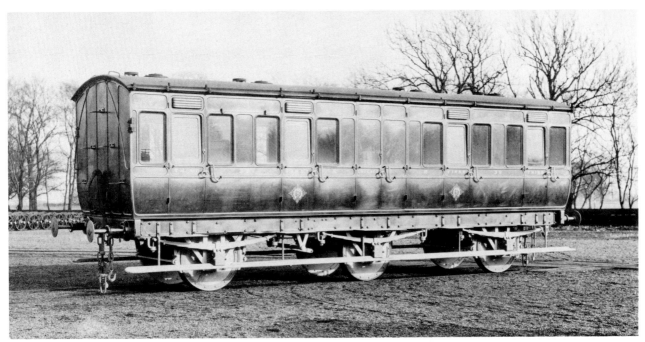

Fig. 66. 30 ft composite No. 39 built 1876 by Brown, Marshalls, one of a batch of 50 constructed as four-wheelers, photographed c.1890 after conversion to six-wheeler and fitting of automatic vacuum brake. (DY 5781)

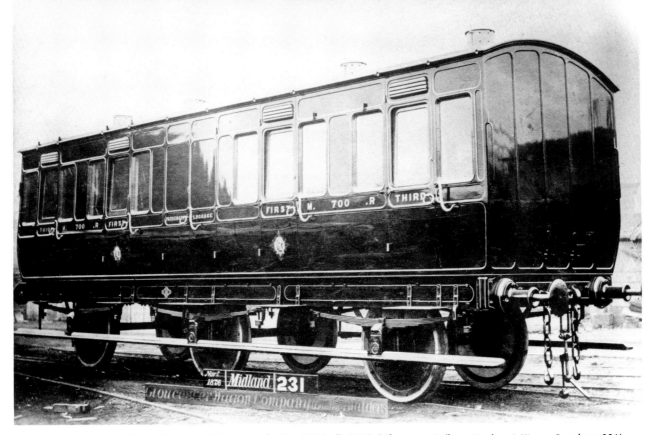

Fig. 67. Gloucester Wagon Company 30 ft composite No. 700, built 1876. (Gloucester Railway Carriage & Wagon Co. photo 231)

Fig. 68. No. 688, another 30 ft composite of the same batch as No. 700, photographed in 1890 and by now provided with brakes and modified lettering on the waist. *(DY 6456)*

appearance of No. 39 in about 1890 after the automatic vacuum brake had been fitted.

On 17th August 1875 forty more were ordered from the Gloucester Wagon Company (CW 332) for use on the Settle-Carlisle line. *Fig. 67* shows No. 700 at the builder's works in November 1876, delivery not taking place until well after the opening of the line. The main difference to be seen between its appearance as built and that of No. 688 in about 1890, when the photograph in *Fig. 68* was taken, are the absence of brakes and the rather more elaborate original style of lining and lettering in the first-named. A minor point is that when new, corner lamp brackets were fitted at one end only; this may have been a mistake on the part of the makers.

The numbers of the Gloucester carriages were almost certainly 679-718, but those of the Brown, Marshalls batch are uncertain. It is thought that originally they had scattered numbers from 701 upwards, being given the numbers of the old carriages they replaced, increased in each case by 700, but that in 1878 they were renumbered, reduced by 700, so that former No. 739 became No. 39. CW 975 mentioned earlier, which lists carriages fitted with various forms of brake during 1874-8, embraces composites which appear to have included some of these 30 ft vehicles. Those having Westinghouse automatic brake were: 725, 727, 729, 730, 732, 866, 904, 910, 867, 913-5

and those with Sanders automatic brake were: 680, 691, 709, 704, 689, 698 and 710.

Of the Gloucester carriages, No. 687 had been withdrawn by mid-1897 and not replaced; a new bogie carriage built then to capital account was given this number, which was then vacant. Apart from this, the carriages were all replaced in 1898-1900 by new composites. Many must have remained in service for some years as duplicate stock, but there is now no record of them.

When the discussions about four or six wheels were in progress, nothing was said about altering the numerous 28 ft and 29 ft carriages then on order. It was not until 1879 that anything was done about them. In that year two drawings, Nos. 423 and 424 of 16th and 17th July, were prepared, showing details of the alterations of composite carriages from four- to six-wheeled. The work must have been done at Derby in 1879-80. As with other types of carriages built with four wheels, the original link-end suspension of the springs was retained for the outer axles, while the middle axle had springs with J-type hangers to give a measure of flexibility. The only ones not altered to six-wheeled were the 20 slip-composites Nos. 524-44.

It will be remembered that because of the cancellation of the orders for the so-called 60 ft bogie carriages in March 1875, material prepared for them was left unused.

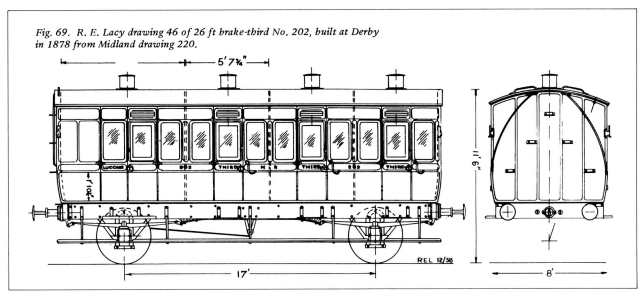

Fig. 69. R. E. Lacy drawing 46 of 26 ft brake-third No. 202, built at Derby in 1878 from Midland drawing 220.

It was decided to employ this for the construction of some new third-class carriages and three separate designs were prepared. The first, drawing No. 184 dated 1st September 1875, was for a six-wheeled 30 ft carriage with five third-class compartments; the second, drawing No. 206 of 17th November 1875, was for a similar but shorter vehicle 29 ft 2½ in long over panels. Both drawings were marked 'not built'. The design eventually adopted was to drawing No. 220 of 2nd December 1875, on which *Fig. 69* is based. This was for a four-wheeled 26 ft brake-third with three passenger compartments 5 ft 7¾ in long between partitions, as in the previous design. Like the other carriages of the period, it had an inside height of 7 ft 1 in, a wheelbase of 17 ft and link-end springs and is further illustrated in *Fig. 70*.

These brake-thirds were, in fact, not built until 1878, when the new works at Derby were open and, strictly speaking, should be dealt with in Chapter V but their story can more conveniently be completed here. Twenty-five of them were ordered in lot 10 of November 1877. It

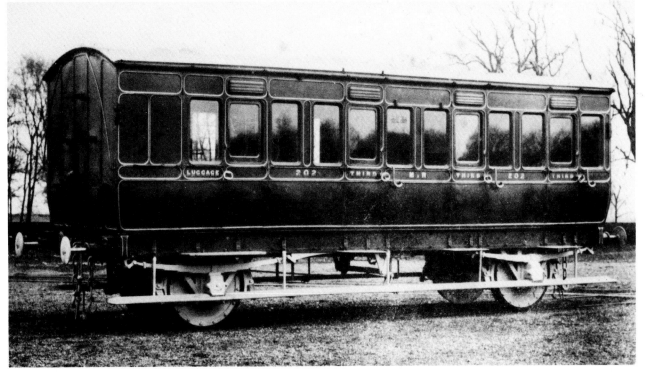

Fig. 70. Brake-third No. 202 of 1878. *(DY 5821)*

is not clear whether they were counted as capital stock, but they carried scattered numbers, two being Nos. 202 and 666. The Lot Register is endorsed 'to use up materials prepared by the Ashbury Co. for 60 ft bogie carriages'. In appearance they resembled the earlier Clayton carriages, rather than the modified ones which began with lot 5. It is not apparent why the 26 ft design was chosen rather than the longer one with five third-class compartments. The solebar timbers for the bogie carriages would have been suitable for carriages up to 31 ft long. There may be a connection with the decision of 1875 that future carriages should be four-wheeled or bogie, but some 30 ft six-wheeled composites had previously been built, so the decision was already ignored.

The brake-thirds were due for replacement in 1898-9 and it is known that No. 202 was replaced by a new 48 ft brake-third of lot 432. The numbers of the other carriages of this lot suggest that some of the 26 ft vehicles were numbered 103, 118, 128, 131, 132, 168, 186, 205, 221, 243 and 234. The one numbered 666 was replaced about 1902 by a short buffered 48 ft brake-third, the later renewal being due to a delay in delivery. As No. 0666 it was altered into a motor trailer for use on the Harpenden-Hemel Hempstead branch (CW 4467 of 17th August 1905), being converted into a corridor carriage by making an opening in the internal partition between each compartment, that to the guard's compartment being fitted with a door. There was no connection to any adjoining carriage. The arrangement is shown on official diagram D 23.

A sudden application of brakes on the locomotive of a train travelling between Dronfield and Dore & Totley on 16th October 1872 resulted in the breakage of a tyre. When the subsequent Board of Trade report was considered by the Traffic Committee fifteen days later it was agreed to follow the suggestions made and once again experiment with continuous brakes in an effort to find the best way of securing a uniform retarding force throughout trains. At the suggestion of Allport, the General Manager, just back from a tour of American railways, the current production of the Westinghouse Brake Company was selected.

Trials under normal working conditions were successively carried out on the Melbourne-Trent line in March

1873 and, during 1873 and 1874, simultaneously on the Leeds-Bradford and St. Pancras-Bedford lines. For eight months from 15th March 1874 a Westinghouse-fitted train operated a return trip daily between St. Pancras and Manchester. In the early part of 1875 further extensive trials with sets of carriages fitted with the brake began on London-Bedford, London-Manchester and London-Liverpool services. One rake of 16 carriages in public service between St. Pancras, St. Albans and Luton was equipped with a new version of the Westinghouse brake, which was completely automatic in action and was under the control of the guard as well as the driver. It proved to be a curtain raiser to the Newark brake trials of 9th-16th June 1875.

These were held under the auspices of the Board of Trade and took place on the Nottingham-Newark line of the Midland. Six railway companies participated, the Midland providing three trains and the others one each to demonstrate eight different braking systems, each train consisting of 15 vehicles. A full account of the Newark brake trials and of the brakes employed was compiled by C. H. Carruthers and reproduced in *The Railway Gazette* of 3rd and 10th July 1908. Suffice it here to say that the Midland train equipped with Westinghouse automatic brake came off best, the comparative results being given at the bottom of the page.

This painted a rosy prospect for the Westinghouse automatic brake, but it did not enjoy the support of the Midland technical officers concerned. At this time, with the opening of the Settle and Carlisle line only months away, neither Johnson nor Clayton favoured the fitting of the Westinghouse brake beyond the minimum number of locomotives and carriages necessary to work the new Scotch services. They submitted a report on the subject of brakes to the Board in mid-February 1876, in which they declared that the ideal continuous brake had not yet been found. They pleaded for uniformity in the type of brake to be adopted and went so far as to say:

'Our present view is that an efficient steam brake can be arranged for the engine and tender, and that this, together with the ordinary guard's brake power, would be found to meet the requirements of ordinary passenger working. We also recommend that the block system be so worked that no express or fast passenger train shall be permitted to pass a station until the main line through the station in front, at which it is not

Train weight with loco Tons cwt		Owning company	Brake employed	Speed on application mph	Distance run; application to halt in ft.	Time occupied secs.	State of rails
203	4	Midland	Westinghouse automatic	52	913	19	dry
198	3	Midland	Clark's hydraulic	52	1,212	22¾	dry
186	13	L & Y	Fay's mechanical	44½	1,165	27½	wet
262	7	GN	Smith's vacuum	49½	1,448	29	dry
241	10	LNW	Clark & Webb's chain	47½	1,337	29	dry
210	2	Midland	Barker's hydraulic	50¾	1,549	32	dry
204	3	LBSC	Westinghouse vacuum	52	1,728	34½	wet
197	7	Caledonian	Steel & McInnes	49½	1,603	34½	wet

booked to stop, is clear of trains; that is — trains, if shunting, must be clear of the main line before block is released, or if not shunting they must have left the station . . . . '

Despite this escape clause offered to them, the Directors decided to use the Westinghouse brake on the locomotives and carriages needed for the Scotch traffic and at the beginning of March 1876 authorised its provision on 88 carriages at a cost of £2,904. Nevertheless, the scope of the trials was widened. In November 1876 it was ordered that two trains and the locomotives for working them were to be fitted with Smith's vacuum brakes; two trains between London and Manchester were also equipped with Smith's vacuum brakes in mid-1877; and in August of that year an additional train was provided with the Sanders & Bolitho vacuum brake. Monthly working reports of each type of brake were rendered to the Board; they showed the number of trains operated, the percentage using each type of brake, the number of failures, the minutes lost thereby in each case and the cost of maintenance.

This yardstick of performance was to play an important part when the time came for the final decision on the standard all-line braking system to be made.

At the end of the period just reviewed the Midland added the Swansea Vale Railway to its hopes and responsibilities. This South Wales mineral line, which had grown out of ancient tramroads along the River Tawe, was registered in 1845 and incorporated in 1855. Passenger trains were not operated until 21st February 1860, when a service was started between Swansea St. Thomas and Pontardawe. The line was leased to the Midland from 1st July 1874 and on 11th August two years later it was vested in that company, when a handful of coaching vehicles was acquired. Illustrations of Swansea Vale rolling stock are extremely rare and the third-class four-wheeler built by the Gloucester Wagon Company and shown in *Fig. 71* is the only known photograph of one of the passenger carriages. Details of the livery do not appear to have survived.

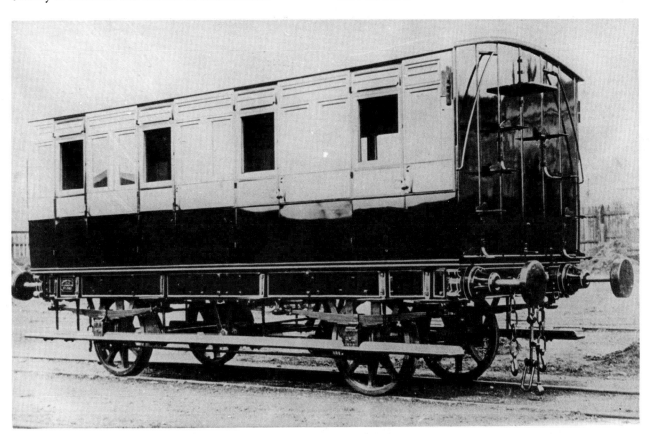

Fig. 71. Third-class carriage of the Swansea Vale Railway. *(Gloucester Railway Carriage & Wagon Co. photo 97)*

Fig. 72. Pullman sleeping car Enterprise for the Midland Railway. From Engineering of 2 April 1875. (George Dow Collection)

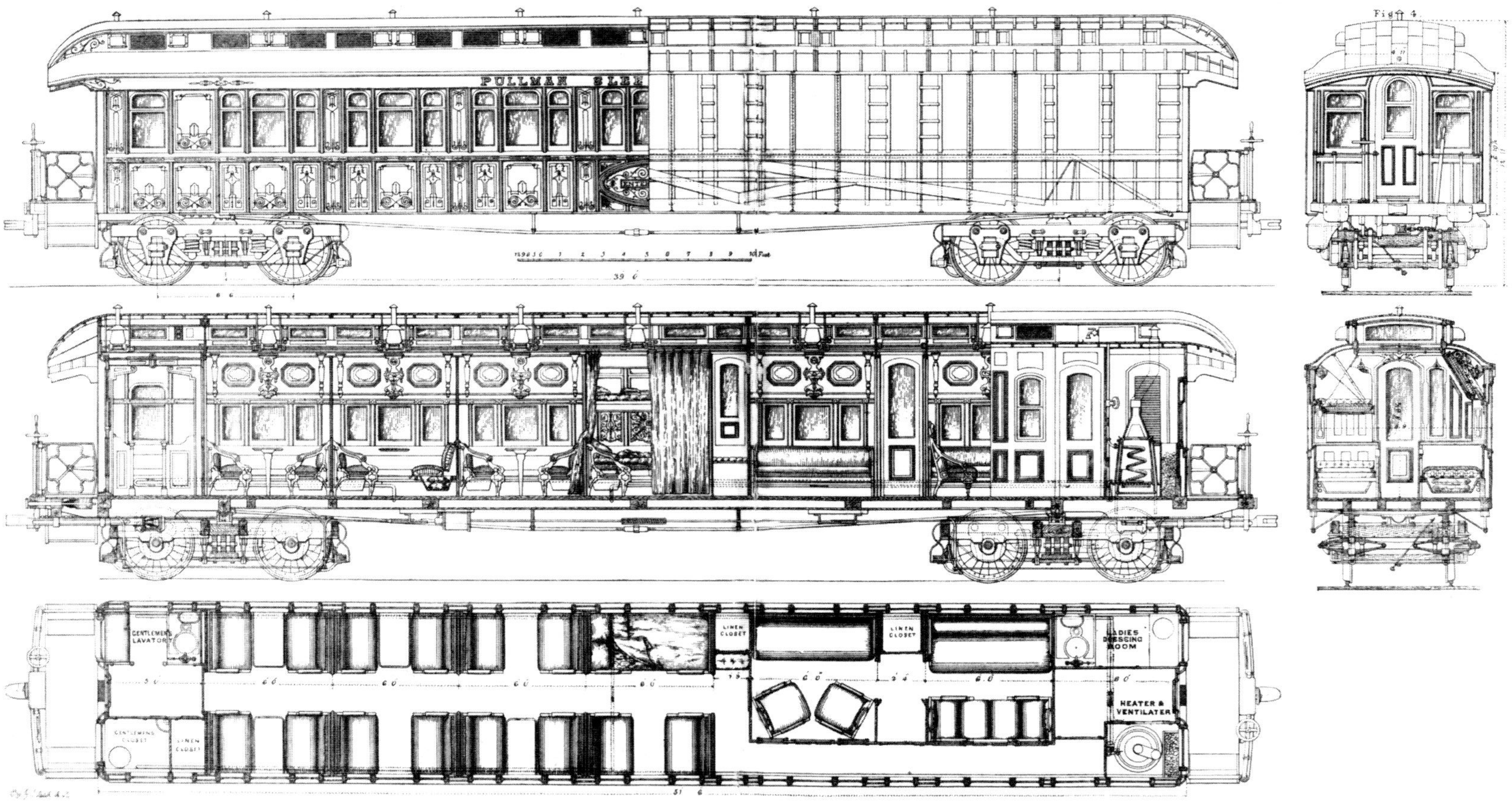

CHAPTER IV

PULLMAN CARS

ALTHOUGH Pullman cars made their British début on the Midland during the first crowded years of Clayton's régime at Derby, they are given a chapter of their own because they were not products of Midland design and construction and their story extends some years beyond the middle 1870s.

The purpose of Allport's tour of America in 1872 had been to enable him to see first-hand what the railways there had to offer. He had met George Mortimer Pullman and returned favourably impressed by journeys he had made in the parlour and sleeping cars then being built by his Pullman Palace Car Company. He was determined to introduce them on the Midland, and on 5th November 1872 the Traffic Committee considered their use. The interest of Price, Chairman of the Board, was thoroughly aroused and it was decided to invite Pullman to attend the next meeting of shareholders, with models of his vehicles.

This took place on 18th February 1873, when the shareholders were first told about Pullman before it was revealed that he was present. In introducing him, and expressing the hope that Pullman cars would soon be running on the Midland, Price added, 'I ought to say that it is not proposed that we should bring over bodily the carriages now running on the Canadian and American railways, because probably they would not be altogether adapted to our service; but that carriages specially adapted to our requirements will be constructed upon the Pullman principle and as early as possible will be tried, I ought to say at his (Mr. Pullman's) own risk, upon our railway.' The contemporary *Herepath's Journal* account of the meeting also reported that Pullman described how the Midland, without cost, could run coaches 'equal to a first-class hotel.' He would bear the cost of the new carriages; and he would also build them; all he asked the Midland to do was to attach them to its trains! His reward would, of course, be derived from the supplementary charges levied upon passengers for the privilege of travelling in his 'first-class hotel'.

It was agreed that Pullman would construct the cars in Detroit, take them to pieces and ship them across the Atlantic to Derby for reassembly in a shed erected by the Midland, solely for that purpose, at the carriage works. The vehicles were to be of two designs, parlour car and sleeping car (easily convertible for day use), the latter embodying a kitchen and a buffet in which meals were served. One car of each design was to be assigned to each of the selected trains, with Midland carriages making up the rest of the rake. This prompted Allport to request Pullman to build at Derby works some more coaches of the same exterior design as the parlour and sleeping cars but with ordinary seats, for passengers not wishing to pay the supplement. This would enable all-car sets to be run instead of mixed trains of American and British style vehicles which Allport thought would not look good aesthetically. Pullman accepted the proposal, it being agreed that the Midland would purchase the cars, which became known as 'day coaches', as soon as they were completed, the parlour and sleeping cars remaining Pullman-owned and maintained.

Eight day coaches were built in Detroit, shipped over and reassembled in Derby. They had bodies 58 ft long and 8 ft 7 in wide, clerestory roofs and end platforms matching those of the Pullman cars and were carried on 4-wheeled bogies. Four of them, Nos. 1-4, were brake-thirds, their bogies set at 36 ft 2 in centres; the other four, Nos. 5-8, were first/second-class composites, their bogies at 32 ft 6 in centres. All had a centre gangway with seats on either side, those in the first-class being trimmed in blue cloth, the second-class with green and the third-class with red. The cost of these day coaches to the Midland was: brake-thirds £4,730 4s. 10d., first/second-class composites £7,875 17s. 1d. When second-class was abolished on 1st January 1875 the second-class compartments were altered, trimmed with blue cloth and made first-class; all smoking compartments in the composites were done away with and provison for first-class smokers was made in one end of the third-class coaches, trimmed and fitted up as first-class (CW 234).

On 25th January 1874 the first Pullman, a sleeping car, was ready for traffic. It was one of the pioneer standard gauge bogie vehicles in the British Isles and the first Pullman in Europe. Appropriately named *Midland*, it measured 58 ft 5 in long over platforms, 8 ft 9 in wide over mouldings and 13 ft 2 in high overall, weighed 21 tons 9 cwt and slept thirty. It was carried on two 4-wheeled wooden-framed bogies with 3 ft 6 in diameter Mansell wheels on a 6 ft wheelbase set at 39 ft centres. Its internal arrangements originally embodied ten sofa sections and two cross sections. The latter was the usual Pullman layout of two transverse facing seats with a folding berth above; in a sofa section the two were replaced by a sofa, convertible into a berth, with its back to the windows. *Excelsior*, another sleeping car which followed on 15th February, had eight cross sections in the main saloon and two compartments, each made up of one cross section and one sofa section, which was a layout frequently adopted. It is illustrated in *Fig. 72* of the sister sleeping car *Enterprise*, from which it will be seen that lavatory and water closet compartments for gentlemen occupied one end and a ladies dressing

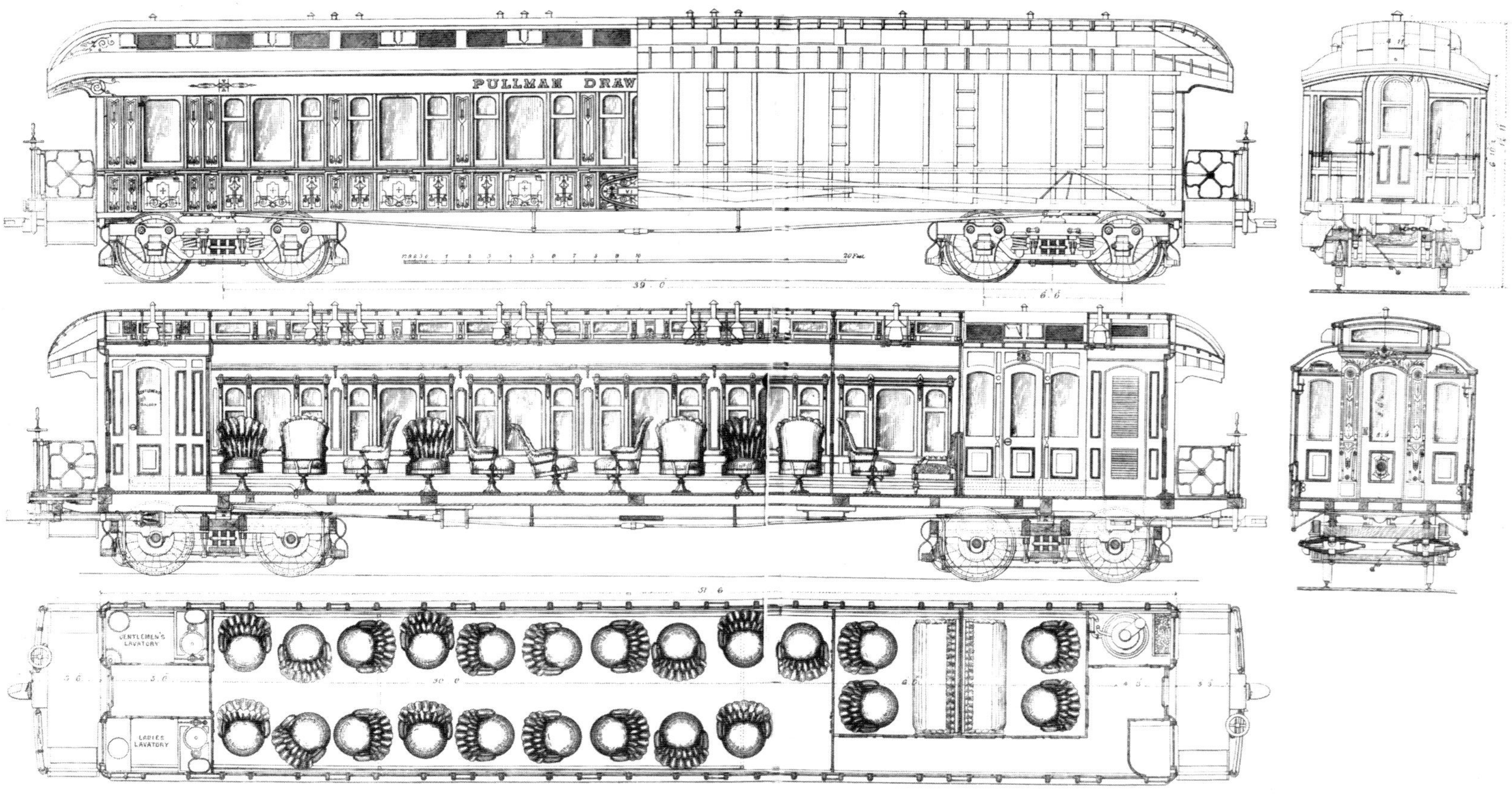

Fig. 73. Pullman drawing room car Victoria for the Midland Railway
From Engineering of 2 April 1875. (George Dow Collection)

room and heating boiler the other. Hand pumps supplied water for the lavatories from low level tanks and there was a separate tank for drinking water. The open entrance platforms, with their wrought iron gates and hooded roof-ends, typified contemporary American practice.

The first trial trip was run on 17th March 1874, when *Midland* and *Excelsior* carried Midland directors and officers from Derby to St. Pancras, hauled by 2—4—0 locomotive No. 906. Originally the Traffic Committee had thought that some kind of match carriage would be needed on trains including Pullmans, because of the incompatibility of British and American couplings, but this problem was at first overcome by fitting the tenders of some of the locomotives, of which No. 906 was one, with the Miller automatic coupling. Four days later, on 21st March, with the addition of parlour car *Victoria*, illustrated in *Fig. 73*, and a day coach, some eighty passengers were guests of the railway company on the first all-car train to be run, this being from St. Pancras to Bedford and back. It was also the first train in this country on which refreshments were obtainable, the caterers being Spiers & Pond.

By June 1874 six vehicles had been completed, the parlour cars *Victoria*, *Britannia* and *Leo* and one more sleeping car *Enterprise*, just mentioned. They were accompanied by the Midland day coaches Nos. 1-8. John H.

White Jr., in his monumental *The American Railroad Passenger Car* (Johns Hopkins University Press, 1978) mentions that *Victoria* and parlour cars sent over later by Pullman were not newly made; they were existing cars that had been refurbished especially for overseas service. *Midland* was designed with an eye to overseas business and was transferred to the Continent in July 1874. Upon its return to the Midland in June 1877 it was altered to conform to the layout of the other sleeping cars.

On 1st June 1874 the first regular passenger service to include Pullman cars went into operation. This was between Bradford and London, the southbound train leaving at 8.30 a.m. and arriving at St. Pancras at 2.05 p.m. The return train departed from St. Pancras at midnight, passengers being able to join the sleeper at 10.00 p.m., and on arrival at Bradford at 5.50 a.m. the sleeper was shunted to a quiet spot where its occupants could sleep through until 8.00 a.m. According to George Behrend in *Pullman in Europe* (Ian Allan, 1962) there were five cars in the set working this service: third-class with baggage, first/second class composite, Pullman sleeping car, Pullman parlour car, third-class with baggage.

The parlour cars originally consisted of a long saloon, with revolving chairs which could be tilted back as much as 45°, and two private compartments each having two

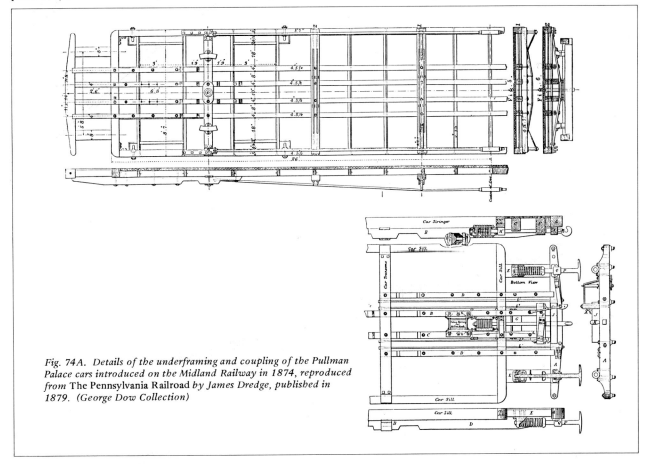

Fig. 74A. Details of the underframing and coupling of the Pullman Palace cars introduced on the Midland Railway in 1874, reproduced from The Pennsylvania Railroad *by James Dredge, published in 1879. (George Dow Collection)*

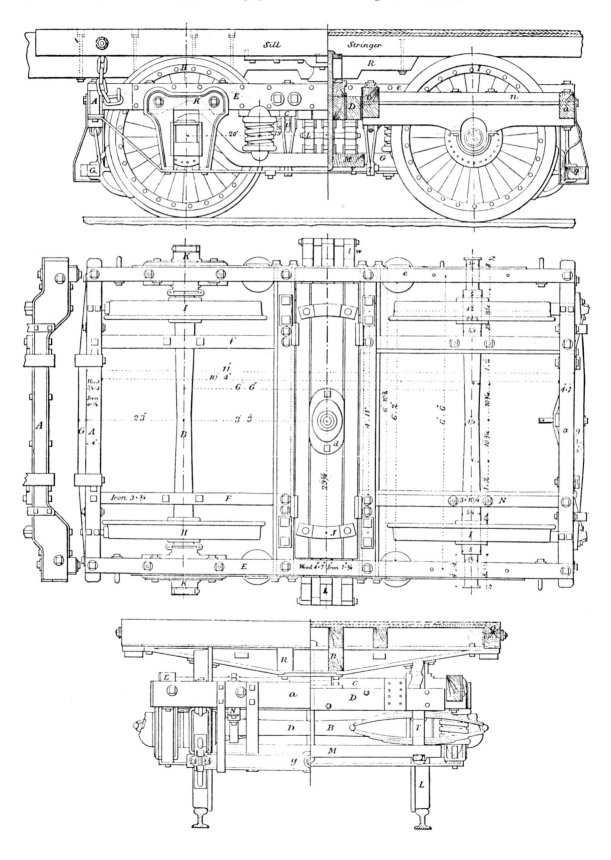

Fig. 74B. *Details of the truck of the Pullman Palace cars introduced on the Midland Railway in 1874, reproduced from* The Pennsylvania Railroad *by James Dredge, published in 1879. (George Dow Collection)*

armchairs and a sofa. Internal woodwork was American walnut with gilt chamfers. The paraffin lamps, with Argand burners separate from the reservoirs, so casting no shadows, and the light luggage racks were bronze, the remaining fittings being nickel-plated. Ceilings were lined with quilted American cloth, florally decorated. Upholstery was plain, quilted or buttoned-in, the trimmings usually being in crimson or maroon Utrecht velvet. The windows were fitted with spring roller blinds and the decklights were pivoted to provide ventilation, being protected externally by gauze screens. The Baker heater, which consisted of a small coil-tube boiler serving a closed circuit of hot water pipes girdling the car, provided warmth in cold weather.

With their external livery of a rich chocolate-mahogany brown, as C. Hamilton-Ellis described it in *Nineteenth Century Railway Carriages* (1949), the Pullman cars presented to British eyes an entirely new departure in coaching stock. Constructionally it was the same story. Body and frame formed a single entity. The underframe of two wooden solebars was strengthened by iron truss-rods and four longitudinals, with transverse timbers giving lateral support. The body and floor of the assembled cars possessed considerable strength which stood them in good stead when they were involved in accidents. Details of the bogie truck, underframe and coupling are shown in *Figs. 74A and 74B.*

But the running of the Pullman cars was not altogether satisfactory at first and CW 305 of 6th July 1875 mentions Clayton's observations on the operation of the 4-wheeled bogies, which did not run as cool as they should. Again, in April 1878, Clayton reported continual trouble with hot boxes due, he said, to their bad construction, mode of lubrication and great weight bearing upon the journals. These difficulties were, however, eventually overcome.

The use of special couplings became an irritating source of inconvenience and delay. Clayton told the Carriage & Wagon Committee on 30th June 1874 that he wanted the Pullman couplings altered to the Midland pattern but, surprisingly, his plea was apparently ignored because CW 941 of 17th December 1878 reported difficulties in coupling Pullman cars and bogie carriages (which also had the special couplings) with ordinary carriages; and there had been cases of couplings breaking loose so that the carriages depended on the side chains. Spring side buffers and ordinary couplings were recommended and it was ordered that six cars be so fitted as an experiment. And so 1879* marked the end of the American type couplings.

On 1st April 1875 another all-car train was put on, this time between St. Pancras and Liverpool Central. It left St. Pancras at 4.00 p.m. and arrived at Liverpool at 9.40 p.m., the train in the reverse direction departing Liverpool at 9.30 a.m. and being due to reach St. Pancras at 4.05

*The year 1876 is given on page 203 of Peter Baughan's authoritative *North of Leeds*, but this is a typographical error.

p.m. The St. Pancras-Leeds and Bradford all-car train was withdrawn not long afterwards, having been on trial for nearly two years. Although the St. Pancras-Liverpool service, like its predecessor, contained the supplement-free Midland day coaches, the mass of travelling public was wedded to the compartment carriage and, after some thirteen months, compartment stock was substituted for the day coaches. One more experiment was made with an all-car service in March 1878 between St. Pancras, Liverpool and Manchester, but again the public preference for compartment carriages could not be ignored. Nevertheless, there was some demand for Pullman accommodation and this was met by attaching the Pullman cars to existing expresses. When the Settle and Carlisle line was opened for passenger traffic in 1876 Pullman cars were included in the make-up of the Scotch expresses, one each for the Glasgow and Edinburgh portions. Supplementary fares from St. Pancras to the following cities in May 1878 were: Leicester 1s. 6d.; Derby 2s. 0d.; Sheffield 2s. 6d.; Leeds or Manchester 3s. 0d.; Liverpool 3s. 6d.; Carlisle 4s. 0d.; and Glasgow or Edinburgh 5s. 0d.

Despite all the delays arising from hot boxes, incompatible couplings and couplings which misbehaved, the whole compounded by the foibles of the young Westinghouse brake with which they were fitted, the Pullman cars greatly enhanced the Midland's growing reputation for enterprise. Their impact upon the public was considerable. Of all that has been written about them, there is probably no better contemporary description that that of the *Railway News* correspondent, who travelled by the first Anglo-Scottish train to run from St. Pancras via the Settle and Carlisle line when it was opened on 1st May 1876. This was the express which left unostentatiously at 10.30 a.m. and contained the parlour cars *Juno* and *Britannia*, of which he wrote:

'The drawing room car is a large saloon, fifty-eight feet long and nine feet broad, divided into several compartments, a main or general saloon upwards of thirty feet long, two private rooms with couches and armchairs, each about six feet long, and various smaller chambers forming lavatories. The main saloon, an altogether magnificent apartment, superbly painted, decorated and mirrored, with plate glass windows, from the ceiling to the bottom [sic], has sixteen armchairs, eight on each side, with a passage between them. The chairs, covered in scarlet velvet, with handsome anti-macassars against the backs, swing on pivots all round, and the sitter, therefore, may turn his face whichever way he chooses, towards the windows on either side, backward or forward, the seat fastening, by the touch of a spring, whenever desired. By the touch of another spring the chairs fall back to any angle down to forty-five degrees, allowing, with feet on stool, any amount of comfortable positon or change of position. Thus reclining in the most luxurious ease, with the daylight moderated or increased at will by self-acting curtains (roller blinds) — one of the thousand cunning devices to be found in the Pullman cars, which really show the strain of ingenious thought in every nook and corner, being, so to speak, brimful of brains — the traveller may survey the landscape under a sense of enjoyment from which nothing detracts.'

Fig. 75. Interior of Pullman sleeping car. Note longitudinal berths in large saloon made up for sleeping. *(DY 4279)*

He waxed even more lyrically about the Pullman sleeping cars, in one of which he must have made a journey on another occasion:

'The large compartment, a beautiful saloon about 26 feet long, exceedingly well lighted, and equally well ventilated, has during the day two rows of seats, with a table between the seats of each pair. By a series of very ingenious mechanical appliances all that is necessary to transform the saloon into a sleeping carriage is to remove the tables and convert each pair of seats into a bed, while a second bed above is formed by letting down a shelf, which, looking like a part of the ornamental ceiling, hangs obliquely against the roof of the carriage. The mattresses and bed linen, all exquisitely neat and proper, are, during the daytime, stowed away on the upper shelf, while a box beneath the seats holds the pillows. All the seats and couches are covered in Utrecht velvet, while the whole of the woodwork is of American walnut, which looks very chaste as a background of much tasteful gilding and painting. Numerous other comforts, great and little, including a system of warming by hot water pipes, and abundance of curtains, and lavatories for both ladies and gentlemen, raise travelling in the Pullman Palace Train from a fatigue into a positive pleasure.

'But, apart from all the luxurious upholstery and the many contrivances which add to the comfort of the temporary inhabitants of the travelling palace, there are two other things which make the Pullman Train the perfection of all railway trains. The first is the admirable service of the carriages. There are no porters taking delight in opening and slamming doors, either playfully or dutifully asking for tickets, but in their stead act well-trained servants in livery, polite and courteous, obeying the behests of Mr. Pullman's guests and patrons as if waiting upon Mr. Pullman himself. This is a change which must be felt to be appreciated.'

His second point was the noticeably smooth and quiet running due to the bogies and he went on:

'A bed in a Pullman car means an actual place to sleep. Indeed it is asserted on good authority that there are persons who, like the great German Chancellor, suffering from insomnia, find immediate relief during a night's trip in a Pullman sleeping car.'

The great German Chancellor was, of course, Bismarck. A large saloon, with its longitudinal berths made up for sleeping, is depicted in *Fig. 75*.

The Midland day coaches, which were equipped with the Westinghouse non-automatic air pressure brake in 1874, were never popular with the public, despite their through gangways and lavatories; the last-named were the first in this country for third-class rail passengers. A contemplated order for a dozen more day coaches, first/third composites, was never fulfilled. All eight day coaches were taken out of traffic in July 1876 for internal improvements costing an estimated £1,340. In August 1878 it was directed that ordinary carriage roof lamps were to be installed in them and CW 1020 of 1st July 1879 reported that all were out of service, having been found unsuitable even after alteration. Before they could be used for excursion or branch line traffic the handbrake power had to be increased and this was done at a cost of some £70.

Nevertheless, CW 1675 of 17th December 1883 records a proposal to convert one of them into a spare dining car, and No. 8 was so altered at a cost of £716. The quarterly reports show that it was being remodelled on 4th January 1884 and a subsequent report reveals that six months later it was still in the shops and had been named *London*. Two more day coaches were converted into dining cars, authorised by CW 1747 of 17th July 1884. The quarterly report of 3rd October 1884 notes that car No. 7 had been altered to dining car No. 17 and car No. 6 to dining car No. 18. It seems that neither was given a name. The October report is the last in which the day coaches appear, and it is not apparent what happened to the third-class cars. In a memoranda book at Derby of *circa* 1890, No. 19 is listed as an old first-class car and it would appear that it was old No. 5 because 6, 7 and 8 when converted to dining cars became respectively Nos. 18, 17 and 16.

As mentioned earlier, the Pullman company maintained the cars owned by them and operated by the Midland, but on 20th August 1878 (CW 880), under a new agreement, the railway company was to take over the maintenance, under the supervision of a Pullman representative, in the two sheds at Derby occupied by the Pullman company. The Midland was to allow reasonable facilities for Pullman to erect cars for other railways. The agreement also stated that the Midland was to discontinue running the cars between Leeds and London and between Leeds and Bristol; any cars of which Pullman could dispose were to be valued by Clayton and another assessor, the Midland to pay Pullman for any dilapidations. It was minuted that Pullman was to take back two sleeping cars, *Germania* and *India*, the Midland paying £31 5s. 0d. and £40 6s. 0d. respectively for refurbishing them. According to Behrend, both cars were transferred to the Great Northern in the same month.

During the ensuing years up to 1883 further transfers took place. Parlour car *Victoria* of June 1874 went to the London & South Western in 1880, the name thereupon being changed to *Alexandra*. Parlour car *Ariel* of October 1876, *Adonis* of January 1877 and *Ceres* of May 1877 were transferred to the London Brighton & South Coast in October 1881, their names being changed to *Louise*, *Victoria* and *Maud* respectively. In May 1882 parlour car *Jupiter* of August 1875 was moved to the London, Chatham & Dover, and in January 1883 sleeping cars *Castalia* and *Australia*, of April and June 1876 respectively, migrated to Italy; they were replaced by *St. Andrew* and *St. Mungo*. In addition, sleeping car *Enterprise* of June 1874, which was burned out in an accident at Hunslet on

29th October 1882, was replaced by sleeping car *Missouri* in September 1883.

The much travelled sleeping car *Midland*, the first Pullman in this country, returned from the Continent in June 1877. For reasons unknown it was lent to the Great Northern on 26th April 1879, returning to Midland metals on the following 10th July, during which period it ran 33,952 miles. In 1973 R. H. Offord discovered that the Pullman body grounded for many years at Skipton carried on the centre oval panel the name *Midland*, which had been overpainted with the numerals 21. The body was soon rescued by the Midland Railway Trust, in whose safekeeping it now rests at Butterley station for preservation.

In May 1882 parlour car *Leo* was altered to an hotel car, which was current Pullmanese for dining car, and renamed *Delmonico*. Sister car *Britannia* was similarly converted in the following July and renamed *Windsor*. This brought the number of dining cars on the Midland to five, which remained unchanged until the construction of others to Clayton's design was taken in hand in 1892.

Two of the last Pullman cars to appear on the Midland were *St. Louis* and *St. Denis*. They were lightweight six-wheeled sleeping cars 36 ft 3 in long and 8 ft 7 in wide, originally built speculatively for operation on the Western Railway of France between Paris and Trouville. Unlike their predecessors, they had no end platforms or vestibules. Furthermore, their entrance doors were located centrally, flush with the sides, and opened outwards. Each side of the entrance were sleeping sections separated by a 3 ft 6 in compartment containing a WC on one side and washbasin and locker on the other side of the centre

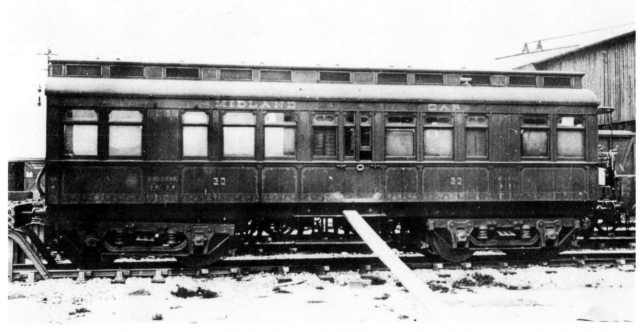

Fig. 76. Midland picnic saloon No. 30, originally built as six-wheeled Pullman sleeping car *St. Denis*. *(George Dow Collection)*

Fig. 77. Midland drawing room car No. 8, originally Pullman parlour car *Albion*, photographed before it was converted to a picnic saloon in 1894. Note that the elaborate lining-out has survived. *(DM 4248)*

Fig. 78. Interior of car No. 8, before conversion to a picnic saloon. *(DM 4153)*

Fig. 79. Typical Midland express train formation of the late 1880s, consisting of 43 ft brake-third, former Pullman dining car, 54 ft composite and 25 ft passenger van. *(George Dow Collection)*

gangway. Curtains were transverse across the gangway. The cars were offered to the Midland which, after some unsatisfactory trial running, rebuilt them as bogie vehicles on underframes constructed to lot 72 of 25th January 1882; these embodied 6 ft 6 in wheelbase instead of the standard 8 ft wheelbase bogies. They went into service on the Midland to and from Greenock on 1st July 1883. They were altered to picnic saloons in 1894 and No. 30, formerly *St. Denis*, is so illustrated in *Fig. 76*.

Lot 72 was for 4 underframes. The other pair was for two more Pullman sleepers of the same design, *Balmoral* and *Culross*, which had been sent to the Great Northern as six-wheelers and put into service between Kings Cross and Edinburgh, where they had proved unpopular. Pullman had them brought back to Derby, where they were converted to bogie vehicles and placed on the Highland Railway, *Culross* being renamed *Dunrobin*. They worked the night service between Inverness and Perth, leaving at 10 p.m. and arriving at 7 a.m., the supplement being five shillings.

The maximum number of Pullman cars in operation on the Midland was 33. From CW 772 of 6th November 1877 and later minutes, it is possible to form a complete list of them, although in some cases the Midland numbers which eventually supplanted the Pullman names have to be deduced. The data is set out in Appendix 10 and it is appropriate here to mention that neither the parlour car *Ocean*, nor the sleeping car *Ohio*, illustrated on page 667 of F. S. Williams' fourth edition of his Midland history, was ever in use on the Midland; both were built in 1875 for working on the Great Northern.

In October 1883 (CW 1647, B 3408) the Board came to the conclusion that it would be advisable to purchase the Pullman parlour cars, 15 in number, then running on the company's system. Allport was authorised to negotiate an arrangement with Pullman on the basis of a payment by the Midland of £1,600 for each car, plus an amount to be ascertained, being the conversion of two parlour cars into dining cars. The latter were, of course, *Delmonico* and *Windsor*. It seems that the 15 cars retained their names for a while, as they continued to be referred to by them in the quarterly reports. The first to be numbered was *Windsor*, which in CW 1778 of 3rd October 1884 is referred to as 'No. 15, originally *Windsor*'.

With the expiry of the agreement with Pullman due to take place on 18th February 1888, the Carriage & Wagon Committee was requested 'to consider what type of sleeping carriages it will be desirable to adopt in the event of it being decided to run such carriages upon the line, either in lieu of or in conjunction with the Pullman cars.' As recorded in the next chapter, Clayton duly submitted plans and four different sleeping carriages were built, but in fact the Midland bought the Pullman sleeping cars and no further vehicles of this kind were needed for some years. CW 2213 of 15th March 1888 notes the purchase of the 14 Pullman sleeping cars and directs the removal of the Pullman names, the substitution of the word *Midland* for *Pullman* on the sides of the vehicles and the introduction of Midland running numbers. But the elaborate external décor and other Pullman features were retained for some years, as shown in *Figs. 77 and 78* of No. 8, formerly parlour car *Albion*, before conversion to a picnic saloon in 1894.

In March 1888 (CW 2211) it was suggested that two of the parlour cars should be converted into sleeping cars, but nothing came of it and in January 1894 (CW 2924) Clayton asked for disposal instructions of 13 parlour cars which by now had been withdrawn and put into storage. There is no record of the decision taken, but it is likely that all were altered that year to picnic saloons. In May 1895 CW 3047 records the proposed conversion of six sleeping cars, no longer required, into picnic saloons by removing the upper berths at a cost of £48, the cars involved being Nos. 20-22, 25, 30 and 31. Former parlour

Fig. 80. Midland 4—4—0 No. 1338 with 25 ft passenger van, 29 ft composite, 40 ft family saloon, former Pullman lettered MIDLAND DRAWING ROOM CAR, 43 ft composite, 31 ft third-class carriage and 25 ft passenger van. Photographed at Castle Donington between 1884 and 1887. *(DY 4270)*

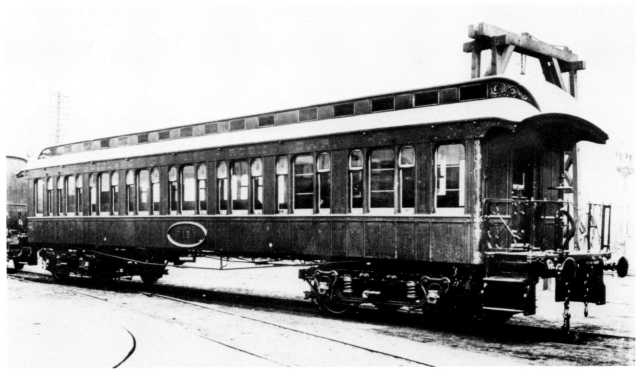

Fig. 81. Former Pullman car *Eclipse*, as converted to picnic saloon No. 13. Back of longitudinal seats then fitted can be seen above window sills. The eaves lettering MIDLAND RAILWAY DRAWING CAR is still carried. *(Leicester Museums, Art Galleries & Record Service 200/83/8)*

car No. 10 is known to have worked in an excursion train on 10th July 1894 and this is believed to be the earliest record of the use of one of the Pullmans as a picnic saloon.

The following table, copied from an old manuscript in Derby carriage and wagon drawing office, compiled, it is thought, in 1895, includes the 18 picnic saloons then in use:

Description of vehicle	Bogie centres	Bogie wheelbase	Total wheelbase
Parlour car No. 1, picnic saloons Nos. 2-13, 20-22, 25, sleeping cars Nos. 23, 24, 26, 27	37 ft 2 in	8 ft 0 in	45 ft 2 in
Dining cars Nos 14, 15	35 ft 1 in	10 ft 6 in	45 ft 7 in
Dining cars Nos. 16-18	32 ft 4 in	11 ft 6 in	43 ft 10 in
Sleeping cars Nos. 32, 33	35 ft 1 in	8 ft 0 in	43 ft 1 in
Sleeping cars Nos. 28, 29	36 ft 1 in	8 ft 0 in	44 ft 1 in
Picnic saloons Nos. 30, 31	23 ft 8 in	6 ft 6 in	30 ft 2 in
Old first-class car No. 19	37 ft 9 in	6 ft 6 in	44 ft 3 in

Picnic saloon No. 13, once parlour car *Eclipse* and still lettered MIDLAND DRAWING ROOM CAR, is shown in *Fig. 81*. It is probable that the picnic saloons were replaced by the twenty 48 ft third-class saloons of lots 447 and 517. The eight sleeping cars Nos. 23, 24, 26-29, 32 and 33 were doubtless replaced by a like number of sleeping carriages built in lots 520-522.

Many of the Pullman cars enjoyed great longevity. In 1906 four of them were adapted for motor train working on rural branch lines, as described in Volume 2. Several others were found useful as lineside offices, messrooms and stores for the railway staff. They were scattered all over the Midland system and were often to be seen at locomotive depots. They did not, however, represent the only venture of the Midland into the field of American passenger car design. Four Pullman sleeping cars were ordered in 1899, but these were the property of the railway company from the start and the bogies, buffing gear and drawgear were provided by the Midland. They therefore take their place in Chapter VI.

Fig. 82. Decorative 8 3/4 in x 4 7/8 in cast iron ventilator grille from Midland Pullman car of the 1870s. Lettering on one end gives maker's name: H. D. CARROLL & CO SPRINGFIELD MASS. *(George Dow Collection)*

Fig. 82A. An excursion train of Clayton four-compartment six-wheelers at Butterley, c.1912, provides an interesting view of carriage roofs. (*George Dow Collection*)

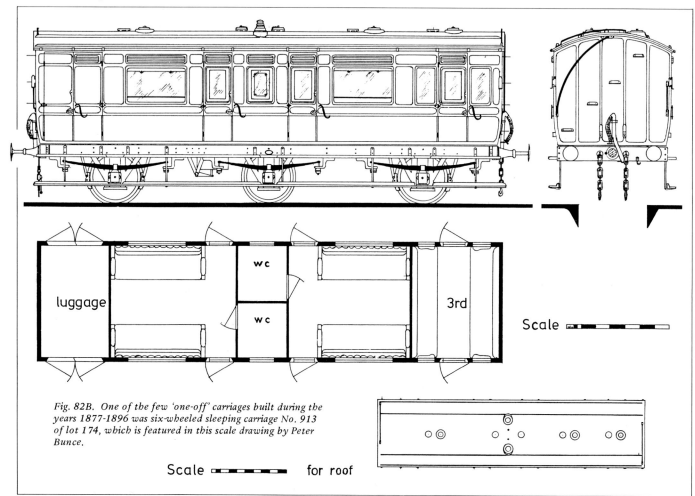

luggage

w c

w c

3rd

Scale

Fig. 82B. *One of the few 'one-off' carriages built during the years 1877-1896 was six-wheeled sleeping carriage No. 913 of lot 174, which is featured in this scale drawing by Peter Bunce.*

Scale   for roof

CHAPTER V

MAIN LINE CARRIAGES
1877–1896

AS soon as the new works at Derby were ready, the construction of carriages and wagons began in earnest. A Lot Register was opened on 4th April 1877 and its coaching stock contents began with lot 3. Many vehicles in the earliest lots were additions to stock, relatively few being renewals. It is not known whether the 25 four-wheeled brake-thirds of lot 10, already dealt with on page 63, were counted as additions to stock or renewals, but from lot 27 onwards most carriages built were renewals of old ones.

It is not possible to estimate precisely the total number of replacements because the renewal of passenger-carrying vehicles was not usually on a one-for-one basis. During one period each bogie carriage replaced two old four-wheeled ones. Subsequently, renewal was on a basis of compartment-for-compartment, but this was complicated by the fact that some hundreds of first-class compartments were replaced by thirds. For instance, large-scale renewal of Kirtley first-class carriages began in 1880, but very few new first-class vehicles took their place; most of the old carriages were replaced by composites or even third-class carriages. Some may have been altered to third-class in the late 1870s, there being a recommendation that 50 should be so dealt with in CW 746 of 14th August 1877. From available data it appears that the approximate numbers of carriages constructed as renewals in the period 1877-96 were: first-class 4, composite 530, third-class 850. In the same period additions to stock were: first-class 125, composite 92, third-class 230. These figures reveal a considerable expansion in the carriage fleet, some 25% of the passenger-carrying vehicles built being additions to capital stock.

The main-line carriages produced during the years 1877-96 were, with few exceptions, highly standardised, with first-class compartments 7 ft 3 in long between partitions and third-class compartments 6 ft 0 in long. Door and window sizes and moulding arrangements showed little variation, so that the dimensions of most can be estimated from photographs or simple sketches once the basic dimensions are known. The higher arc-roof with an internal height of 7 ft 4 in was used. The principal exceptions were lots 3 and 7, which had clerestories on a low arc-roof; lots 27 and 36, which had 6 ft 6 in long third-class compartments; and lot 201, which comprised carriages for the West Bridge branch, with bodies only 7 ft 8 in wide. Where ordinary compartments were incorporated into saloon carriages, dining carriages and so on, they had normal dimensions.

In 1875 Clayton had twice drawn attention to the shortage of carriages, particularly first-class and composite. On an average 222 vehicles were under or awaiting repairs at a time, including some 6.2% of first-class and composite carriages, as compared with 12.5% on other leading railways. Clayton considered that to keep the stock in good repair there should be 360 regularly in shops for attention (so giving plenty of time for paint and varnish to harden) and he suggested that 200 additional carriages should be ordered. He was not helped by the labour situation. In February 1876 (CW 548) he reported a shortage of both skilled and unskilled men and a reluctance to go on piece-work.

There is no minuted discussion on the additional carriages sought, but CW 628 of 19th December 1876 records a request of the General Purposes Committee for 150 more carriages, these vehicles to be carried on four-wheeled bogies 'and to be 40 feet long with raised roof, same as the 12 wheel bogie carriages are and that they be built in the Company's own shops.' The estimated cost of them was £102,208 and by 31st July 1877 their construction had started, the order being divided as follows:

Lot No.	Date of order	Dwg. No.	Type	Date built	Number built	Numbers allotted
3	4/77	294	Clerestory roofed brake-thirds with four compartments	1878	30	236/48/74/9/80/2/6/9, 291/4/6, 301/2/3/5/6, 316/21/3/4/36/43/5/6, 351/7/9/62/70/2
5	"	294 & 386	Arc-roofed brake-thirds with five compartments	"	40	Probably 1401-1440
16	7/78	332	Composite (3rd, 3rd, 1st, 1st, 3rd, luggage)	1879	50	" 737-786
17	"	331	Composite (3rd, 1st, 1st, 1st, 3rd luggage)	"	30	" 787-816
					150	

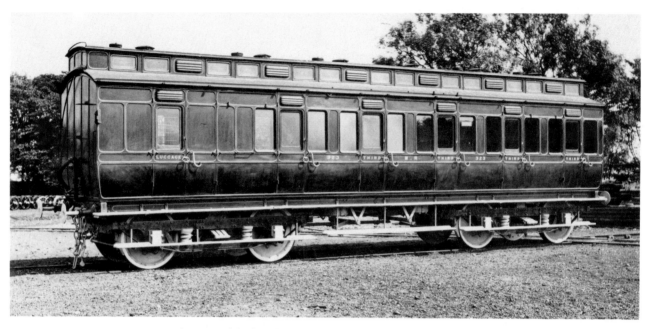

Fig. 83. 40 ft brake-third No. 323 of lot 3, built 1878. *(DY 5749)*

All were 40 ft in length. Clayton had stated in 1875 that he favoured bogie carriages 45 ft to 48 ft long and actually built two 47 ft composites. The reduction in length to 40 ft in the new carriages is therefore surprising and may indicate that experience had shown that the 54 ft carriages in use were for some reason too long. Certainly very few of the longer carriages were built in the next twenty years, the length of most of the bogie vehicles being 40 ft, 43 ft or 45 ft.

The luggage compartments in lots 3 and 5, the first to be built, were to be 14 ft 9 in and 8 ft 9 in in length respectively and be provided with handbrake; those in lots 16 and 17 were to be 6 ft and 5 ft long respectively and have no handbrake. Taking into account existing stock, the allocation between first- and third-class accommodation had been calculated, reported Clayton and Needham in CW 746, so as to enable future London-Scotland and London-Liverpool-Manchester expresses to be formed exclusively of bogie carriages. They also expressed the opinion that the proportion of first-class carriages to third-class was greater than the traffic on the system warranted and that the best remedy would be to renew first-class with third until the right balance had been secured.

A question which arose at this time concerned continuous footboards (or stepboards) on carriages. Hitherto Midland carriages had been provided with an individual step of chequer-plate iron, two feet long, below each carriage door. Clayton pointed out to the Carriage & Wagon Committee on 4th September 1877 that 'the Board of Trade have expressed some decided opinions on the subject of continuous stepboards on carriages as recommended by the Royal Commissioners on Railway

Accidents' and asked for a ruling. The General Purposes Committee dealt with it, issuing a vaguely-worded instruction (CW 753) to the effect that stock coming into the shops for general repair 'be constructed in this respect as heretofore.' This seems to mean that no change was to be made, but photographs of carriages built after this time show them with continuous wooden footboards attached to the solebars. Most older carriages with iron steps seem not to have been altered, some running as late as 1907 in this condition.

The comfort of the third-class compartments in the new carriages evidently left something to be desired because on completion of the initial 30 in lot 3 the General Purposes Committee asked for all in the order to be improved in accordance with a sample prepared by Clayton. This improvement work was also to be carried out in the third-class compartments of bogie carriages already in use as they came in for repairs. The cost is given as £9 9s 7d per compartment, charged to capital.

Cost as well as illumination problems influenced the supercession of the clerestory roof by the plain arc-roof. There is evidence that there was difficulty in giving sufficient light with the oil lamps in clerestory-roofed carriages, but CW 832 of 16th April 1878 reveals that with the completion of the first 30 with clerestory roofs £25 per carriage could be saved if the remainder were given arc-roofs. So the latter returned. Amendments in red ink on drawing No. 294 show the alterations made to the brake-thirds of lot 5 as compared with those of lot 3. S. W. Johnson makes it clear in his presidential address of 1898 that the 40 ft composites of lot 17 had an inside height of 7 ft 4 in, 3 in greater than that of Clayton's earlier carriages. This increased height was obtained by making the roof radius 8 ft instead of 10 ft, whilst keeping the height at the sides unchanged. The brake-thirds of lot 5 were built with this higher roof.

By mid-November 1878 Clayton was turning out three bogie carriages each week and 54 had so far been completed (CW 924). The 30 brake-thirds of lot 3 had been fitted with the Sanders & Bolitho automatic vacuum brake and he was anxious for a decision to be taken on the type of brake to be standardised: he had no wish to waste time bringing the carriages back into the shops for fitting brakes. A month later the Midland Board resolved to fit the remaining 120 bogie carriages with the Sanders brake (CW 939).

There is no record of the completion of the 80 composites and little is known of their history. By CW 2264 of 20th September 1888 it was agreed that 50 bogie composites with luggage compartments should be fitted with handbrake, communication wheel, etc. so that they could be used as guard's brakes when required; no doubt vehicles of lots 16 and 17 were among those altered. CW 3066 of 18th July 1895 records that '40 of the existing bogie carriages containing three 1st and two 3rd compartments' were to have one first-class compartment converted into third-class at a cost of £13 5s. 0d. per compartment but no photograph of a carriage so altered appears to have survived.

All 150 carriages, with the possible exception of some of the arc-roof brake-thirds, appear to have been renewed in 1898-1900. It seems that the carriages in lot 3 were replaced by 6 lavatory brake-thirds of lot 432, 14 lavatory thirds of lot 437 and 8 corridor thirds of lot 439; the replacements of two of them, Nos. 306 and 351, have not been traced. The composites were replaced, it is thought, by new carriages numbered in the series 3001-3289 in 1900-1901; No. 762 was still running with its original number on 6th July 1901, when it was damaged in an accident.

After having been in the duplicate lists since replacement, most had been withdrawn by about 1914. No. 372 was damaged in a collision at Esholt Junction on 9th June 1892 and No. 0346 was similarly involved in an accident elsewhere on 8th February 1906. A tracing at Derby, numbered 386A, shows that two brake-thirds of lot 5, Nos. 001 and 002, were fitted up for fruit traffic and a diagram, D263, indicates that a few composites of lot 16 were still running as late as 1910-11. All had gone by 1918.

As far as can be determined, all the other bogie coaches built up to the end of 1888 were renewals of old carriages, with the exception of the six family carriages of lot 7, which are dealt with in Volume 2.

It is unfortunate that the records of carriages given in the minute books are not only incomplete but sometimes misleading. For example, if one compares the proposals in the minutes for new carriages during 1879-83 with the lots under which carriages were built in the same period it is apparent that many do not appear in the proposals at all, whilst two series of 54 ft carriages requested under CW 1325 were built as first-class and brake-thirds in lots 88 and 89, differing appreciably from the proposals. Even

Fig. 84. 40 ft brake-third No. 1409 of lot 5, built 1878. *(DY 5798)*

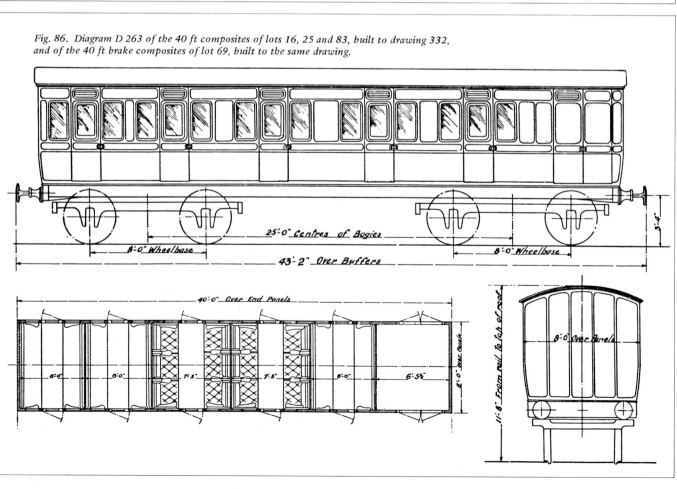

Fig. 85. Diagram D 261 of the 40 ft brake-thirds of lot 5.

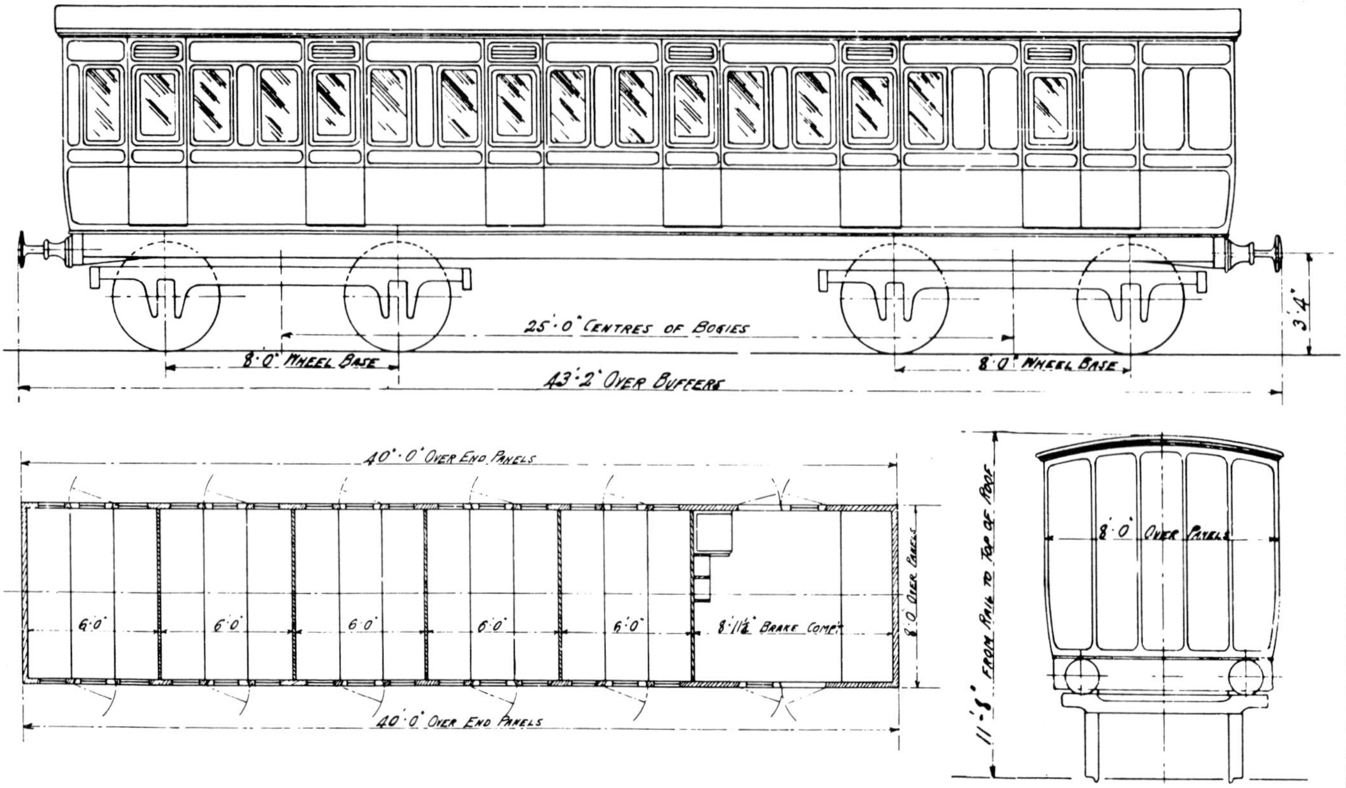

Fig. 86. Diagram D 263 of the 40 ft composites of lots 16, 25 and 83, built to drawing 332, and of the 40 ft brake composites of lot 69, built to the same drawing.

the Lot List does not always tell the full story and must be used with caution. There were at least two copies of it at Derby, one of which appeared to be a late copy of the original and which omitted details of the individual orders. It is believed that the Lot List records all vehicles built for the Midland at the new works at Derby, except for 45 Midland Scotch Joint Stock carriages in 1883 and 250 other carriages in 1897-1902. The order of the works lot numbers can conveniently be followed in this and other chapters.

After the 150 additional carriages were completed, 30 composites were built for Midland Scotch Joint Stock, as described in Volume 2, the last being finished in September 1879. They were followed by four batches of 40 ft carriages, lots 27, 36, 50 and 58, amounting to 120 vehicles. All appear to have been replacements of old carriages and no doubt their construction was taken in hand without special authorisation, because no minutes about them have been found.

Lot 27, ordered in January 1879, and lot 36, ordered in the following November, each consisted of 50 bogie third-class carriages to drawing 383 and illustrated in *Fig. 87*. They were unique among the arc-roofed carriages in that the compartments were 6 ft 6 in long, six inches more than the standard third-class compartment. It is likely that they were all completed in 1880-1 and that those numbered in the 1400 series were replacements of old first-class vehicles. No. 01482, after ten years on the duplicate list, was sold in 1912 to become No. 32 of the

Stratford-upon-Avon & Midland Junction and LMS No. 18891 in 1923. It is probable that the whole of lots 27 and 36 were replaced in 1901-2, but like No. 01482, some remained in service for several years as duplicate stock. The scrapping records show that one was broken up in 1900 and ten more in 1905-13. At least one was still in Midland service in 1915, being listed as available for War Office requirements, but its number is not recorded.

The 120 vehicles were completed with lot 50 for ten 40 ft composites in July 1880 to drawing No. 331 and a further ten in March 1881, lot 58, all being identical with those of lot 17. It is thought that they were built in 1881, fitted with wood-framed bogies, and that all were replaced in 1900-1.

Next to be ordered were the 50 bogie third-class carriages in lot 60 of July 1881. This time it was decided to make the carriages 43 ft long so that seven standard 6 ft compartments could be accommodated exactly. A new 8 ft wheelbase bogie with iron frames was designed for them, and used on all subsequent eight-wheeled carriages. It had leaf springs to the axleboxes, in place of the helical springs and compensating beam used on the earlier bogies. The leaf springs to the bolster remained, as before. On 25th April 1882 the order was increased by 40 third-class carriages and 10 brake-thirds, making 100 in all. The extra carriages were called for to make good a seating deficiency and to meet a request for 10 third-class and 10 brake-thirds by the Traffic Committee (CW 1362 of 3rd January 1882). The brake-thirds were to be built to the same

Fig. 87. 40 ft third-class carriage No. 1466 of lots 27 and 36, built in 1880-1. *(DM 5979)*

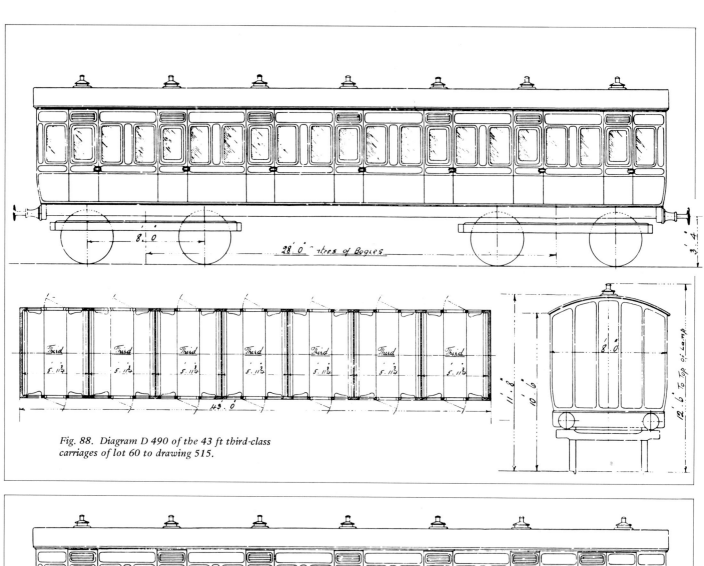

Fig. 88. Diagram D 490 of the 43 ft third-class
carriages of lot 60 to drawing 515.

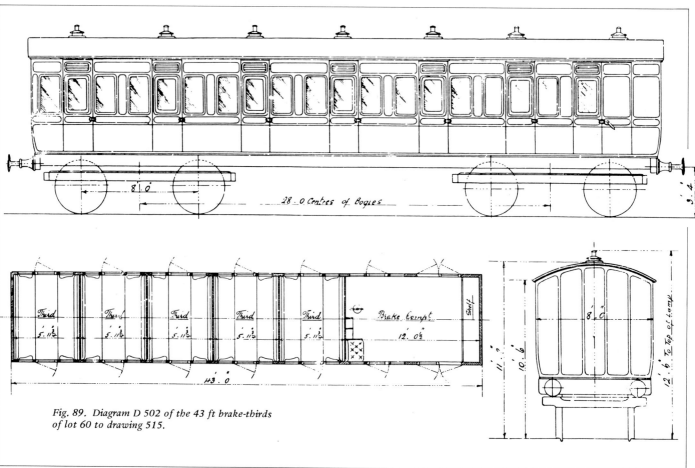

Fig. 89. Diagram D 502 of the 43 ft brake-thirds
of lot 60 to drawing 515.

Fig. 90. 43 ft brake-third No. 537 altered in 1892 to include two lavatories. *(DY 6505)*

drawing as the thirds, No. 515, but had only five passenger compartments, the remaining space being taken by a long guard's compartment. The thirds are illustrated by D 490 in *Fig. 88* and the brake-thirds by D 502 in *Fig. 89*.

When built, the first 50 were given solebars of wood, 3½ in thick by only 9 in deep, strengthened on the outside by a soleplate of iron angle 9 in by 4 in and ³/₈ in thick. This was soon found to be insufficiently rigid, and the remainder were given angle ½ in thick, the amendment on the drawing being dated 28th April 1882. This too proved to be inadequate, and on 16th August 1888 a further amendment was made, a steel plate 9 in x ¼ in being fastened to the back of the angle by ⁵/₈ in rivets. Yet more stiffening was added to the underframes of some of the carriages from about 1890, when truss rods like those used on the 48 ft carriages of 1898 were added. This alteration is shown in pencil on the drawing of the 43 ft carriages, but is not dated.

All the carriages in lot 60 were built during 1882 and many of them had a long life. Although replaced about 1904, there were still 42 of the thirds and 2 of the brake-thirds in service in 1918, being reduced to 24 and 1 respectively by 31st December 1922. There is no certain information about their numbers. Two of the thirds may have been numbered 14 and 577 and one of the brake-thirds 156.

The middle third-class compartment of 29 43 ft brake-thirds was altered to a pair of lavatories in 1892. *Fig. 90* shows No. 537 so converted, but there is no record of the lot numbers of the carriages involved. Two others were numbered 1702 and 1708. The reason for renumbering some of these rebuilt lavatory brake-thirds into the series

1699-1708, or thereabouts, is not recorded. These numbers in the capital list would be reached in about 1891-2, which suggests that the carriages were renumbered when altered from ordinary brake-thirds in 1892, this date being quoted in the index to the Carriage Photograph Album. It is difficult to think of a plausible accounting reason for the action, which presumably would leave vacant a like amount of capital numbers elsewhere in the third-class list.

During the years 1909 to 1920 the Midland & South Western Junction Railway bought 16 old bogie third-class (D 490) and 4 brake-third carriages (D 502) from the Midland at £150 each for use between Cheltenham and Southampton (CW 4966). Great Western records give the date of construction as 1882, and if this actually applies to every one they must all have been from lot 60. Several photographs of these carriages awaiting scrapping at Swindon were taken in 1924-5. Some had strengthened underframes, some had torpedo roof ventilators over all passenger compartments, others only over smoking compartments, and this was probably the state in which they had been sold by the Midland. The original Midland numbers cannot be traced, but on the M & SWJ the third-class carriages became Nos. 5-7, 11-14, 17, 18, 20, 21, 24, 25, 57, 61, 62 (later GW Nos. 4473-85 and 4497-9) and the brake-thirds Nos. 8, 15, 60, 63 (later GW Nos. 4648-51). Subsequently 13 horse-boxes (dealt with in Volume 2) and 16 brake-composites (D 528) were acquired, the latter becoming M & SWJ Nos. 1-4, 10, 50-56, 58-9, 64-5 (GW Nos. 6345-9 and 6358-68). The brake-composites were of at least two varieties, probably being rebuilt from luggage composites of lot 83 (Fig. 91) or brake-composites of lot 69, both of which were built to drawing 332 with compartments arranged 3rd, 3rd, 1st, 1st, 3rd, luggage and 3rd, 3rd, 1st, 1st, 3rd, brake respectively. Many were altered to 3rd, 3rd 1st, 1st, brake, so becoming operationally identical with lot 106 (D 528), but differing externally in the position of luggage doors and moulding details.

Renewal of carriages in 1878-81 was made on the basis of one-for-one, except that one bogie carriage replaced two of the old four-wheelers. This was the basis on which Clayton made his original comparison of ordinary and bogie carriages in 1874 and it inevitably led to a reduction in the total seating capacity of the carriage stock. On 4th October 1881 the Chairman of the Traffic Committee called attention to this loss and it was agreed that Allport and Clayton should confer and submit their suggestions for rectifying the deficiency and for the type of carriage which should be built for that purpose. It was also decided that in all future renewals 'an equal seating capacity shall be preserved'. The General Manager's report given in CW 1325 of 18th October shows that 30 new carriages were needed to meet the seating deficiency. The 15 third-class carriages were built as proposed, doubtless as part of lot 60, but the 54 ft carriages of lots 88 and 89 differed from those laid down in the minute. Instead of 3 composites with a total of 9 compartments, 3 first-class carriages each with 6 compartments were built (lot 89). The proposals would have provided 15 third-class compartments in the composites and 84 in the 54 ft thirds which, with 105 in the fifteen 43 ft carriages, made a total of 204 third-class compartments, or 213 with the first-class added.

In fact only six 54 ft third-class were built (lot 88), each with seven compartments and a guard's compartment. It is likely, therefore, that to make up the full number of compartments, 22 of the 43 ft thirds were built, so giving a total of 196 third-class and 18 first-class compartments, 214 in all and one more than the original proposal.

Although the decision to change the basis of renewal was taken in October 1881, it is not until October 1882 that the returns of the carriages broken up and renewed given in the minutes begin to be presented in the form of compartments instead of carriages. For the first three months the returns are only of the total number of compartments, but from January 1883 the number of each class of compartment is given separately, so it is often possible to deduce what types of carriage have been built.

The problem of standardisation of brakes had by now been resolved, and the Locomotive Committee appears to have had the final say. At the end of September 1879 it expressed preference for the improved Sanders & Bolitho automatic vacuum brake which, it stated, fully equalled the power of the Westinghouse automatic brake to stop a train. Furthermore, the simplicity of its construction not only made it less vulnerable to failure because of disuse or arduous weather conditions but cheaper in first cost and maintenance. The Board did not commit itself, but decided that any trains subsequently fitted with an automatic brake would have the Sanders & Bolitho. A report by Johnson and Clayton dated 4th January 1881 shows that there were by then 11 trains working over the Settle and Carlisle line, including two each way between London and Carlisle, provided with Westinghouse brake;

Fig. 91. 40 ft brake-composite No. 164 of lot 69 built to drawing 332 in 1882. (DY 5811)

Fig. 92. 45 ft composite with luggage compartment No. 6 of lot 79, built in 1883. *(DM 1421)*   *George Dow Collection*

47 trains in service between main centres on the system had Sanders & Bolitho brake, together with 6 engines so fitted on the Bradford-Leeds local trains; in London 12 engines working the suburban services to and from Moorgate Street had been equipped with Smith's non-automatic vacuum brake; and 2 trains between London and Bedford had Barker's hydraulic brake. Carriages were involved to the following extent: Westinghouse 155, and 56 having through pipes; Sanders & Bolitho 940, and 325 having through pipes; Smith's 115 and Barker's 20.

When in September 1882 the Board directed that the automatic vacuum brake was to be fitted to 352 horseboxes and 316 carriage trucks the Midland virtually became a fully automatic vacuum line. Vehicles in the joint services which were operated with the Glasgow & South Western and North British via Carlisle were dual-fitted with automatic vacuum and Westinghouse brakes. From 1886, however, all new G & SW passenger locomotives were given vacuum brakes and six years later all G & SW goods tender engines were dealt with likewise. The North British remained a Westinghouse line.

Following the carriages of lot 60 were the fifty 40 ft brake composites of lot 69, ordered by CW 1349 of 15th November 1881. They were constructed to drawing 332, which was used earlier for the composites of lots 16 and 25, but whereas those were built with a simple luggage compartment, lot 69 had handbrake and accommodation for the guard. They closely resembled the vehicles of lot 106 (page 95), which had a longer brake compartment

and one less third-class compartment. It is believed that all were completed in 1882, being provided with the then new iron bogies. The only running number known is No. 164 in the official photograph of the class, reproduced as *Fig. 91*. Records show that 11 were still in service in 1918 and 4 on 31st December 1922, by which time some had one third-class compartment taken into the brake compartment.

Next came a new design, the thirty 45 ft composites of lot 79 referred to in CW 1349 and 1357, which were ordered in June 1882. They were turned out of the Derby works in January to April 1883, being built to drawing 563, and each had 3 first-class, 3 third-class and 1 luggage compartment. No. 225 is illustrated in *Fig. 92*. The Lot Register is endorsed 'Shop drawing compiled. See drawing 589', which implies that a shop drawing was made up from other similar ones, the master drawing, which still exists, not being prepared until later. On 2nd May 1890 the Traffic Committee asked for lavatory accommodation to be provided in ten '48 ft bogie carriages' (CW 2468). The length given in the minute includes the length over buffers, the carriages concerned being the 45 ft composites of lot 79. There is no mention in the minutes of any other alterations, but the index to the Photograph Album shows that in addition to having 1 first-class compartment converted into a pair of lavatories, the luggage compartment was altered to a guard's brake compartment. These changes took place in 1890 and are represented by *Fig. 93*. A further modification, probably carried out at the same

Fig. 93. No. 6, as altered in 1890 to embody a pair of lavatories and a guard's brake compartment.   *George Dow Collection*

time, was the fitting of truss rods to the underframe. No diagram was prepared of these carriages and nothing further is known of them. They were probably replaced around 1904.

Also completed in 1883, between March and July, were the thirty-seven 40 ft composites of lot 83 to drawing 332. Ordered in October 1882, they were similar to lot 16, but differed in that they had iron-framed bogies. No. 114 is illustrated in *Fig. 94.* It is likely that some, perhaps all of them, like lot 69, had the luggage compart-

ment enlarged by taking in the adjacent third-class compartment some time after construction, the modification being shown in diagram D 528 in *Fig. 95.* In 1918 six of of the lot were still in service, but all had been withdrawn by 31st December 1922. It is the only batch of bogie composites not specifically referred to in the minutes, but there is no doubt that all were renewals of old carriages. They themselves would have been replaced in about 1904.

The eighty 40 ft brake-thirds asked for by the Traffic Committee on 15th November 1881 (CW 1349) were not

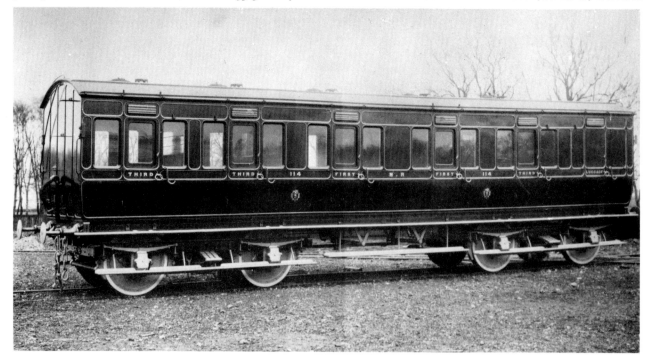

Fig. 94. 40 ft composite No. 114 of lot 83, built 1883, similar to lot 16 of 1878-9, but with iron-framed bogies instead of wooden ones. (DM 5980)

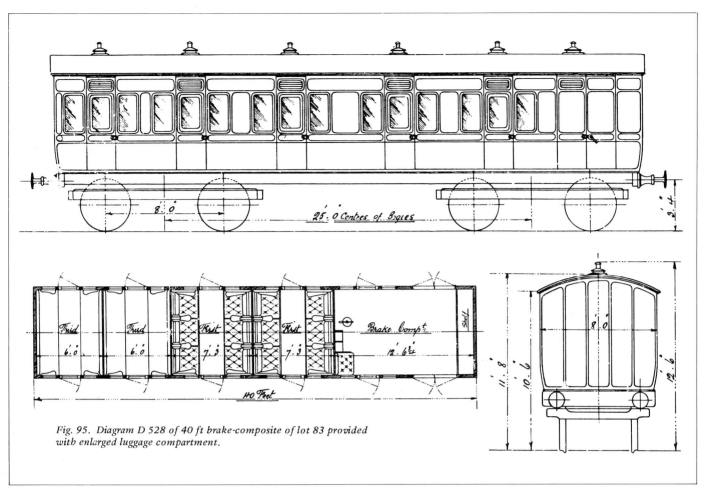

Fig. 95. Diagram D 528 of 40 ft brake-composite of lot 83 provided with enlarged luggage compartment.

Fig. 96. 43 ft third-class carriage No. 33 of lot 85, built to drawing 515. (DY 6470)

Fig. 97. 43 ft brake-third No. 1254 of lot 85, also built to drawing 515. *(DY 5750)*

built; instead eighty 43 ft brake thirds, ordered in December 1882, were constructed in their place as lot 85. The considerable delay was no doubt due to the amount of work created by the immense renewal programme which had been undertaken. The lot also included twenty 43 ft third-class carriages, and some confusion has been caused because the second copy of the Lot Register states that

this lot consisted of 100 third-class carriages. One of the third-class carriages, which were similar to those of lot 60 to drawing No. 515, was No. 33 and is shown in *Fig. 96*; two others may have been Nos. 91 and 101, all three being replaced in 1907. The brake-thirds, represented by No. 1254 in *Fig. 97*, were also similar to those of lot 60 to drawing 515. Some were probably numbered 475, 500,

Fig. 98. 43 ft composite with luggage compartment, No. 316 of lot 86 built 1883. *(DY 6464)*

521, 413, 419, 444, 447, 485, 537, 560 and 582. They were replaced by carriages of lots 610, 679 and 680 in 1905-7.

More bogie composites were ordered in January 1883 as lot 86, which consisted of ten 43 ft vehicles to drawing 579, all of which were completed in December 1883. Their four third-class and two first-class compartments were supplemented by a very short luggage compartment, which was unusual in that the double doors folded in the middle, the door nearest the end of the carriage having the other hinged to it. No. 316 is illustrated in *Fig. 98*. No diagram of this lot was prepared and all must have been replaced in 1904-5. According to diagram D 809 one was made available for War Office use in 1915. The plan shows that no alterations had been made to the carriage, the weight of which was given as 18 tons.

The next two lots to be ordered, 88 and 89 of January 1883, were the 54 ft carriages introduced to make good the loss of seating capacity caused by the old method of replacement mentioned earlier. On 2nd January 1883, at a meeting of the Traffic Committee, it was agreed that from 1st May next two express trains each way between Liverpool and London were to be run at suitable times independently of the Manchester and London service. These were to be formed of 3 three-car sets, brake-third, first and brake-third, all carried on six-wheeled bogies (GP 3744 of 1st February). The 9 brake-thirds needed formed lot 88 and they were all completed by August 1883. Their drawing 580 does not appear to have survived, but diagram D 809 shows the plan of one of them which was available for War Office use in 1915. The lavatory compartment measured only 2 ft 8 in by 3 ft 9 in and was fitted in a corner of the third-class compartment next to the guard's compartment. Its opaque window can be seen in the official photograph of No. 1369, reproduced as *Fig. 99*. The arrangement must have been far from convenient and, so far as is known, it was not repeated in any other Midland carriages.

Other numbers carried were 1370 and probably 1365, 1367, 1376 and 1381, all seemingly taken from old carriages altered from second-class in 1875. Nos. 1369 and 1370 were replaced in 1910 by carriages of lot 714 and No. 1365 in the same year by one of lot 715. Although they were replaced so late, and must therefore have been in the capital stock of 1905, no diagrams of them were prepared, possibly because they were due for renewal, having attained the age of 21½ years. A note on D 809 shows that at least one of these carriages survived until 1915, presumably in the duplicate stock, but no further information is available about them.

The trio of 54 ft first-class carriages which formed lot 89 were also completed in August 1883 and so the new independent express service between London and Liverpool must have used existing carriages when it was inaugurated on 1st May. The new vehicles were built to drawing

Fig. 99. 54 ft brake-third No. 1369 of lot 88, built 1883. (DY 5776)

Fig. 100. 54 ft first-class carriage No. 36, with luggage compartment each end, of lot 89, constructed in 1883 to drawing 581. (DY 5823)

581 and contained 6 first-class compartments supplemented by a luggage compartment at each end, as will be seen from *Fig. 100*. This illustrates No. 36; another was No. 29. Apart from Directors' saloon No. 1, they had the distinction not only of being the sole arc-roofed *bogie first-class* carriages built but also the only first-class carriages turned out as renewals in the period under review. There is no record of any alterations to them, but it is thought that they were given Nos. 2502-4 in 1902. No diagram was prepared and they were replaced in 1908 by carriages of lot 677.

No photograph of these new trains of six-wheeled bogie carriages has been traced, nor is it known how long they were operated in three-car sets or whether the similar six-wheeled bogie carriages of the Cheshire Lines which appeared in 1881 had had any influence on the Midland. Although given the same type of underframe (drawing 372) as the Midland Scotch Joint Stock composites of lot 24 built in 1879, lots 88 and 89 had a new type of steel-framed six-wheeled bogie, with 11 ft 6 in wheelbase (drawing 539 of 23rd January 1882) instead of the 11 ft wheelbase wooden-framed bogie used on the MSJS vehicles. It was set at 35 ft centres and all subsequent 54 ft carriages up to lot 359 had the same underframe arrangement.

Lot 95, which followed next, represented the largest batch of 43 ft thirds to be built; ordered in June 1883, it consisted of 100 carriages which were constructed in 1883 and 1884 to diagram D 490 on page 84. Neither photographs nor numbers of any of this batch can be found but it is believed that No. 918 may have been one. In 1918 there were 58 still in service and this had been reduced to 24 by 31st December 1922.

By the beginning of 1884 the final stage of the vast renewal programme had been reached. On 23rd January Clayton informed the Traffic Committee that some 500 old third-class carriages and 150 old composite and first-class carriages needed replacement. After one or two changes of mind (CW 1708 and 1760), this was achieved by the construction of 158 bogie carriages (lots 105, 106 and 108-110) and 350 six-wheelers made up of 100 composites (lot 111) and 250 thirds (lot 112). The six-wheelers are dealt with on page 104.

Lot 105, comprised of twenty-five 45 ft composites, each with 3 first, 2 third and a luggage compartment, was ordered in February 1884, but in the following August it was decided to fit them with lavatories by dispensing with the luggage compartments, the first ordinary carriages to be so equipped. This was carried out but the batch was, in fact, turned out with three third-class compartments in each instead of two. They are illustrated in *Figs. 101* and *102*. The arrangement of a pair of lavatories between two compartments became a standard practice on the Midland until the large-scale introduction of the corridor carriage; even after this it was continued in some suburban stock.

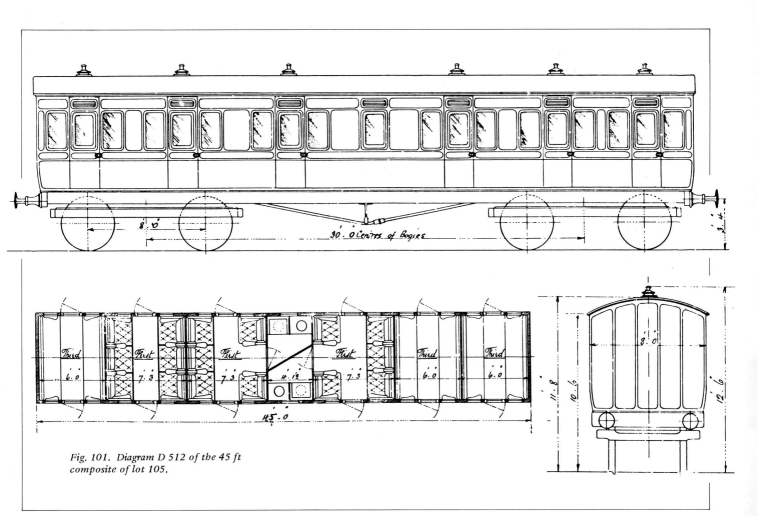

Fig. 101. Diagram D 512 of the 45 ft composite of lot 105.

Fig. 102. No. 487, 45 ft composite of lot 105, as built with two lavatories in 1884. The water tank partly above the roof was put inside by 1900. (DY 5775)

Fig. 103. 45 ft lavatory-composite No. 395 of lot 105 photographed c.1889 when it had been fitted with electric lighting. The dark blue SMOKING window labels had replaced the SMOKING boards, the roof brackets for which are still *in situ.* (DY 6492)

George Dow Collection

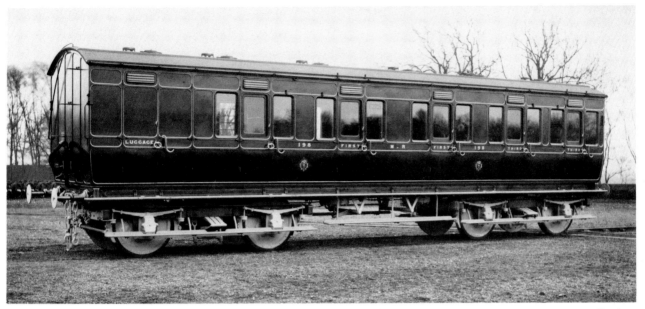

Fig. 104. No. 198, 40 ft brake-composite of lot 106, completed in 1884 to drawing 606. *(DY 5795)*   *George Dow Collection*

The water tank was carried partly above the roof, which made it vulnerable to frosty weather, but a similar arrangement was followed with some carriages built during the next two or three years: the tanks were put inside before 1900. By December 1884, twenty-one of lot 105 had been completed, the remaining four being finished in the following April.

In its issue of 5th October 1883 *The Engineer* stated that the Midland had decided to fit its coaches with the Pintsch system of compressed oil gas illumination, of which mention was made on page 58. 'The Midland Railway Company thus once again takes the lead in one of the most desirable railway improvements' ran the report, 'but in this case the credit deserved is perhaps not quite so great as for some of the improvements made on the Midland line, in as much as this system of lighting by gas costs considerably less per year than the troublesome, sinnermaking oil lamps.' An odd expression, the last one, but that the report as a whole was over-optimistic is borne out by CW 1955 of 18th February 1886. This contains a Traffic Committee resolution that two lavatory carriages were to be fitted with the Pintsch system of illumination by gas for working in the Scotch services, the cost being £100 16s. 0d. These must have been two of lot 105 and it is evident that the wholesale provision of oil-gas lighting in carriages had not yet started.

Although built only a short while after lots 88 and 89, these 45 ft composites were given a diagram in 1905. No. 487 in *Fig. 102* replaced one of the last Kirtley carriages; it was renumbered 3539 in 1902 and replaced in 1910 by a bogie composite of lot 757. Most will have been renewed by this time, but a dozen were still running in 1918 and three on 31st December 1922. No. 395 in

Fig. 103 is shown newly painted outside Derby works in about 1889. It is fitted with battery boxes below the underframe and with a flexible electric cable at the end. Some experiments were made with electric lighting on trains in the London-Bradford service and No. 395 may have been one of the carriages involved, although fittings for oil lamps are still in place.

These experiments had been preceded by others of a similar character. *Engineering*, in its issue of 31st May 1889, reported:

'This week the Midland Railway Company began to use the electric light on their system, the light being used for the first time on the London and Manchester and Liverpool express. The dynamos are situated in the rear guard's van, the driving gear being attached to the axle of the front pair of wheels. The speed of the dynamos was to be very quickly and easily regulated, and during the run from London to Leicester the light was quite steady and brilliant. During the stoppage of the train to change engines the light was kept perfectly steady by the accumulators.'

Unfortunately, these initial attempts of the Midland to obtain an improved system of train lighting did not enjoy the success they deserved. At the company's half-yearly meeting at Derby on 12th August 1894, the then Chairman, G. E. (later Sir Ernest) Paget, said that it had been a great disappointment to the Board to have to do away with electric light. It was a beautiful light, he said, but unreliable and very costly. If it were possible to have a dynamo worked from the engine which would illuminate all the carriages as soon as they were attached, he believed near-perfection in train lighting would be attained.

Lot 106, consisting of eight 40 ft brake-composites, was ordered in March 1884; they were completed in the following August. The vehicles were nominally of a new

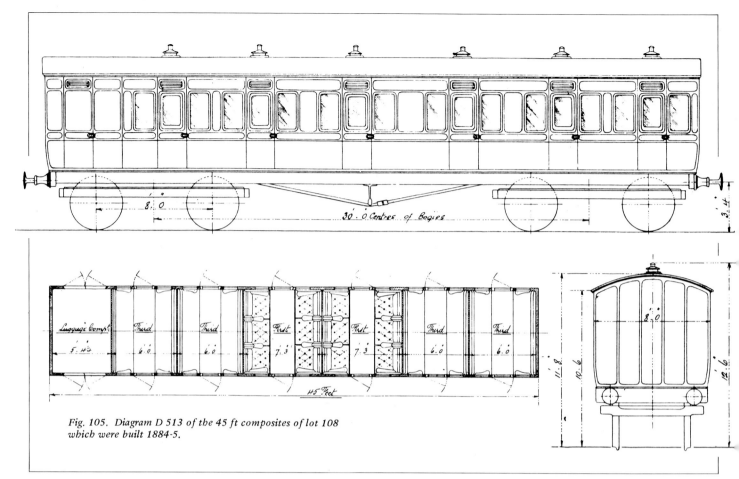

Fig. 105. Diagram D 513 of the 45 ft composites of lot 108
which were built 1884-5.

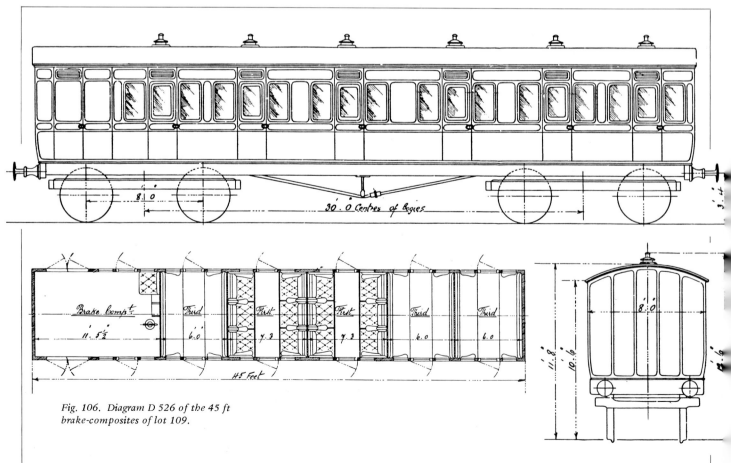

Fig. 106. Diagram D 526 of the 45 ft
brake-composites of lot 109.

type, to drawing 606, but they were, in fact, generally akin to the earlier brake-composites of lot 69, with an enlarged guard's compartment taking in what was a third-class compartment in the older carriages. As noted earlier, many of the older ones also had this compartment subsequently taken into the guard's, so making them similar to lot 106, No. 198 of which is shown in *Fig. 104*, its applicable diagram being D 528, reproduced in *Fig. 95*. These brake composites can be distinguished from the earlier ones by the position of the double doors in the guard's compartment, which were set some 1 ft 9 in from the end, as compared with about 9 inches in the predecessors. They were the last batch of 40 ft carriages to be built and, from this time onwards, no composites shorter than 45 ft were produced. They had quite a long life, four still being in service in 1918, but all had gone by 31st December 1922.

The eighty 45 ft bogie composites of the next batch, lot 108, which were also ordered in March 1884, contained 2 first-class, 4 third-class and a luggage compartment. They were built during 1884-5 to a new drawing 617 and are illustrated in their diagram D 513 in *Fig. 105*. There is no official photograph of them and no more is known of them, except that 56 were still in operation in 1918 and 14 on 31st December 1922.

Lot 109 was made up of twenty 45 ft brake composites ordered in March 1884 to the same drawing as the preceding lot, but embodying a longer guard's compartment and one third-class compartment less, as shown in *Fig. 106* of diagram D 526. No official photograph of them was taken when new but one appears in the motor trains chapter in Vol. 2. Five subsequently had a third-class compartment altered to a pair of lavatories; the compartment selected was the second one from the end, so allowing one first- and one third-class lavatory to be made. One was altered in December 1898 to a slip-composite and in 1907 seven were adapted for use in motor trains. When built in 1885 four were numbered 469, 491, 515 and 520, becoming 3521, 3543, 3567 and 3572 in 1902, and another was renumbered 2925 at the same time. It is not known how many were still in service in 1918 or at the end of 1922, but it is unlikely that they can all have been withdrawn by the latter date.

The 25 bogie composites of lot 110 were elegant 54 ft twelve-wheelers embodying 3 first, 4 thirds and a luggage compartment and were originally provided with oil lighting. No. 430 is illustrated in *Fig. 107*. Ordered in March 1884 and built to drawing 618 in 1886, their diagram D 507 is shown in *Fig. 108*. They were among the last bogie arc-roofed carriages to be constructed without lavatories and in 1892 twenty of them were altered to lavatory composites, including No. 279, shown in *Fig. 109*. Unusually, a separate diagram, D 507A, was drawn for the conversion, which was of two varieties. The diagram shows the first-class compartment nearest the luggage compartment altered to first- and third-class lavatories; in the case of No. 279 the first-class compartment at the

Fig. 107. 54 ft composite with luggage compartment No. 430 of lot 110, built in 1886. (DY 6467)

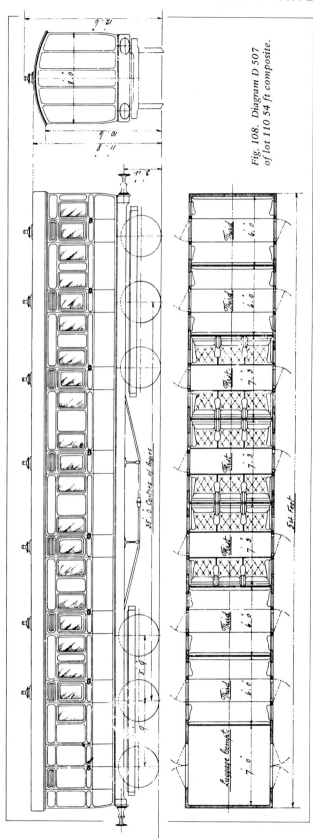

Fig. 108. Diagram D 507 of lot 110 54 ft composite.

other end of the vehicle was converted. No. 279 was fitted with gas lighting at the same time.

According to the Drawing Office copy of the Diagram Book, all 25 of the carriages were in service in 1918 and 21 on 31st December 1922. This is the annotation on D 507, but a note on D 507A in the same book reads '11 of lot 110 left at Dec 1922', implying that 11 of the lavatory carriages were left. The further implication is that there were 10 of the non-lavatory type, although there should be not more than five if in fact 20 were altered. The discrepancy cannot, unfortunately, be resolved. No. 481 was renumbered 3533 in 1902, and replaced in 1923 by a new carriage of LMS lot 33, together with about 45 other composites, some of which were doubtless also from lot 110. Others must have been replaced at an earlier date, since four had been withdrawn before 1923.

The thirty 43 ft third-class carriages of lot 113, ordered in March 1884, were similar in all respects to those of lot 60. They were probably built in 1886, but nothing further is known of them, except that 25 were still in service in 1918 and 14 on 31st December 1922. For some unaccountable reason a couple of 43 ft Post Office vehicles were turned out in the same lot, although the only thing common to the two types was the underframe; they are dealt with in Volume 2.

On 4th February 1887 Clayton was able to report (CW 2084) that during the six months ending 31st December 1886 all arrears of renewal of Midland carriages had been cleared after nine years, these at one time, June 1884, having amounted to 310 vehicles. He added that there were now 62 third-class compartments in excess of the capital stock and that the only Midland coaching vehicles which had not been rebuilt to the new standards were 93 carriages, 210 horseboxes, 161 carriage trucks and 9 passenger vans. Some 85 further carriages were renewed in 1887-92 and these will doubtless be those mentioned by Clayton.

It had been noted in March 1886 that the continuance of carriage stock renewal on a compartment for compartment basis would result in the creation of more first-class compartments than prevailing traffic levels warranted (CW 1973). The decision was therefore taken to renew only 50 of the next 300 first-class compartments to be broken up, and to replace the remaining 250 by third-class compartments. This was to be accomplished by the construction of 10 bogie brake-composites, 20 bogie brake-thirds, 30 six-wheeled brake-thirds and 15 six-wheeled composites of lots 149, 150, 151 and 141 respectively. These 75 carriages contained 300 compartments, 40 of which were first-class.

Although ordered in May 1886, drawing 755 of lot 149 was not made until 29th August 1887 and the vehicles themselves were not built until 1889. No official photograph of these ten 45 ft lavatory-brake-composites has been traced, but their general appearance and internal

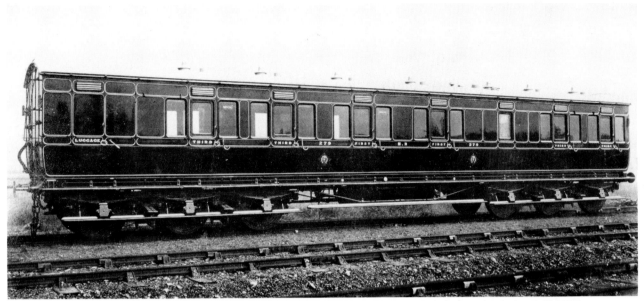

Fig. 109. 54 ft composite No. 279 of lot 110 in 1892 when a compartment had been converted to two lavatories. *(DY 6508)*
George Dow Collection

layout are shown in *Fig. 110* of their diagram D 527. The layout reflects the wish expressed by the Traffic Committee in September 1888 for the inclusion of one first-class compartment instead of the two originally envisaged. The vehicles were the first to be built with third-class lavatories since the brake-thirds of lot 88 and all subse-

quent bogie arc-roof carriages were so provided. In 1918 there were nine still in service and seven on 31st December 1922; all had gone by 1933.

In May 1886 the twenty-two 43 ft brake-thirds of lot 150 were ordered. According to CW 1973 twenty were to be regarded as renewals and it is presumed that the extra

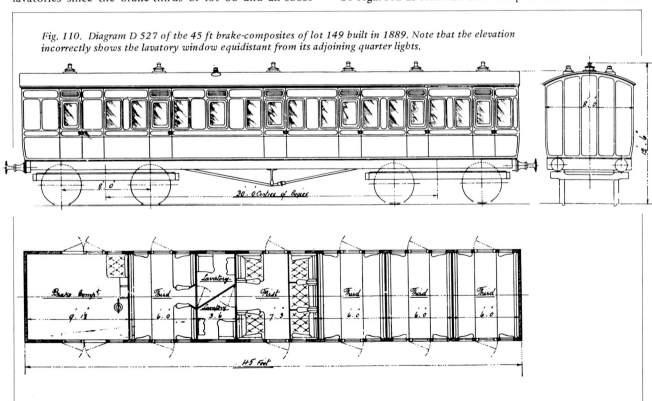

Fig. 110. Diagram D 527 of the 45 ft brake-composites of lot 149 built in 1889. Note that the elevation incorrectly shows the lavatory window equidistant from its adjoining quarter lights.

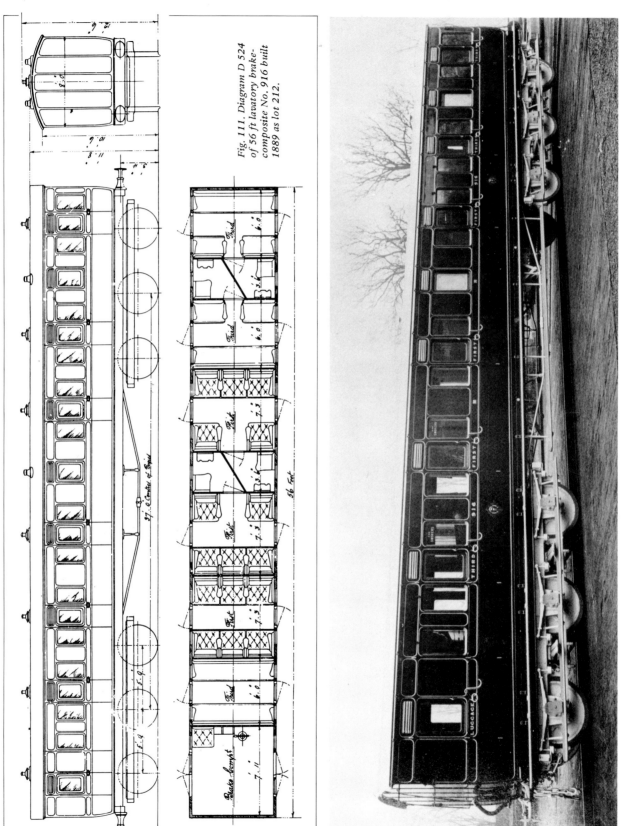

Fig. 111. Diagram D 524 of 56 ft lavatory brake-composite No. 916 built 1889 as lot 212.

George Dow Collection

Fig. 112. No. 916 deservedly won a Grand Prix medal at the Paris Exhibition of 1889. (DY 6572)

Bogie Carriages built at Derby as renewals 1879-89

Lot No.	Date	Drawing No.	Diagram No.	Number built	Type
27	1/79	383	—	50	40 ft third-class, six 3rds
36	11/79	,,	—	50	,, " " "
50	7/80	331	—	10	" composite, 3rd/1st/1st/1st/3rd/luggage
58	3/81	,,	—	10	" " " " "
60	7/81	515	490	50	43 ft third-class, seven 3rds
,,	4/82	,,	,,	40	" " " "
,,	,,	,,	502	10	" brake-third, five 3rds
69	11/81	332	—	50	40 ft brake-composite 3rd/3rd/1st/1st/3rd/brake
79	6/82	563	—	30	45 ft composite, 3rd/3rd/1st/1st/3rd/luggage
83	10/82	332	—	37	40 ft " same as lot 16
85	12/82	515	490	20	43 ft third-class, same as lot 60
,,	,,	,,	502	80	" brake-third, " " "
86	1/83	579	—	10	" composite 3rd/3rd/1st/1st/3rd/3rd/luggage
88	,,	580	—	6	54 ft brake-third, seven 3rds
89	,,	581	—	3	" first-class, luggage/six 1sts/luggage
95	6/83	515	490	100	43 ft third-class, same as lot 60
105	2/84	620	512	25	45 ft lavatory-composite 3rd/1st/1st/lavs/1st/3rd/3rd
106	,,	606	528	8	40 ft brake-composite 3rd/3rd/1st/1st/brake
108	3/84	617	513	80	45 ft composite, 3rd/3rd/1st/1st/3rd/3rd/luggage
109	,,	,,	526	20	" brake-composite, 3rd/3rd/1st/1st/3rd/brake
110	,,	618	507	25	54 ft composite, 3rd/3rd/1st/1st/1st/3rd/3rd/luggage
113	,,	515	490	30	43 ft third-class, same as lot 60
149	5/86	755	527	10	45 ft lavatory-brake-composite, 3rd/3rd/3rd/1st/lavs/3rd/brake
150	,,	515	502	22	43 ft brake-third, same as lot 60

two were also renewals. Their diagram number was D 502 (*Fig. 89*), so they were apparently identical with lot 60. All were completed in 1888 and all were still at work in 1918, twelve remaining on 31st December 1922. It is possible that one of them was numbered 228, which was replaced by a new vehicle in 1907 and renumbered 0228. It was allocated 22845 in the LMS renumbering list of 1933 but withdrawn in December 1932.

In the table above are summarised the bogie carriages built at Derby as renewals over the years 1879-89. No less than 240 third-class carriages to D 490 and 112 brake-thirds to D 502 were constructed, but their running numbers or duplicate numbers (which contain the prefix 0) are known positively in only a few cases. They are given below, with the year of replacement shown in parentheses:

Third-class   188 (1904); 14, 0458, 577 (1905); 33, 91, 101,
D 490:   0582 (1907); 673 (1908); 760, 878, 918, 356, 399,
           522 (1910); 780, 791 (1911); 1372 (1912); 312,
           646 (1913); 31 (1922)

Brake-third   1708 (1903); 156 (1904); 0475, 0500, 521 (1905);
D 502:   0228, 0233, 0334, 0413, 419, 429, 0444, 447, 485,
           537, 560 (1907); 695, 746, 1131, 01174, 1254
           (1909); 1272 (1921); 1283 (1922); 1702 (1924)

Brake-thirds Nos. 537, 1702 and 1708 had one compartment altered to a pair of lavatories in 1892; No. 0233 was sold in 1912 to the Stratford-upon-Avon & Midland Junction, becoming No. 31 and, in 1923, No. 18992 of

the LMS; and No. 0228 was allotted LMS No. 22845 in the list of 1933 but was withdrawn in December 1932.

The remaining bogie passenger carriages built during the years 1877-96 were lots 212, 224 and 359. All were additions to capital stock and can conveniently be noted before turning to the six-wheeled renewals and additions of the same period.

On 20th September 1888 CW 2268 reported that the Board had agreed to exhibit at the Paris Exhibition of the coming year a locomotive and a carriage. The latter had, in fact, already been ordered the previous month as lot 212 and was to consist of the 56 ft lavatory-brake-composite No. 916 depicted in *Figs. 111* of diagram D 524 and *112* of the official photograph.

No. 916 was unique, being the only one of its kind and the only carriage of its length to be built by the Midland. The underframe was of oak, the floor, partitions, roof and inside casing red deal, the outside panelling and mouldings Honduras mahogany. The six-wheeled bogies were chiefly wrought iron, the tyres and axles Bessemer steel, the wheel discs being teak segments with cast iron bosses. The axleboxes were so arranged that the brass bearings could be removed without lifting the carriage. Internally No. 916 was electrically lit and in the guard's compartment was a hand-brake, a valve for applying the vacuum continuous brake, a switch for controlling the electric light and appliances for communicating by cord with the driver.

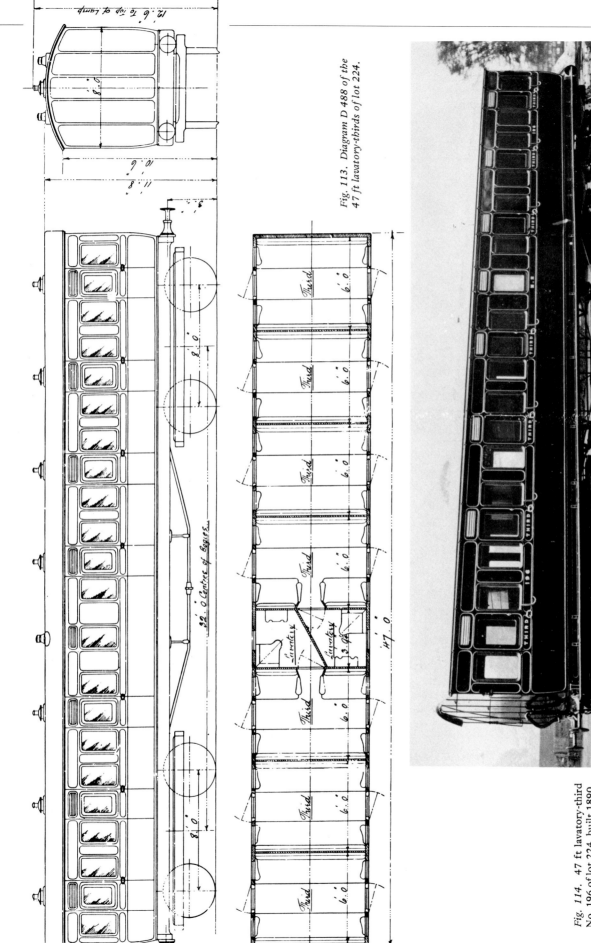

Fig. 113. Diagram D 488 of the 47 ft lavatory-thirds of lot 224.

Fig. 114. 47 ft lavatory-third No. 196 of lot 224, built 1890. (DY 6514)

The three first-class compartments each had a different style of furnishing, exemplifying those adopted for Midland carriages. The non-smokers' compartments were upholstered in blue woollen carriage cloth, the smokers' in crimson morocco and the ladies' in brown plush.

The labels on the windows of the two smoking compartments (the third-class and first-class nearest to the guard's compartment) were unusual in that they read 'FOR SMOKERS' in two lines instead of the usual 'SMOKING'. Similar labels, 'FOR LADIES', distinguished the two ladies compartments (the first class and adjacent third-class at the opposite end of the coach). No. 916 must have been one of the first carriages to use smokers' labels instead of the boards which had hitherto been dropped as necessary into holders above the compartment doors. It was also provided with holders on the roof for the newly-adopted larger destination boards.

This beautiful railway carriage, which added lustre to the enviable reputation the Midland was earning for itself, was deservedly awarded a Grand Prix medal at the Paris Exhibition. It is believed to have been renumbered 3716 in 1902 and was replaced twenty-three years later.

Lot 224 consisted of six bogie lavatory-thirds which were built instead of a like number of six-wheeled lavatory-thirds. They were 47 ft long, the only Midland vehicles of this length apart from the two experimental vehicles constructed in 1876. They were generally similar to the 43 ft third-class carriages, but it will be seen from the diagram D 488 in *Fig. 113* that a pair of lavatories was embodied between the third and fourth compartments. The order for them was made in February 1889 and all six were completed in 1890 to drawing 776, which is of interest in that the end view shows that torpedo ventilators were at 3 ft 6 in centres when fitted; the red-ink amendment giving this detail is dated 20/3/05.

These were the last bogie carriages to be turned out with oil lighting. The official photograph in *Fig. 114* shows No. 196. This was replaced in 1928 by an LMS lavatory-brake-third of lot 448, the first six of which were numbered 73, 125, 184, 196, 254 and 292, and it is likely that these were the numbers of the lot 224 vehicles. They were built as additions to stock so the six numbers were presumably ones that had been ruled out but now brought into use again.

The bogie lavatory-brake-composites of lot 359 were the last arc-roofed carriages to be built. They were asked for by the Traffic Committee in July 1895, at an estimated cost of £817 5s. 0d. each. Twenty were ordered as addi-

Fig. 115. Clayton four-wheeled bogie. *(DM 7165)*

tions to stock in August 1895 and all were built to drawing 1071 in the following year. *Fig. 117* of D 522 gives their leading dimensions and internal layout. They were generally similar to previous designs, with all the handsome lines of a Clayton twelve-wheeler, but had gas lighting and the improved third-class furnishings introduced in 1891. It will be seen from *Fig. 118* of No. 484 that the door handles differed from those used before, the ring handles being in a plane perpendicular to the body side. An external lever was fitted to the righthand door of the luggage compartment.

It is likely that all twenty carriages were still at work on 31st December 1922, although this is not recorded in the Diagram Book. Only three of the original numbers are known, Nos. 484, 535 and 542 which respectively became Nos. 3536, 3587 and 3594 in 1902, when Nos. 3378, 3423 and 3430 were also allocated to others of lot 359. The LMS list of 1933 showed the following:

MR No.	LMS No.	Date of withdrawal
3378	25926	January 1936
3423	25927	February 1933
3430	25928	January 1933
3536	25929	February 1934
3587	25930	May 1955
3594	25931	December 1933

Neither No. 3536 nor No. 3587 carried their LMS numbers but the second of them actually survived long enough to appear in a British Railways list of May 1955, where it is shown as 'missing'. It was soon officially written off!

Six-wheeled carriages built during the years covered by this chapter must now be given attention, beginning with those regarded as renewals. CW 1708 of 17th March 1884, which recorded the decision to build 140 replacement bogie carriages, also referred to the need for 50 non-bogie twin-composites, the residue in 5-bodied third-class carriages for excursion traffic. It was in CW 1708 that mention of six-wheeled long-buffered carriages was first made in a Midland minute, although in fact carriages of this type had appeared in the previous year as Midland Scotch Joint Stock. The Glasgow & South Western had built, to Midland drawings, ten of the third-class five-compartment type, whilst the North British had constructed 25 of the composites. Except for the brakes, they were exactly the same as the subsequent Midland vehicles.

The archaic expression '5-bodied' appears several times in the minute books. It is derived from the earliest days of railways, when a 5-compartment carriage would, in effect, be made of 5 carriage-bodies on a common underframe. The reference to twin-composites is to the compartment

Fig. 116. Clayton six-wheeled bogie. (DM 9437)

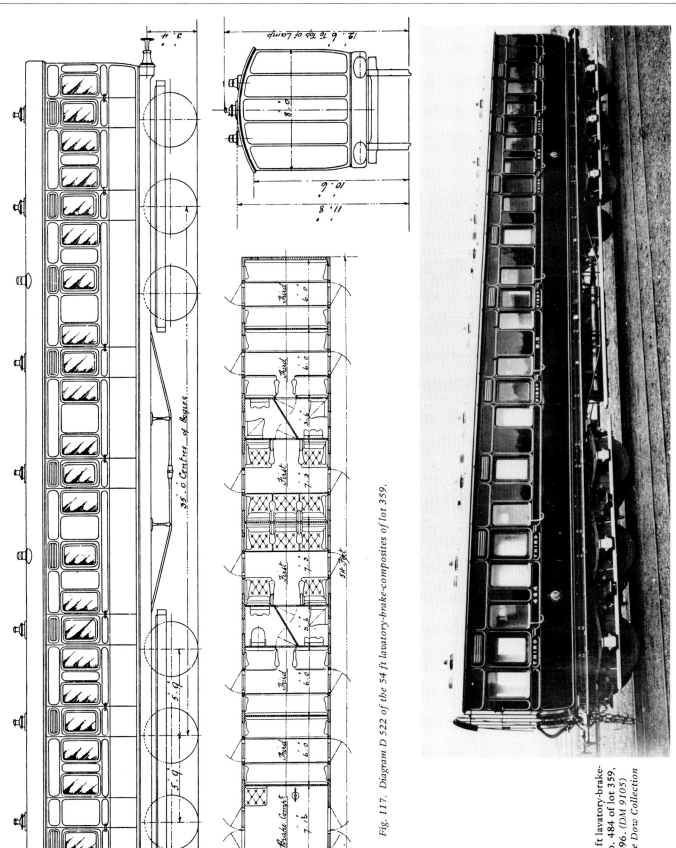

Fig. 117. *Diagram D 522 of the 54 ft lavatory-brake-composites of lot 359.*

Fig. 118. *54 ft lavatory-brake-composite No. 484 of lot 359, completed 1896. (DM 9105)*
George Dow Collection

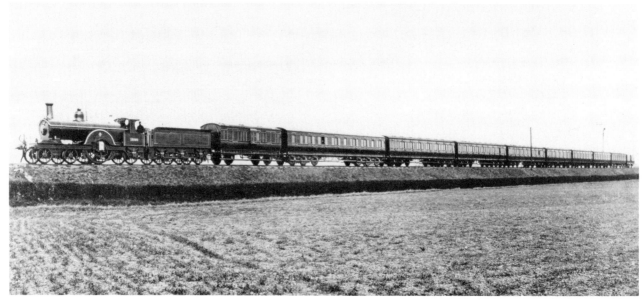

Fig. 119. A Midland express of c.1889, hauled by 4—2—2 No. 1860 and consisting of 25 ft passenger van, No. 361, 56 ft Paris Exhibition composite No. 916, 54 ft composite No. 210, two 54 ft brake-thirds, a 43 ft composite, three 43 ft thirds and a 25 ft passenger van. *(DY 7098)*

arrangement of these vehicles, which had a first and a third on either side of a central luggage compartment. Because of the more generous dimensions of the passenger compartment, the luggage compartments were smaller than those of the 29 ft and the 30 ft composites of 1874-5; in consequence, the new twin-composites had odd-size luggage doors, the lefthand one having the usual width of two feet, the other being 1 ft 8 in wide. Although the composites were of a new design, the third-class and brake-thirds were generally similar to the short-buffered close-coupled carriages already under construction for suburban services and dealt with in Volume 2.

Initially 100 composites, not 50, and 250 third-class carriages were built, these forming lots 111 and 112 respectively of March 1884. They were followed in November 1885 by 100 more composites and 50 third-class of lots 141 and 142, the former being specially referred to in CW 1926 of 4th December 1885. This stated that the Traffic Committee had resolved that thirty first-class carriages of 90 compartments now on the broken up list were to be renewed as 45 composite carriages each containing 2 first, 2 third and 1 luggage compartment, the third-class carriages being made up from the third-class carriages already broken up. It is probable that the extra carriages in the lots were not specifically mentioned because they were straight replacements of old carriages, compartment for compartment. Altogether 551 long-buffered six-wheeled arc-roofed carriages were built at Derby as renewals over the years 1884-88 and they are summarised on page 121. The largest contingent consisted of 314 third-class vehicles, illustrated in *Figs. 120* and *121*, followed by 200 composites, *Fig. 122* and 30 brake-thirds, *Figs. 123* and *124*.

The remaining seven vehicles were for trains operated to and from West Bridge station, the Leicester terminal of the old Leicester & Swannington Railway. These consisted of 1 third-class, 2 composite and 4 brake-third carriages which, because of restricted clearances in Glenfield tunnel, were made only 7 ft 8 in wide over panels and were provided with bars across the droplight openings to prevent passengers putting their heads out. Drawing 741 applied to all seven carriages, which formed lot 201. Their appearance when new is shown in official photographs *Figs. 125, 126* and *127* and it is believed that they may have retained their oil lamps until renewed around 1928. In 1928-9 it is known that a couple of them, Nos. 1247 and 929, were replaced by new carriages with the same numbers, but the old carriages may have been withdrawn before this.

Some of the six-wheeled composites (D 516) had their luggage boxes converted to a pair of first-class lavatories. This was carried out in 1892 and *Fig. 128* illustrates No. 877 so altered. It is not recorded whether any of the third-class carriages were similarly converted.

The known numbers of six-wheelers built as renewals 1879-89 are given below, most or all of which were long-buffered:

Third-class D 493	11, 30, 54, 395, 492, 504, 524, 563, 606, 619, 622, 626, 705, 736, 744, 756, 0819, 863, 902, 903, 922, 931, 958, 974, 983, 987, 988, 992, 995, 1003, 1022, 1025, 1033, 1061, 01067, 1075, 1087, 1098, 1109, 01119, 1122, 1210, 1217, 1218, 1229, 1243, 1252, 1255, 1264, 1279, 1300, 1333, 1340
Brake-third D 504	64, 71, 73, 149, 154, 204, 207, 865, 0971, 01053, 1182, 1205, 1341, 01368, 01383, 01400, 01441
Composite D 516	488, 877, 03397, 3447, 03451, 3540, 3674, 3684, 3701, 3705, 3706, 3712

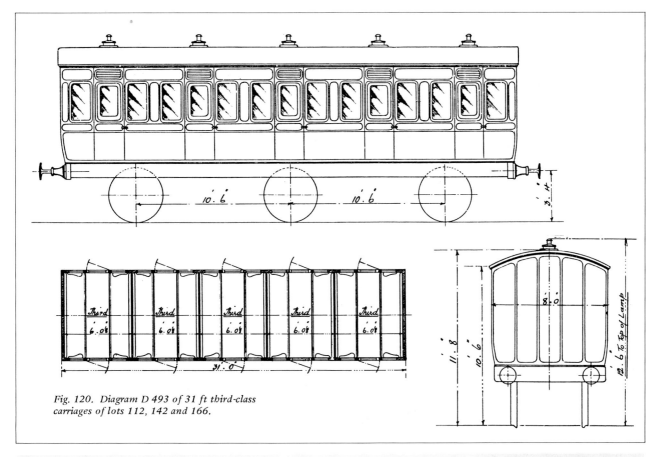

Fig. 120. Diagram D 493 of 31 ft third-class carriages of lots 112, 142 and 166.

Fig. 121. 31 ft third-class carriage No. 1217 of lot 112. (DY 6501)

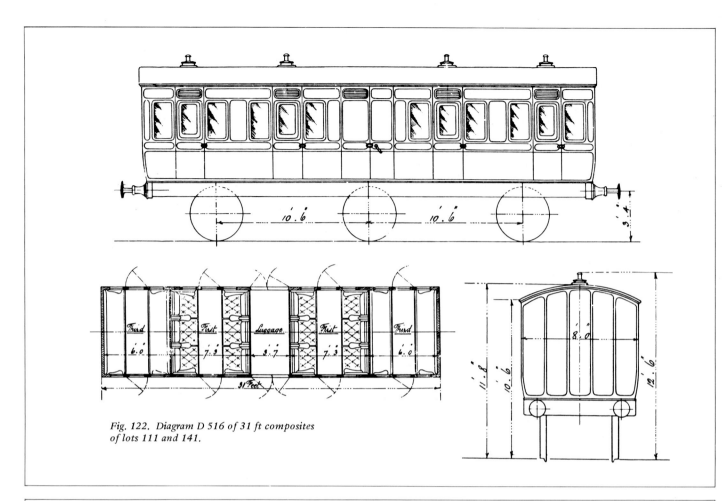

Fig. 122. Diagram D 516 of 31 ft composites
of lots 111 and 141.

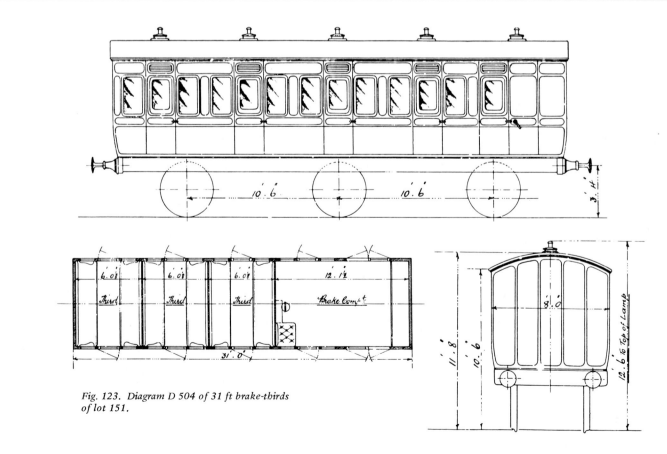

Fig. 123. Diagram D 504 of 31 ft brake-thirds
of lot 151.

Fig. 128. No. 877, 31 ft composite as altered in 1892 by conversion of central luggage box into lavatories. *(DY 6494)*

thirds, which were displaced by the six 47 ft bogie lavatory-thirds of lot 224 already described, twenty-two six-wheeled lavatory-thirds of lot 225, of which No. 874 is illustrated in *Figs. 129* and *130*, and twenty-two ordinary six-wheeled thirds of lot 226. All were ordered in February 1889 and represented some of the earliest lavatory carriages to be built. In June of the same year CW 2370 records the need for 85 five-compartment thirds, 15 'five-bodied brake carriages' and 12 slip carriages. The thirds were turned out as lot 230 but the brake-thirds of lot 241 were not ordered until January 1890.

At the end of that year the biggest order of the period was placed, made up of 28 brake-thirds, 20 lavatory-thirds and 120 ordinary thirds (lots 257-259), six of the last-named, according to the Lot Register, being fitted with short buffers. Finally, there were the 75 thirds and 32 brake-thirds of lots 290 and 291, ordered at the beginning of 1892 for the impending opening of the Dore and Chinley line and, in May 1895, 50 'five-bodied third-class carriages' (lot 357) which were the last of the type to be constructed. On 2nd April 1896 Clayton reported that they were ready for traffic 'except for the photographs for the interior of the compartments', which were doubtless part of the improved internal furnishings introduced in 1892 and exemplified in *Figs 131* and *132*.

These additions to the six-wheeled passenger stock are summarised on page 121. Once again, running numbers are difficult to trace, but it is known that the thirds of 1890, which were withdrawn in 1933-34, included Nos. 931,

988, 992 and 1210 and the brake-thirds of 1891-92, withdrawn in 1933-35, included Nos. 819, 1341, 1368, 1383, 1400 and 1441. Lot 357 was made up of Nos. 1808-57 and one of the brake-thirds took the place of No. 1502, which was destroyed in June 1892 at Esholt Junction. It seems that 241 of the additional thirds and all the lavatory-thirds and brake-thirds took scattered numbers in the third-class list.

Although many of these carriages were doubtless made up into sets with a brake-third at each end, most were probably used as loose vehicles in ordinary trains. Photographs and accident reports show that they were regularly in service with bogie vehicles in express trains right up into LMS days. On 31st December 1922 47 of the composites and 528 of the thirds were still in traffic.

A few of the thirds and composites saw service on the Brecon & Merthyr Railway. CW 6029 of 18th December 1919 authorised the sale of eight of the former and three of the latter, together with three four-wheeled brake vans, to J. F. Wake of Darlington, from whom they were purchased by E. E. Cornforth on behalf of the B & M in the following year. The Midland running numbers are not known, but on the B & M the brake vans (D 529) became Nos. 101-3, the composites (D 516) Nos. 104-6 and the thirds (D 493) Nos. 107-14. The Great Western withdrew them all before the end of 1928.

The contract with the Pullman Palace Car Company was due to end in 1888 and on 10th October 1886 it was decided to build some sleeping carriages. They were in the

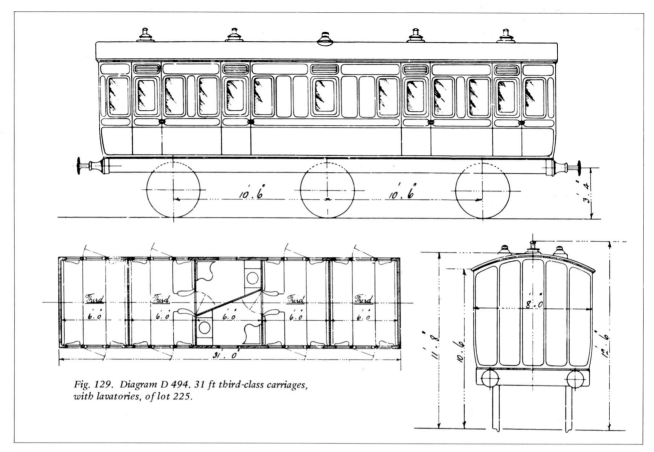

Fig. 129. Diagram D 494. 31 ft third-class carriages,
with lavatories, of lot 225.

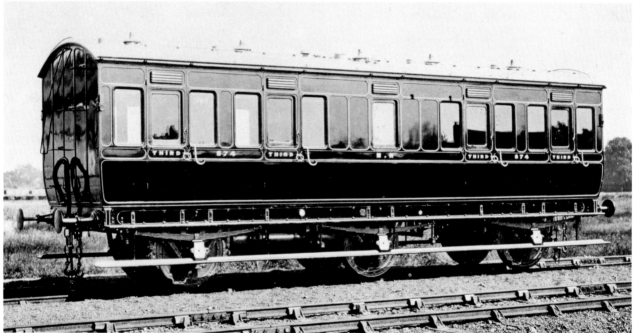

Fig. 130. No. 874, 31 ft third-class carriage of lot 225, built in 1889. (DY 6502)

Fig. 131. First-class compartment in 31 ft composite No. 901 photographed, it is believed, in 1892-3. The woodwork of the ceiling and walls was finished in sycamore veneers with maple margins. Blue leather covered the doors and blue carriage cloth, trimmed with lace, the seats. There was patterned lino on the floor, partly covered by a blue rug. *(DM 7562). Fig. 132.* Third-class compartment in No. 901. The ceiling and upper part of sides were painted white with crimson decoration, the corner motifs being stencilled. Woodwork was mahogany and the upholstery crimson plush. *(DM 7561)*

nature of an experiment to determine the most suitable type to use when the Pullman cars were withdrawn from the Midland. Plans were submitted by Clayton, but not until 17th March 1887 was it decided to take in hand three types, 54 ft, 48 ft and 32 ft in length. In fact, four sleeping carriages were built, the fourth being 43 ft long, and all were ordered in March 1887 as follows:

Lot 171 54 ft with 6-wheeled bogies — No. 356
Lot 172 48 ft with 4 wheeled bogies — No. 357
Lot 173 43 ft with 4-wheeled bogies — No. 358
Lot 174 32 ft with six wheels — No. 913

They were completed in the same year. No reference has been traced of their reception by the travelling public, but no more were built because in March 1888 the Midland bought the 14 Pullman sleeping cars then running on the system and used them until they were replaced by new Derby-built vehicles in 1908. The four sleeping carriages of 1887 are shown in *Figs. 133* to *136*.

No. 356 contained six first-class compartments, each only 6 ft 4 in long and each having accommodation for four passengers by day or by night. Its drawing, 677, is little more than a simple diagram to a scale of half an inch

to the foot, but shows that at night there were two longitudinal berths and two lower ones in each compartment. The upper berths were suspended from the roof by iron scissor-type stays and when not in use could be raised and clamped to the roof; during the day there were four ordinary first-class seats with a central gangway. A door in the middle of each partition gave access to the entrance lobbies and to the two lavatories. Thus the four middle compartments were subject to disturbance by the passing of travellers seeking the latter facilities. The two end compartments had only one door each and so enjoyed greater privacy; one was for ladies and the other was marked 'private' on the drawing. The weight of No. 356 was 26 tons 8 cwt. According to the Weight Book it was altered to a third-class saloon, but it was renumbered 2749 in 1902, which suggests that it was then still a first-class carriage. Presumably therefore it was converted initially to a first-class saloon, maybe in 1894 when Nos. 357 and 358 were altered, and the note in the Weight Book refers to a subsequent change. The last record of it is in a photograph taken in or after 1906, wherein part of No. 2749 can be seen behind a locomotive; it wears the

Fig. 133. The longest of the four sleeping carriages built in 1887, 54 footer No. 356 of lot 171. *(DY 6433)*

post-1906 livery, with word SALOON displayed on the waist.

Drawing 684 shows that the 48 ft sleeping carriage No. 357 contained three compartments, each with two berths, and one compartment with four berths, two upper and two lower. Each of the four compartments was 8 ft 9 in long. There was a separate compartment with W.C. and

washbasin for each sleeping compartment and in the central lobby was a heater and a hinged seat for the attendant. Each sleeping compartment had two external doors, giving an entry and exit either side of the carriage. The two inner compartments also had a door leading to the central lobby but the two outer ones were completely isolated, as will be seen in the plan in *Fig. 137.* The weight

Fig. 134. 48 ft sleeping carriage No. 357 of lot 172. *(DY 6460)*

Fig. 135. 43 ft sleeping carriage No. 358 of lot 173. *(DY 6452)*

Fig. 136. Baby of the sleeping carriage quartette was 32 ft six-wheeler No. 913 of lot 174. *(DM 5934)*

Fig. 137. Internal layout of sleeping carriage No. 357, drawn by Gregory Fox.

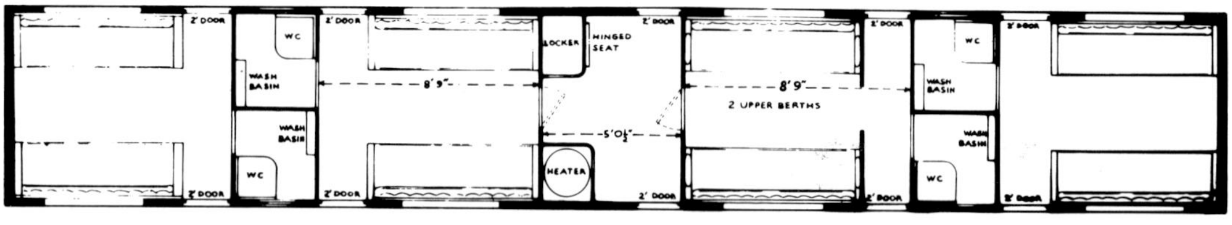

of No. 357 was 20 tons 1 cwt and its life as a sleeping carriage was a short one. On 4th May 1894 (CW 2964) it was agreed to convert it to a third-class carriage and fit it with hot-water pipes. The extent of the conversion was not then recorded, but it is believed that it was furnished with longitudinal seats in each compartment, because diagram D 1253 of 1921 refers to it as a first-class saloon. It is likely that doors were cut through the partitions when it was altered in 1894, in such a manner that two lavatories were retained. It was renumbered 2750 in 1902, converted to a third-class saloon in 1921 and replaced in 1930.

The 43 ft sleeping carriage No. 358 also had four sleeping compartments, but arranged in a different way. Its drawing 685 is missing, but the photograph suggests that the two inner compartments were reached from transverse lobbies partitioned off from them and were therefore less roomy than the others. The two end compartments appear to be arranged similarly to those in No. 357, with individual access from outside only. There was no attendant's compartment and, presumably, no heating. This carriage, which weighed 18¾ tons, was also altered to a first-class saloon in 1894 and fitted with hot-water heating. It was renumbered 2751 in 1902 and replaced in 1930.

These alterations to all three bogie sleeping carriages, when only seven years old, seem to indicate that they were either not satisfactory or surplus to requirements because of the retention of the Pullman sleepers. The minutes are silent on the point.

Six-wheeled sleeping carriage No. 913, which was built to drawing 686, had two sleeping compartments in the middle, each provided with a lavatory, as in the arrangement adopted for No. 357. At one end was a luggage compartment with double doors, and at the other end a third-class compartment for servants, there being no connection between the various compartments. No. 913 weighed 11 tons 17 cwt. Because of the third-class compartment the vehicle was classed as a composite and numbered in the composite series. It was renumbered 3713 in 1902 and replaced in 1925. There is no record of any alteration to it.

In 1890 the Midland built its longest-ever four-wheeled carriages. On 4th July CW 2492 reported that the Traffic Committee required 100 workmen's carriages. In the following month 50 were ordered (lot 251), later increased to 63. They were constructed to drawing 831 and the body seems to have been to the same outside profile as the ordinary 31 ft carriages, but contained six compartments, each 5 ft long between partitions. No record of the interior finish has survived but undoubtedly the seats were of wood, with no cushions. It has been suggested, but not confirmed, that their external finish was a utilitarian dark green, and the official photographs, one of which is reproduced in Fig. 138, show that the square-cornered mouldings were black without lining. A further seven were built in lot 289 of November 1891. As far as can be determined, the carriages of lot 251 were given Nos. 1626-88 and the remainder Nos. 1689-95. No diagram number was allocated.

Accident reports show that these workmen's carriages were made up in trains of various lengths, eight and eleven being used in two trains on 7th October 1899, with a brake at each end in addition. The numbers of the latter on one train, 789 and 794, suggest brake-thirds, possibly old 27 ft London suburban vehicles built in 1876 by Gloucester Wagon Company. The second train mentioned was the 5.08 am from Dronfield to Glapwell and six of the carriages were noted as Nos. 1639/69/41/52/54/92, the other five not being mentioned. On 11th September 1906 the 5.35 am from Dronfield to Alma colliery consisted of workmen's brake No. 6, carriages Nos. 1695/89/58/28/34/1646/45/35/43/91 and workmen's brake No. 0131. A note in the Railway Magazine of July 1908 (page 87) mentions a set of Midland four-wheeled workmen's carriages without lights then in use on the Avonmouth-Hotwells service. They were Nos. 1633/50/58/66 and two brake-thirds Nos. 22 and 0284. The last-named is thought to have been a 27 ft brake-third of lot 100 and, along with No. 22, replaced in 1908-9.

Most of the workmen's carriages were replaced in 1928-29 by new LMS carriages of various types. Nos. 01659, 01676 and 01693 survived in the duplicate list and in 1933 became Nos. 26472-4. No other workmen's carriages were built or ordered by the Midland, it being customary to use old worn-out carriages for the purpose.

At the other end of the scale were the superb dining carriages constructed over the years 1892-96. Up to 1891 the Midland had only the five vehicles converted from Pullman cars in 1882-84 and it was now decided to expand the stock. Drawings for a new dining carriage were requested early in 1891 by the Traffic Committee and although the idea was blessed by the General Purposes Committee there is no record of a discussion about the services on which it was to be employed. On 13th April 1892 Clayton reported that new dining carriage No. 359 was finished and ready for traffic. Its lot number was 278.

This impressive addition to the Midland fleet is illustrated in *Fig. 140*. Built to drawing 857, it was 60 ft long and embodied a kitchen and two dining saloons, the larger of which seated twelve and the smaller, for smokers, eight. The high clerestory roof resembled those used earlier by Clayton, but with a higher profile. The underframe to drawing 858 was a new departure for the Midland, being entirely of steel and much more thoroughly strengthened with truss rods than those used on the earlier 54 ft carriages. The six-wheeled bogies were the same as those carrying the latter, with a wheelbase of 11 ft 6 in. No gangway was provided originally at the kitchen end because at the time there was no other similarly equipped carriage to which it could be coupled. Doubtless the gangway was fitted early in 1893, when two more carriages of the same type were built for the joint use of the Midland and

Glasgow & South Western, together with three third-class cars, all of which had a gangway at one end so that the first-class kitchen serviced both cars of a pair. A gangway was added to the outer end in 1899, for use with the new corridor carriages built in that year. A description of the interior furnishings has not survived, but those of the similar dining carriages for the joint services to and from Glasgow are given in Volume 2. Externally, the vehicle was embellished with a large wyvern as well as the usual armorial devices.

Major alterations to No. 359 were made in 1903-6, when a side corridor was put in past the kitchen. Diagram D 440 in *Fig. 139* shows the final layout, with the pantry taking the place previously occupied by the gentlemen's lavatory, the smoking saloon moved so as to adjoin the main saloon and both lavatories repositioned at the end of the vehicle with a new entrance lobby. No. 359 became No. 2752 in 1902 and retained this number when altered to a common restaurant car in 1910. Three years later there was a proposal, shown in diagram D 713, to alter it to a third-class saloon with longitudinal seats, but this was not carried out. The vehicle remained in service until the autumn of 1930, being shown as attached to the Midland Division of the LMS in the Dining Car Circuit Brochure of July of that year, but it did not appear in subsequent ones.

On 18th July 1895 the question of putting first- and third-class dining carriages on the London-Manchester service came up for consideration. In fact, it was agreed only to build three first-class carriages '63 ft in length and

Fig. 138. **31 ft workmen's carriage No. 1689 of lot 289, built 1892.** *(DY 6472)*   *George Dow Collection*

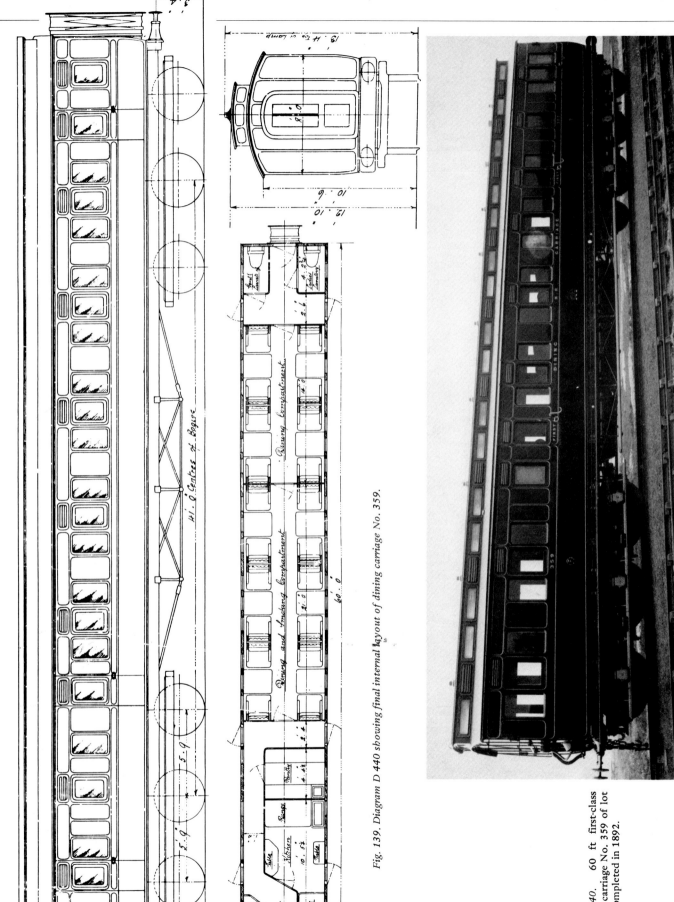

Fig. 139. Diagram D 440 showing final internal layout of dining carriage No. 359.

Fig. 140. 60 ft first-class dining carriage No. 359 of lot 278, completed in 1892.

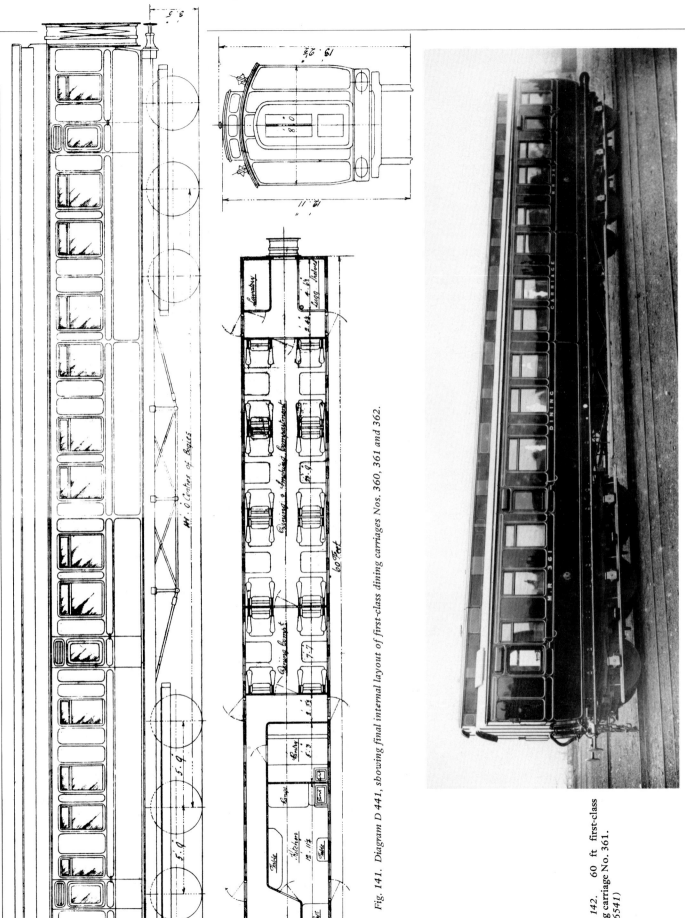

Fig. 141. Diagram D 441, showing final internal layout of first-class dining carriages Nos. 360, 361 and 362.

Fig. 142. 60 ft first-class dining carriage No. 361. (DY 6541)

Fig. 143. Interior of first-class dining carriages of 1896, Nos. 360, 361 and 362, furnished and upholstered by the House of Gillow of Lancaster. *(DY 8508)*

equal in construction and finish to those now running on the L & NWR' (CW 3076). These were to cost £8,000 and they were ordered in lot 365 in the following September to drawing 1085, being 60 ft like No. 359, the 63 ft quoted in the minute being the length over buffers. This time the non-smoking saloon seated only six passengers and the smoking saloon twelve, the reverse of the proportions of the previous type. All three dining carriages, which were numbered 360, 361 and 362, were specially furnished internally in green silk and braid by the House of Gillow of Lancaster and their opulent appearance may be judged from *Fig. 143.* No. 361 is illustrated in *Fig. 142.* An account received from the firm (CW 3215) showed the furnishings and upholstering of Nos. 360 and 361 amounted to £3,581 17s. 8d., the work being carried out in a special shed costing £140 which was erected to cover each carriage as the work was being done. Examination of Gillow's surviving records in the Westminster City Library shows that No. 362 was also furnished by them. No gangways were originally provided because it was intended to operate the three carriages alone. There is no record of the date they were so equipped, but special works order of

11th March 1906 refers to the fitting of a new gangway, a corridor through kitchen and pantry, and a lavatory moved to the end. This new arrangement is shown in *Fig. 141* of diagram D 441.

All three were gas-lit when new, with pendant lamps hung from the centre of the clerestory roof; these were replaced by electric lamps about 1923. The toplights to the fixed lights, and the use of large windows in pairs in the dining compartments, made the carriages intermediate in style between those built in the period 1875-95 and those built between 1897 and 1905. They were the last to have the all-steel underframes, Clayton reverting to composite wooden and steel underframes with subsequent 60 ft carriages.

They were renumbered 2753-5 in 1902. No. 2753 was given a riding test in 1924 and was described as a first class car. All three appeared in the Dining Car Circuit Brochures of July 1929 and 1930 as common cars with kitchen, but not after 1930. No. 2755 was replaced in 1929 and no doubt all were withdrawn in the autumn of 1930.

Long-buffered six-wheeled carriages built at Derby as renewals in 1884-88

Lot No.	Date	Dwg. No.	Diag. No.	No. built	Type
111	3/84	560	D516	100	31ft composite
112	3/84	561	D493	250	,, third-class
141	11/85	560	D516	100	,, composite same as lot 111
142	11/85	561	D493	50	,, third-class ,, ,, lot 112
151	5/86	664	D504	30	,, brake-third
166	2/87	561	D493	14	,, third-class ,, ,, ,, ,,
201	1/88	741	West Bridge	2	,, composite
201	1/88	741	,,	1	,, third-class
201	1/88	741	,,	4	,, brake-third

Long-buffered six-wheeled carriages built at Derby as additions to stock in 1888-95

Lot No.	Date	Dwg. No.	Diag. No.	No. built	Type
193	12/87	561	D493	12	31ft third-class
194	12/87	664	D504	8	,, brake-third
220	12/88	664	D504	10	,, brake-third
225	2/89	782	D494	22	,, lavatory-third
226	2/89	561	D493	22	,, third-class
230	7/89	561	D493	85	,, third-class
241	1/90	664	D504	15	,, brake-third
257	12/90	664	D504	28	,, brake-third
258	12/90	782	D493	20	,, lavatory-third
259	12/90	561	D493	120	,, third-class
290	1/92	561	D493	75	,, third-class
291	1/92	664	D504	32	,, brake-third
357	5/95	561	D493	50	,, third-class

Fig. 143A. Part of carriage repair shop at Derby works in the 1890s and still in use as shop 'C'. In the right foreground, flanking the inspection pit, is the hydraulic mechanism for lifting carriage bodies from their bogies.

Fig. 143B. Down express formed almost entirely of Clayton clerestory square-light carriages and headed by Johnson 4–2–2 No. 2603. The absence of the customary guard's lookout, or ducket, on the leading bogie brake van is explained on page 126. Photographed at Welsh Harp, Hendon, by W. Leslie Good c.1900. (*George Dow Collection*)

CHAPTER VI

THE CLERESTORY HALLMARK
1896-1901

IN 1877 Clayton had set about replacing the whole of the Midland coaching stock and, as related in the previous chapter, had completed the task in mid-1886. By 1896 many of the earliest 'new' carriages were approaching the end of their useful life and, in February of that year, Clayton submitted a report on the subject (CW 3123). He drew attention to the fact that the time would soon arrive when the rebuilding of the company's fleet would have to begin and this opened the important question as to what the carriage stock of the future should be. He gave the following analysis, which embraced the great bulk of the coaching vehicles:

Age of carriages	First	Composite	Third	Pass. vans
21 years or more	–	–	20	–
20 ” ” ”	82	126	40	68
19 ” ” ”	27	124	16	136
18 ” ” ”	–	20	–	8
17 ” ” ”	–	–	54	100
16 ” ” ”	–	66	40	52
15 ” ” ”	–	30	49	–
14 ” ” ”	1	10	50	25
13 ” ” ”	–	72	–	–
12 ” ” ”	3	85	210	3
11 ” ” ”	121	8	336	–
10 ” ” ”	10	237	–	100
9 ” ” ”	–	87	339	30
	244	865	1,154	522

Grand total: 2,785

Clayton pointed out that some of the oldest carriages, those built by contractors between 1873 and 1878, required such extensive repairs that he did not think it economical to spend money on the maintenance of vehicles which may not now be considered up to modern requirements. He said that about ten years ago the carriage stock was well ahead of that of other railways, but since then no ordinary first class or composites had been built, whilst other companies had been going ahead upon what the Midland had previously done, leaving the Midland behind. He welcomed advice upon the subject generally 'as to what alteration in the model or fashion it would be well to adopt in making a fresh start', adding that if designs different from those of the past were to be adopted he would have timber to cut, dry and prepare, all taking time, before rebuilding could be started.

That the Carriage & Wagon Department of the Midland was no self-opinioned watertight one is borne out by the remainder of Clayton's report, which is worth quoting in full:

'I should be glad to get the matter well considered and discussed by each of the Departments interested in the subject, so as to obtain the best ideas and suggestions as to the length, width and height of the carriages, whether the bogie-truck principle should be used either more largely or less so for the future than in the past, whether the carriages should have clerestory roofs or any other shape. I should also like to hear about the windows, doors, blinds, locks and handles, ventilation, lighting and warming. I should also like to get opinions as to the upholstering of the compartments and what, if any, changes. Also regarding the decoration, mirrors, photographs, advertisements etc. Also, as to the seats, whether fixed or detached from the bodies.

'The question of lavatory accommodation should be fully considered and what proportion in number to first and third class compartments. With regard to lavatories, up to 10 years ago, while we were rebuilding our carriage stock, very little provision indeed was made in this respect, but since that date 627 lavatory compartments have had to be put in the carriages. I should like to get opinion expressed as to the best kind of lavatory most likely to suit railway carriages.

'Further, corridor carriages have received a good deal of attention lately, and have been much talked about, and a good deal has appeared in the public papers on the subject, but their adoption would involve the loss of carrying capacity and consequently of additional length and weight of trains by putting on more vehicles to make up for that loss of room.

'Finally, seeing that railway carriages do change fashion considerably in 20 years, which is about their lifetime, it seems desirable that we should, as far as we possibly can, anticipate what railway carriages of ten years hence are likely to be.'

In view of Clayton's remarks about having to cut, dry and prepare timber, one wonders why he did not produce it some two or three years earlier, giving himself more time for preparation of materials. The reason was probably because of the trade recession of the early 1890s, when Derby works was on short time with many men, even skilled cabinet-makers, laid off.

Gangways connecting carriages had been in use for many years on Post Office vehicles and, more recently, on some dining carriages. Corridor carriages proper, however, had not hitherto been contemplated by the Midland, possibly because the narrow carriage bodies would have given little space for the side corridor, while the open saloon-type carriage had not proved popular with the travelling public. Even now, corridor carriages were not introduced immediately, and the first to be ordered in 1898 were only intended to be used in conjunction with dining cars. However, the demand evidently grew rapidly

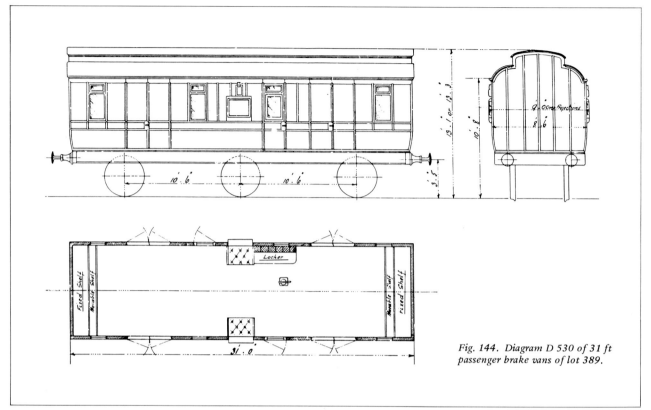

*Fig. 144. Diagram D 530 of 31 ft
passenger brake vans of lot 389.*

and the new non-corridor trains introduced in 1898-9 were replaced by corridor trains from 1904-5 onwards.

In August 1896 Clayton produced another report (CW 3169) in which he complained of the difficulty in getting carriages into the shops for repairs. The Traffic Department was so short of them that it intercepted vehicles *en route* for Derby works and used them! The continued expansion of passenger traffic was demonstrated in the following figures produced by Clayton soon afterwards:

Number of compartments	First-class	Third-class	
June 1886	3,149	8,341	
June 1896	2,966	11,368	

Passengers carried			Seasons
Year ending June 1886	1,452,023	29,539,630	40,000
Year ending June 1896	1,161,865	41,428,669	60,000

In other words, passengers carried had increased in number over ten years by 37.5% and compartments available for them by only 24.75%. He observed that 9.75% of the stock was presently out of traffic for repairs, compared with 14.5% ten years ago, and estimated that 465 new carriages were needed, with a further 177 to give enough to ensure adequate maintenance.

That was the background to the renewal programme which had its genesis in 1896, the first fruits of which were to be the incomparable new style of clerestory-roofed

carriages, destined to become a hallmark of the Midland. The initial order for them was for 18 vehicles forming 3 trains each of 6 carriages for the North and West traffic, namely between Bradford and Bristol. The lots were all dated 21st September 1896 but it was not until the following month that any mention was made of the new carriages in Carriage & Wagon committee minutes. In CW 3184 Clayton referred to them as having been approved by the joint committee, doubtless the Traffic and Carriage & Wagon committees working temporarily in double harness. The cost, £16,800, was soon afterwards ordered to be charged to capital.

Six types of vehicles were constructed, each train being made up in the order of 6-wheeled guard's van (lot 389, Nos. 576-8); 12-wheeled third-class carriage (lot 387, Nos. 1861-3); 12-wheeled third-class dining carriage (lot 385, Nos. 1858-60); 6-wheeled kitchen car with luggage space (lot 388, Nos. 579-81); 12-wheeled composite-first-class dining carriage (lot 384, Nos. 543, 544 and 687); and, finally, 12-wheeled brake composite (lot 386, Nos. 829, 917 and 918). Their respective drawing numbers were 1128, 1122, 1118, 1126, 1115 and 1124 and their diagram numbers are shown in *Figs. 144-149*. Two of the sets, the first of which is illustrated in *Fig. 152*, were used to form the 1.25 pm from Bradford to Bristol and the 2.05 pm from Bristol to Bradford, the third being a spare. When they began running, on 2nd August 1897, M. H. Rollason watched them pass through Birmingham New

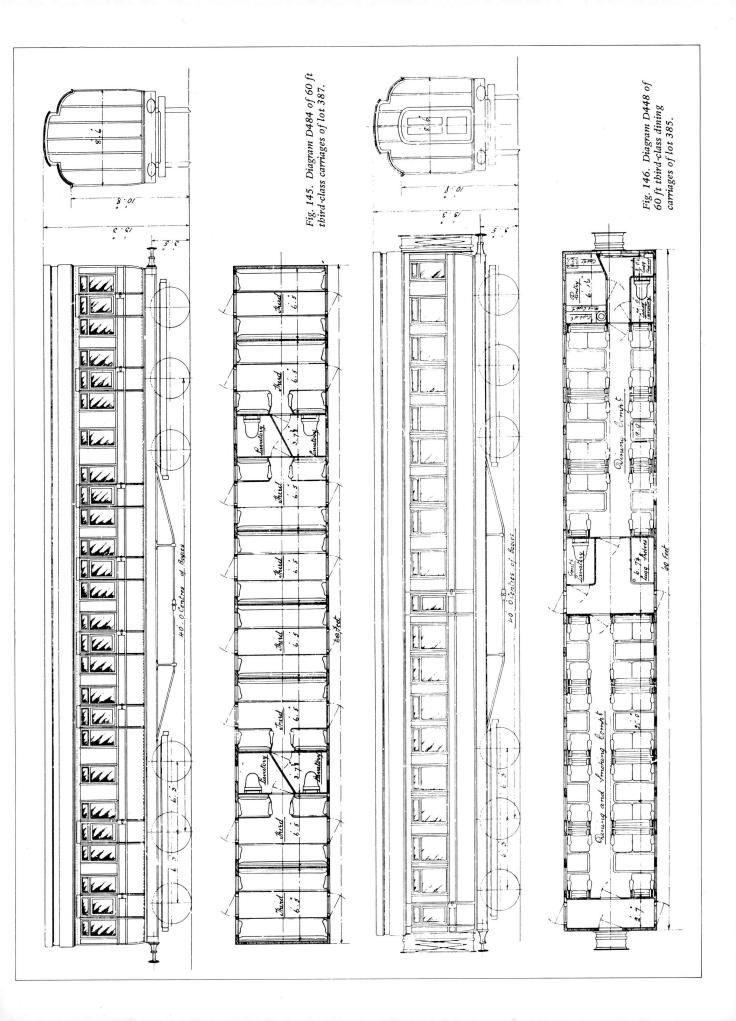

Fig. 145. Diagram D484 of 60 ft third-class carriages of lot 387.

Fig. 146. Diagram D448 of 60 ft third-class dining carriages of lot 385.

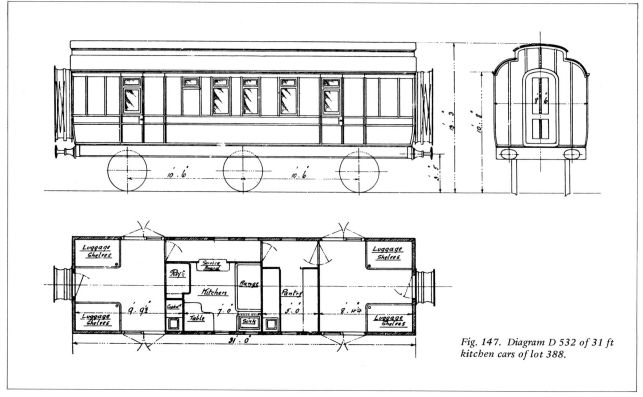

Fig. 147. Diagram D 532 of 31 ft kitchen cars of lot 388.

Street and, many years later, recorded the impression they made upon him in a contribution published in the *Stephenson Locomotive Society Journal* No. 30 of 1954. He tempered his enthusiasm by remarking that in fact there were no less than six classes of passenger on the new trains — first and third diners, first and third non-diners with lavatories and the same without lavatories! The reason for this unusual observation can be obtained from studying the plans in *Figs. 144-149*; it was true save for the first-class travellers, all of whom had access to a lavatory.

Another official photograph of one of the trains, taken soon after *Fig. 152* and reproduced in part as *Fig. 153*, shows the destination information which was by then painted on the roof of every vehicle. This read *Bradford, Leeds, Birmingham & Bristol Express* in sans-serif capitals throughout. A contemporary *Locomotive Magazine* coloured postcard indicates that the letters and border were in gilt on a crimson lake background. Another change in design was to be seen in the door handles, the hitherto ring type having been supplanted by a straightforward bar.

The striking external feature of the new carriages was, of course, the way in which the clerestory roof was made integral with the body endwise as well as lengthwise; it was no longer a box on top of an arc roof, because the end panels were now continuous from top to bottom. Overall height from rail was 13 ft 3 in to the top of the roof, with gas lamp-tops projecting a further 3 in, as in

the case of all the earliest of the clerestory carriages. The guard's vans and brake-composites had large lookouts, or duckets, the total width over which was 9 ft 6¼ in, and the width over steps was 9 ft 3 in. Carriages were built to these overall dimensions until about the middle of 1899, but on 13th June of that year there was an accident at Bakewell, which resulted in the Traffic, Way & Works and Carriage & Wagon committees meeting on 5th July to pass the following resolution: '. . . That the Way & Works committee be requested to report to the Board as to the places where the space between the main lines is less than 6 feet, with the approximate cost of altering the lines where in the open, leaving tunnels for further consideration.' And on 15th July the three committees resolved '. . . That the guard's lookouts be removed as soon as possible from 128 vehicles of new stock. That all the side lamps of the new stock be reduced from 6 to 4 inches in width and be placed lower on the carriage. That the question of side lamps being abolished and replaced by tail-end lamps and of reducing the size of the side lamps be further considered and a report be presented at the Directors' October meeting. And that the question of lessening the outside width over steps be also further considered and experiments made with the object of reducing this width to 9 feet.'

On 3rd November 1899 Clayton reported that he was removing the lookouts (CW 3625) and at the same meeting was quoted B 7489, which recommended that in future the outside width over all projections of new passenger

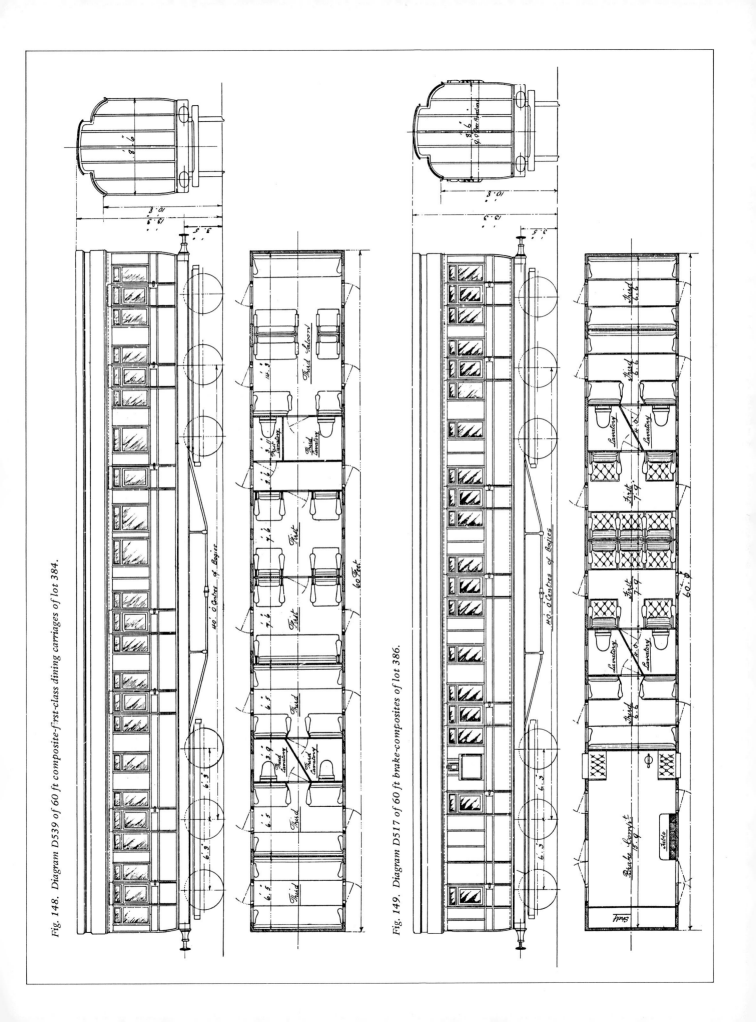

Fig. 148. Diagram D539 of 60 ft composite-first-class dining carriages of lot 384.

Fig. 149. Diagram D517 of 60 ft brake-composites of lot 386.

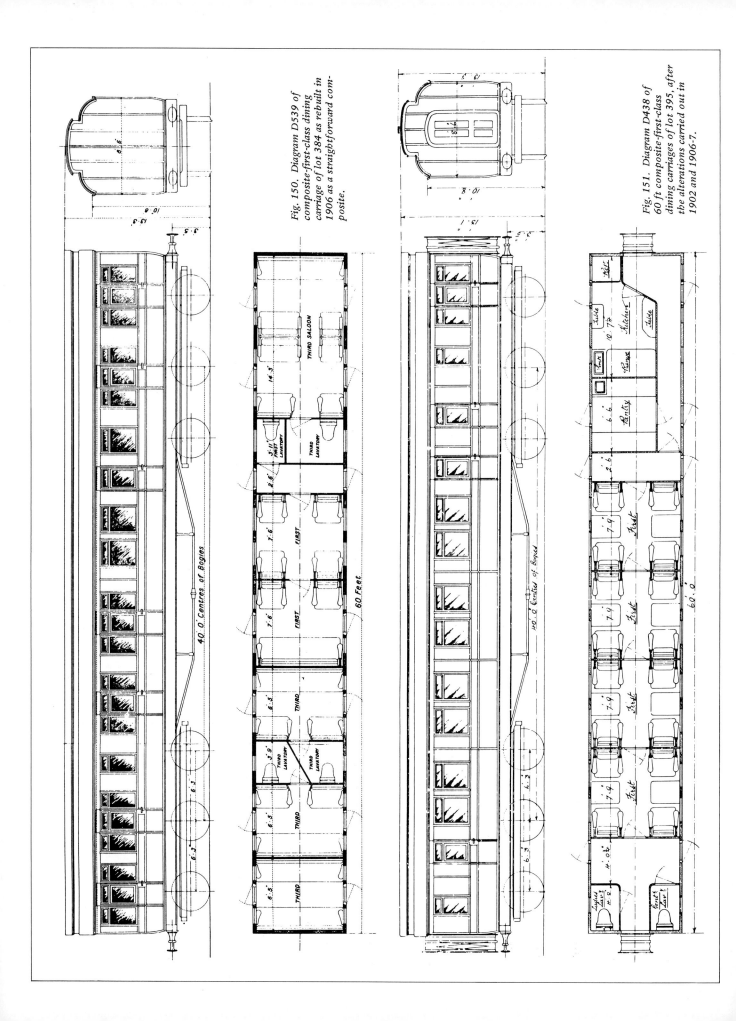

Fig. 150. Diagram D539 of composite-first-class dining carriage of lot 384 as rebuilt in 1906 as a straightforward composite.

Fig. 151. Diagram D438 of 60 ft composite-first-class dining carriages of lot 395, after the alterations carried out in 1902 and 1906-7.

Fig. 152. The first new-style clerestory-roofed train of 1897, photographed probably in July of that year, at the entrance to Derby works. Points of interest are the coat of arms on all vehicles except the leading van and the large lookouts (duckets) on the latter and the brake-composite. *(DY 6302)*

rolling stock should not exceed 9 feet. The existing side lamps of old stock were to be replaced at once by new lamps, a specimen of which was produced, being one inch less in width than present lamps. At the same time it was decided that the width of steps should be reduced and B 7534 approved a Carriage & Wagon committee recommendation to do so by 1½ in each side, so reducing the width over steps to 9 feet. The drawings of earlier clerestory carriages show this amendment, that on drawing 1179 being dated 18th December 1899. A photograph in the carriage and wagon supplement to the *Locomotive Magazine* of 1902 shows brake-composite No. 3004

without the lookouts; unfortunately the negative no longer exists.

It is likely that the three trains were replaced by new gangwayed corridor stock in 1905-6. Certainly the three composite-first-class dining carriages were altered in 1906 into ordinary composite carriages as shown in *Fig. 150.* When they were built they contained 3 third-class and 2 first-class compartments in addition to the first-class saloon, which was connected by gangway to the kitchen car. After alteration the first-class compartments had connecting doors to a lavatory and the saloon became third-class with a lavatory. They were renumbered 3595,

Fig. 153. Part of Bradford, Leeds, Birmingham and Bristol express showing destination information painted on the carriage roofs. The six-wheeler is the kitchen car. *(George Dow Collection)*

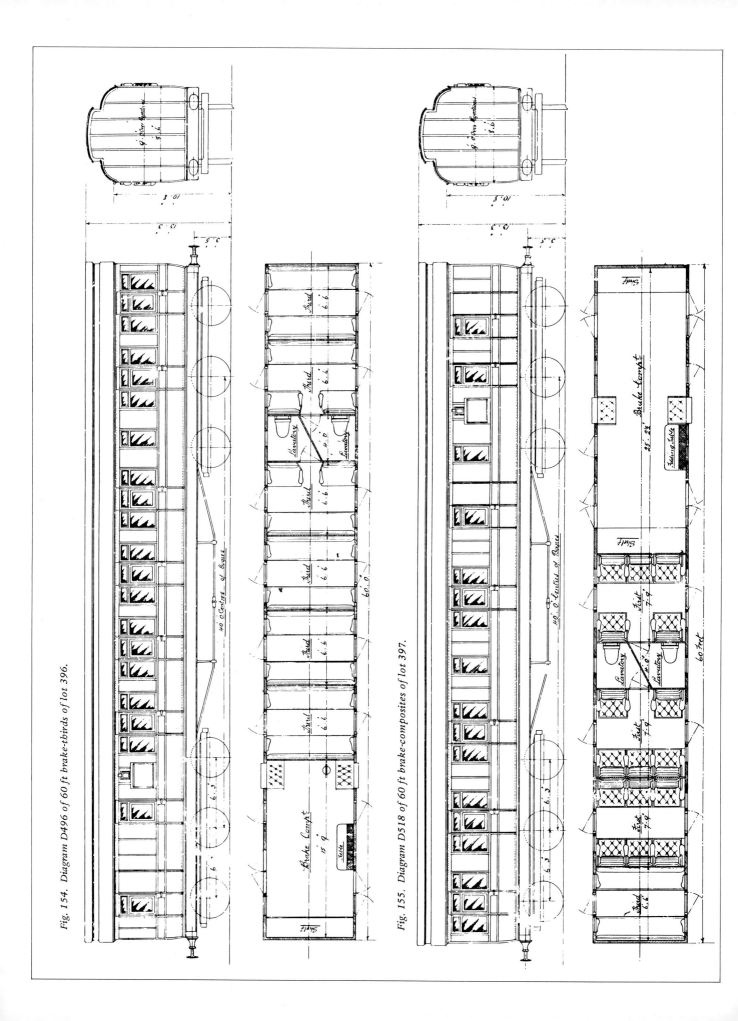

Fig. 154. Diagram D496 of 60 ft brake-thirds of lot 396.

Fig. 155. Diagram D518 of 60 ft brake-composites of lot 397.

3596 and 3647 in 1907 (No. 3595 is known to have been renumbered 03595 in about 1930 and 19807 in 1933), and all were replaced in 1929, No. 19807 lasting until September 1940.

Some time after 1907 the three kitchen cars were altered by having a passage made past the kitchen. At the same time the roof was lowered so that they would pass the Metropolitan loading gauge, with torpedo ventilators at the side, according to a Central Stock Register note. Two of them were used in ambulance trains from 1914 to about 1918, probably Nos. 579 and 581, which are recorded as being reconditioned in 1921, when all three were in traffic. An official photograph of ambulance train No. 11 shows one of the kitchen cars marshalled as the second vehicle, between the officers' carriage and a ward car. Three 'narrow type' kitchen cars appear in Dining Circuit Brochures for July 1928, 1929 and 1930, shown as Nos. 1849-51. It is believed that these were originally Nos. 579-81. They were not allotted new numbers in the 1933 list, so they were presumably withdrawn between September 1930 and late 1932.

The guard's vans were the prototypes of a numerous class which eventually numbered 301 vehicles, but no further examples of any of the other carriages were built. Of the third-class carriages No. 1861 became No. 18892 and No. 1863 was renumbered 18893 in 1933 and both were withdrawn by early 1937. The brake-composites became Nos. 3654, 3717 and 3718 in 1902 and 25938-40 in 1933, No. 25939 being the last of the carriages to remain in ordinary service when withdrawn in August 1946. It was probably survived by guard's van No. 33933, old No. 576, which in 1938 was converted into a staff riding van and may well have been in use for a further twenty years or so.

Two dining car trains for the London-Manchester service, each made up of a quartet of 12-wheeled 60 ft vehicles, followed the Bradford-Bristol sets before any clerestory carriages were built for general use. Each train consisted of a composite-first-class dining carriage to drawing 1146 (lot 395, Nos. 3001-2), a brake-third to drawing 1142 (lot 396, Nos. 3001-2), a brake composite to drawing 1149 (lot 397, Nos. 3003-4) and a third-class dining carriage to drawing 1152 (lot 398, Nos. 1864-5). *Figs. 151* and *154-6* give their diagram numbers and from *Fig. 156* it will be seen that the third-class dining carriage embodied two saloons, one of which was for smokers, and seated a total of 30 passengers. The saloons were embellished with mahogany panels and mouldings, ornamented ivory white Lincrusta-Walton ceilings and linoleum-covered floors. The seats were upholstered in figured crimson moquette and arranged two and one aside a gangway slightly off centre. The kitchen in this vehicle, which also served the adjoining first-class carriage, was equipped with large gas cooking range, boiler, carving table and refrigerator.

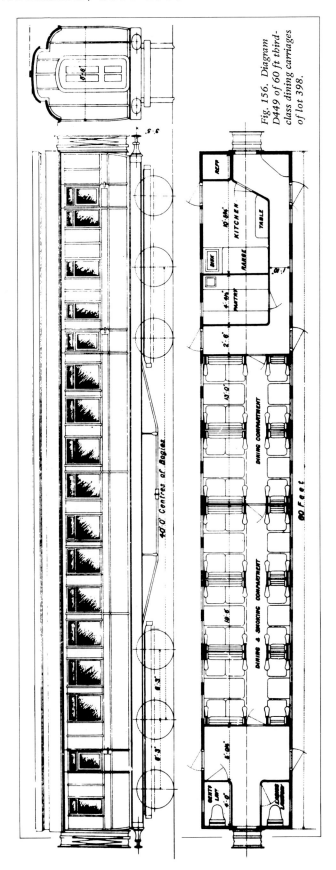

Fig. 156. Diagram D449 of 60 ft third-class dining carriages of lot 398.

Fig. 157. London-Derby-Manchester dining car express, one of two four-car sets built in 1898. *(L.P. Co./Ian Allan Library 2625)*

Dining accommodation for 12 first-class passengers was provided in a composite carriage coupled to the kitchen end of the third-class dining car just described. There were three first-class compartments each containing 4 seats arranged one each side of a central gangway. Their sides, partitions and doors were panelled in walnut wood, with carvings and mouldings decorated with gold tracery, the seats and tables being similarly treated. Upholstery was richly embossed velvet and the ceilings were covered with cream-coloured Lincrusta-Walton, with floral designs in gold leaf. The floors had Brussels carpet laid on a layer of 'Kork' felt and overlaid by a thick rug running down the centre of the car. At the end nearest the kitchen were luggage space and lavatories for ladies and gentlemen. At the other end was third-class accommodation in three compartments, two of which were served by lavatories.

The compartments in the rest of the train, which seated 18 first-class and 86 third-class passengers, were upholstered *en suite* with the dining carriages. Gas lighting by means of lamps suspended from the top of the clerestory was provided in all vehicles, each one of which carried the painted external legend *London Derby & Manchester* in sans serif capital letters at the roof edge on each side. The trains began running on 2nd May 1898.

Unfortunately, few photographs have survived of the clerestory carriages built during 1895-1905 and the minutes do not record any decisions on the change in style. Although there is little doubt that official photographs were taken in those years, only a handful has survived and it has been said that the negatives were given away in the 1930s for use in glasshouses. No prints have been traced and no album corresponding to that for the period 1875-95 is known to exist. But drawings and

diagrams remain and details of the changes made from time to time are given in these pages. Happily, several photographs exist of the London-Manchester clerestory carriages of 1898 in their original form. *Fig. 157* shows well the striking appearance of the complete train, with its four impressive carriages of uniform length and height. Another view of the train is produced in *Fig. 158*, in which ill-fated brake-third No. 3002 may be seen nearest the camera. This vehicle, along with Glasgow & South Western family saloon No. 161, was destined to be smashed up in the Wellingborough accident of 2nd September 1898, when a down express ran into a luggage trolley which had fallen off the platform. The other photographs, *Figs. 159-162*, feature individual vehicles. Negatives of the interiors have not survived but photographs taken inside the two dining carriages were illustrated in the *Locomotive Magazine* of 1898 and are reproduced in *Fig. 163*.

The two composite first-class dining carriages Nos. 3001-2 were extensively altered in 1902, becoming first-class cars with kitchens. There were now seats for 16 in four separate saloons, the new arrangement being shown in general arrangement drawing 1580, according to special works order No. 80 of 26th March 1902. The two cars were given Nos. 2591-2 in the new first-class series of 1902, and were further altered in 1906-7, when a passage by the kitchen was put in, as shown in D 438 in *Fig. 151*. They were replaced in 1929. Of the remaining components of the two sets, it is known that brake-third No. 3001 became No. 952 in 1902, No. 25669 in 1933 and was withdrawn in the following year; brake-composite No. 3003 was replaced in 1932, her sister No. 3004 being renumbered 25937 in 1933 and withdrawn in April six

Fig. 158. One of the London-Derby-Manchester dining car sets of 1898, photographed that year in St. Pancras. Note large ducket on brake-third No. 3002, the left hand vehicle. *(L.P. Co./Ian Allan Library 2693)*

years later; and third-class diners No. 1864 and 1865 were replaced in 1932, the former becoming No. 147 in 1933.

Returning to the development of the main renewal programme, a report by Clayton and W. L. Mugliston, Superintendent of the Line, discussed on 22nd October 1896 (CW 3190) plans to renew, first of all, the London, Manchester and Liverpool trains, 155 vehicles, and then the London and Bradford expresses, about 50 vehicles. Furthermore, 362 additional vehicles were listed, including 180 six-wheeled third-class carriages, 25 composites, 20 lavatory-thirds and 25 brake-thirds. The General

Purposes Committee agreed to their construction on 19th November 1896 (GP 9468), but, after much delay, only 100 33 ft 6 in six-wheeled thirds were ordered. It was decided to have these built by outside contractors to drawing 1199, and on 18th November 1897 (CW 3327) tenders were accepted from Birmingham Carriage & Wagon Company for 50 at £645 each, from the Ashbury Company for 25 at £606 each and from Lancaster Carriage & Wagon Company for the remaining 25 at £650 each.

The contractors were hard pressed at this time and were unable to fulfil their promises for delivery. Only 26

Fig. 159. 60 ft composite-first-class dining carriage No. 3002 of lot 395. *(DM 4150)*

Fig. 160. 60 ft brake-composite No. 3003 of lot 397. (DY 6557)

Fig. 161. 60 ft third-class dining carriage No. 1864 of lot 398. *(DM 4149)*

Fig. 162. Close-up of brake-third of lot 396 (left) and third-class dining carrige of lot 398 (right) of 1898 showing external communication cord. *(DM 10192)*

Fig. 163. First-class dining saloon (left) and third-class dining saloon (right) of London-Derby-Manchester four-car sets of 1898. *(George Dow Collection)*

in all were completed by 1st August 1898, but the last of the Birmingham carriages, No. 1933, was delivered on 1st December and the last Lancaster carriage, No. 1983, on 13th September 1898. Ashburys had delivered only six on 15th December and did not complete their contract until 10th June 1899, Nos. 1946-58 being recorded as built in that year. In design they were akin to the new bogie clerestory carriages already in traffic. They were 13 ft 3 in high to the top of the roof, the lamps projecting a further 3 in above this. D 491 in *Fig. 164* shows their general appearance and the summary below gives their numbers:

Builders	Numbers	LMS numbers allotted those remaining in 1933
Birmingham C & W Co.	1884-1933	26475-96, 26515
Ashbury Co.	1934-1958	26497-502, 26516-23
Lancaster C & W Co.	1959-1983	26503-14 and probably 27099

No. 1910 was renumbered 2258 in 1912 in order that the new Royal saloon built in that year could carry as its number the year of the accession of King George V. Some confusion has arisen over how many were constructed because the Diagram Book indicates 99. This, however, refers to the total in use *circa* 1918; one of them, No. 1916, was destroyed at Cudworth in 1905.

Two contemporary developments deserve mention. In February 1897 responsibility for carriage cleaning and washing was transferred from the Superintendent of the Line to the Carriage & Wagon Superintendent. The other development was the initiation of experiments in the heating of trains with hot water or steam from the loco-motive. At first these were carried out under the aegis of the Locomotive and Carriage & Wagon committees, but in July 1898 a new Carriage Heating committee was set up to pursue the work.

In discussing renewals the Board made an important decision which is recorded in CW 3299 of 16th September 1897. It was that in future the Carriage & Wagon Super-intendent was to submit to his committee at the March meeting each year a statement of each description of vehicle due for renewal in the year following (1st January to 31st December), showing the age of stock, probable number which will be entirely broken up and probable number which may remain for some time in duplicate stock. The statement was to be sent at once to the Traffic Committee to approve the type of replacement vehicles and that as soon as the approval had been given the Carriage & Wagon Committee should authorise the Carriage & Wagon Superintendent to start the work. Renewals were, as far as possible, to be undertaken in advance and no stock was to be taken out of traffic until it could be replaced by renewed stock. It was thought that these arrangements would save the Traffic Department much inconvenience in empty haulage and loss of traffic through shortage of stock, but Clayton pointed out diffi-culties and was asked to make a report.

While he did so, the Board decided to raise his salary from £1,750 to £2,000 as from 1st October 1897. This put him much higher than anyone else in his department, his chief draughtsman ranking next with only some £250. Thomas Peter Osborne, Assistant Carriage & Wagon Super-intendent, was not appointed until 1st November of the following year.

After studying Clayton's report the Board cancelled their minute on renewal policy and substituted another (B 7117), which is given in CW 3429 of 4th August 1898. In it the Carriage & Wagon Committee was requested to obtain from their Superintendent an annual statement in each month of March showing coaching vehicles which have reached 21.5 years of working life prior to the

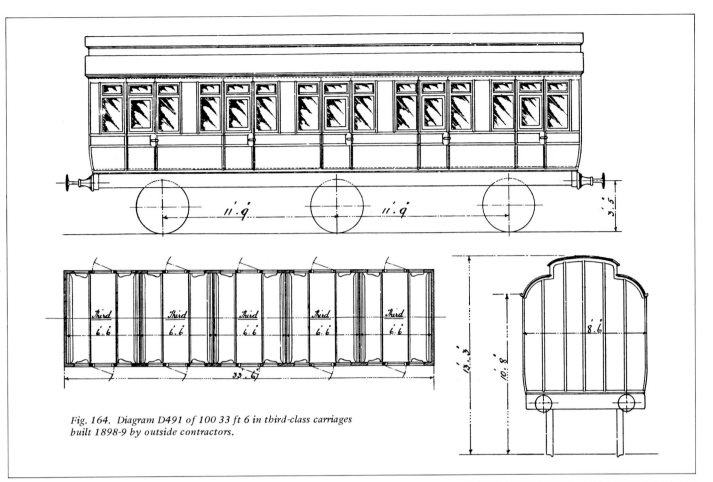

Fig. 164. Diagram D491 of 100 33 ft 6 in third-class carriages
built 1898-9 by outside contractors.

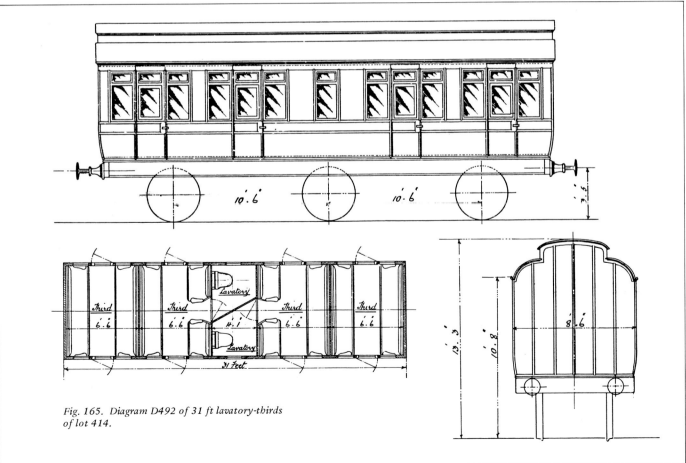

Fig. 165. Diagram D492 of 31 ft lavatory-thirds
of lot 414.

preceding 1st January and which therefore fall due for renewal in the next succeeding year. The statement was to be sent to the Traffic Committee, which would say without delay what was wanted. The succeeding minute 3430 contains a further report by Clayton that on 1st January 1898 135 first, 248 composites, 73 thirds and 205 guard's vans, amongst other coaching vehicles, had reached a life in excess of 21.5 years. This is a considerable increase in all classes of vehicle compared with the situation in 1896, given at the beginning of the chapter.

Not long afterwards CW 3452 of 7th October 1898 records a Board resolution that no new pattern of carriage stock was to be built until a drawing showing all outside dimensions had been submitted to and signed by the General Manager and Chief Engineer. As already related, in the following year the overall dimensions of the new carriages were reduced, whilst carriages built from October

1898 onwards had the height of the clerestory reduced by 2 inches.

On 15th September 1898 the General Purposes Committee agreed (GP 10305) that in future only bogie carriages were to be built for express passenger trains. This meant the construction of bogie vehicles in place of the other six-wheeled third-class carriages authorised by GP 9468, but no mention is made of those six-wheelers whose construction to capital account had been agreed to in the same minute. Evidently they too were cancelled. When this decision was taken a number of other six-wheeled carriages had already been ordered as renewals, and were under construction in the company's works. On 6th May 1898 these were listed in CW 3398 as part of the 269 vehicles approved by the Traffic Department and ordered to be built on Revenue Account. Besides the six-wheeled carriages of lots 414, 424, 425 and 429 it

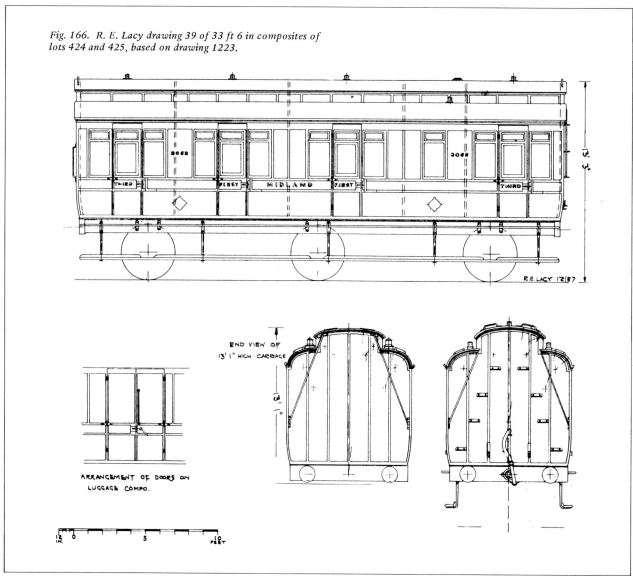

Fig. 166. R. E. Lacy drawing 39 of 33 ft 6 in composites of lots 424 and 425, based on drawing 1223.

included three more 33 ft 6 in six-wheeled thirds, which do not appear to have been built, no lot number having been given them. Presumably their construction had not been started before the decision just mentioned had been taken, and the order was cancelled.

The 11 vehicles of lot 414 were 31 ft lavatory-thirds, Nos. 3019-3029, as illustrated in *Fig. 165* of diagram D 492. With underframes to drawing 1129, all were completed in 1898, five going to the London-Manchester and six to the London-Bradford services. Known new numbers of 1902 are 138, 178, 455, 769, 831, 979, 1146 and 1191; assigned Nos. 27417-24 by the LMS in 1933, all had been withdrawn by mid-1939.

Lots 424 and 425 embraced twenty-seven 33 ft 6 in composites, each built in two batches to drawing 1223, upon which *Fig. 166* is based, both being given underframes to drawing 1179. The first batch in each lot, lavatory-composites Nos. 3056-63 and luggage-composites Nos. 3064-3073, represented by the photograph of No. 3062 in *Fig. 167*, were 13 ft 3 in high, with gas lamps in the clerestory like the other six-wheeled carriages. The second batches, Nos. 3108-11 and 3112-16, were given the 13 ft 1 in high roof and gas lamps in the lower deck, the handrails on the ends being extended to terminate immediately below the clerestory. Leading dimensions of the two lots are shown in *Figs. 168* and *169* of diagrams D 514 and D 515 respectively. The numbers of these

vehicles were not changed in 1902 and in 1933 the LMS allotted Nos. 27443-8 to the lavatory-composites and 27198-204 to the luggage-composites still in service.

The final lot, 429, for eleven 33 ft 6 in brake-thirds (Nos. 3030-40) to drawing 1235 is represented by D 503 in *Fig. 170* and was also given underframes to drawing 1179. London-Manchester trains were allotted seven of them and the rest went to London-Bradford trains. Originally they were fitted with large lookouts, which were removed in 1899, and the vehicles ran without them until the new smaller pattern was provided in 1902-3. In 1902 the numbers were altered to 13, 24, 36, 61, 68, 85, 97, 781, 796, 856 and in 1933 the LMS assigned Nos. 27740-9 to them. Withdrawal from service took place between January 1933 and September 1936, Nos. 27740 and 27748 being the last to go.

All the vehicles in lots 424, 425 and 429 (and also the 100 supplied by outside contractors) were fitted with long buffers for main line working. Those built with lamps in the clerestory tops had them removed and replaced in the lower deck from about 1903 onwards. As far as is known, two sets of steps were fixed only on one end of each vehicle. All were regarded as renewals for London, Manchester and Bradford expresses and no reason is given in the minutes for proceeding with their construction after the decision to run only bogie vehicles in express services. In fact, for some time afterwards, six-wheeled

Fig. 167. No. 3062, 33 ft 6 in lavatory-composite of lot 424, built in 1898. *(DY 55/1)*

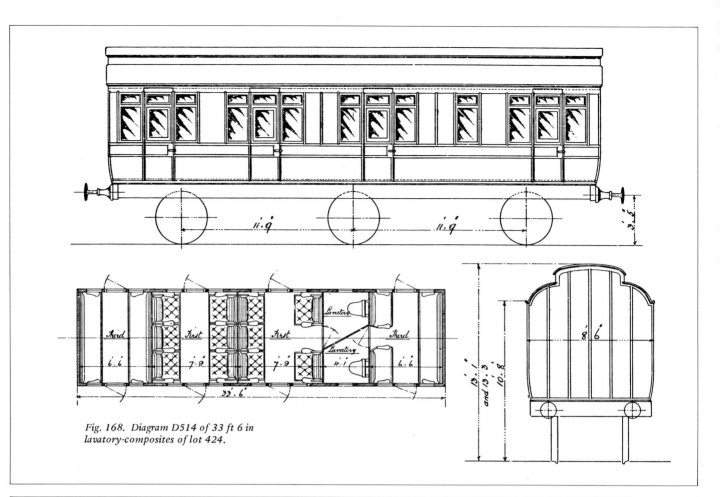

Fig. 168. Diagram D514 of 33 ft 6 in
lavatory-composites of lot 424.

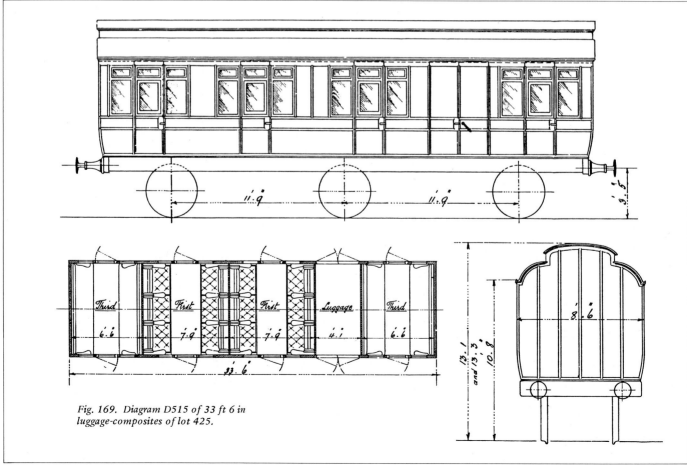

Fig. 169. Diagram D515 of 33 ft 6 in
luggage-composites of lot 425.

carriages continued to be so used, doubtless because of shortage of bogie stock; and six-wheeled guard's vans were to be seen on fast trains until the end of the company's existence.

A manuscript note in the Diagram Book in the Central Stock Register states that in 1907 four third-class, ten brake-thirds and twelve luggage-composites, all six-wheelers, were altered to short-buffered stock for use on Leeds and Bradford suburban trains. In a couple of the composites the luggage compartment was altered to half a third-class compartment, or coupé. These converted carriages would make up into five sets, each with two brake-thirds and two composites. The formation of the sets is not recorded officially, but no more than four could have had a third-class carriage, unless the fifth had two rebuilt composites, making it a six-coach set. Some of these sets were eventually transferred to other parts of the system, notably Sheffield and Birmingham. One of them photographed in Birmingham in July 1934 (*Fig. 171*) was made up of two brake-thirds, two luggage-composites and one third-class, their numbers being noted as 97, 3073, 3069 and 1949, that of the other brake-third being

believed to be 36. It will be noticed that one set of steps had been removed from the end of brake-third No. 97. It was normal Midland practice to have two sets of steps on the outer ends of close-coupled rakes of carriages; there were, of course, none between the vehicles.

Many of the six-wheeled clerestory carriages achieved longevity, about half of them lasting long enough to receive new numbers from the LMS in 1933. It is not known how many actually carried them; thirds 26488 and 26504, lavatory-thirds 27419 and 27423, together with composite 27443, are known to have done so. Lavatory-third 27423 was by then electrically lit, but most still had gas lighting. In January 1935, just before they were withdrawn, thirds 1921 and 1951 were noted as rough riders; the latter still had glass toplights to the doors, but those in No. 1921 had been replaced by louvre ventilators. It is likely that the few which survived until 1937-9 were renumbered, but that most of the others were withdrawn with their old numbers.

From April 1899 onwards seats in all first-class compartments were retrimmed with blue cloth in place of the velvet which had been a feature of the earliest new

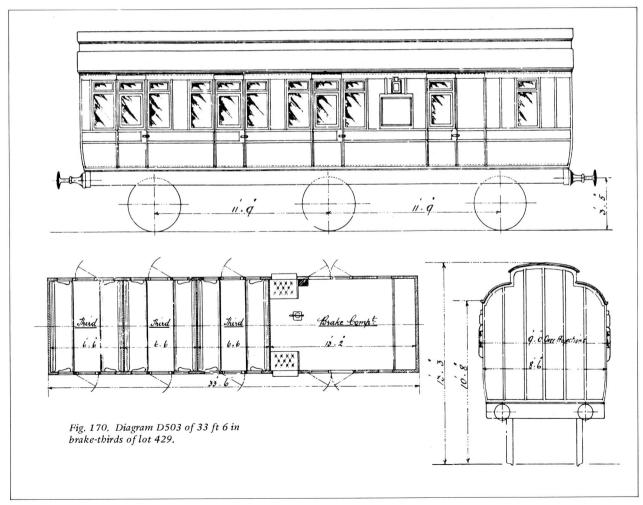

Fig. 170. Diagram D503 of 33 ft 6 in brake-thirds of lot 429.

Fig. 171. Former 33 ft 6 in clerestory six-wheelers made up into five-coach close-coupled set. Photographed at Birmingham in July 1934.

clerestory carriages (CW 3524). Soon afterwards a proposal to exhibit a carriage at the 1900 Paris Exhibition was abandoned when it was found that the railway exhibits would be situated a long way from the main displays (CW 3535).

Clayton now began to experience difficulties in meeting the short notice demands of the Traffic Department, and there was talk of tenders being invited from builders in England and America for some of the stock still awaiting construction; at the time there were four Pullman sleeping cars, described later in the chapter, being built in the United States for the Midland. In the event, it was decided to have 100 bogie thirds and 50 composites, all for short-buffered close-coupled trains, constructed by contractors; they are dealt with in Volume 2. The emphasis was now on bogie vehicles, which cost only one-third more than six-wheeled or four-wheeled carriages, the actual figures, noted in CW 3566 of 7th July 1899, respectively being £900 and £609 each if built in the company's works. The same minute records that the Midland then possessed 958 four-wheelers and 1,874 six-wheelers.

On 21st September of that year it was reported that agreement between the railway companies had been reached on the standard means of communication between passengers and the train crew; this was to be achieved by the partial application of the air or vacuum brake. In mid-1900 the Carriage & Wagon Committee was asked to fit the equipment on Midland carriages (CW 3730), but progress was slow because the manufacturers had been overwhelmed with the demand from all the railways. In April 1901 176 carriages had been equipped and 70 were

in hand. Photographs of carriages taken about this time show a T-connection on the brake stand-pipe, ready for coupling to the gear when it became available. Drawings of old carriages have had added to them the guide-tubes conveying the chains running above the windows inside the compartments. Hitherto, a cord running in guides on the edge of the roof, connected to a bell in the guard's van and to a whistle on the locomotive, had been employed.

The style of the Bradford-Bristol and London-Manchester dining car sets of 1896-98 was followed for all the carriages built in the next few years. It seems that the intention was to standardise the length of bogie carriages at 60 ft, but in fact only one further lot of 60 ft carriages was turned out in the period, apart from dining cars. Nearly all other Clayton-designed express train non-corridor coaches were 48 ft long. Thus history repeated itself, because in the 1870s Clayton began by constructing 47 ft and 54 ft bogie carriages, but when series production started in 1877-78 most were built only 40 ft long. It is assumed that the reduction in length was made in both cases because it gave greater flexibility in planning trains. It cannot have been due to engineering difficulties because 54 ft carriages were built at intervals from 1879 onwards, and 60 ft dining carriages from 1893.

Lot 406 of 4th April 1897 was the 60 ft exception just mentioned. It consisted of ten composites Nos. 3005-14, six being for the London-Manchester and four for the London-Bradford services. Principal dimensions are given in D 506, reproduced in *Fig. 172*, and a photograph of No. 3014 forms *Fig. 173*. These composites were com-

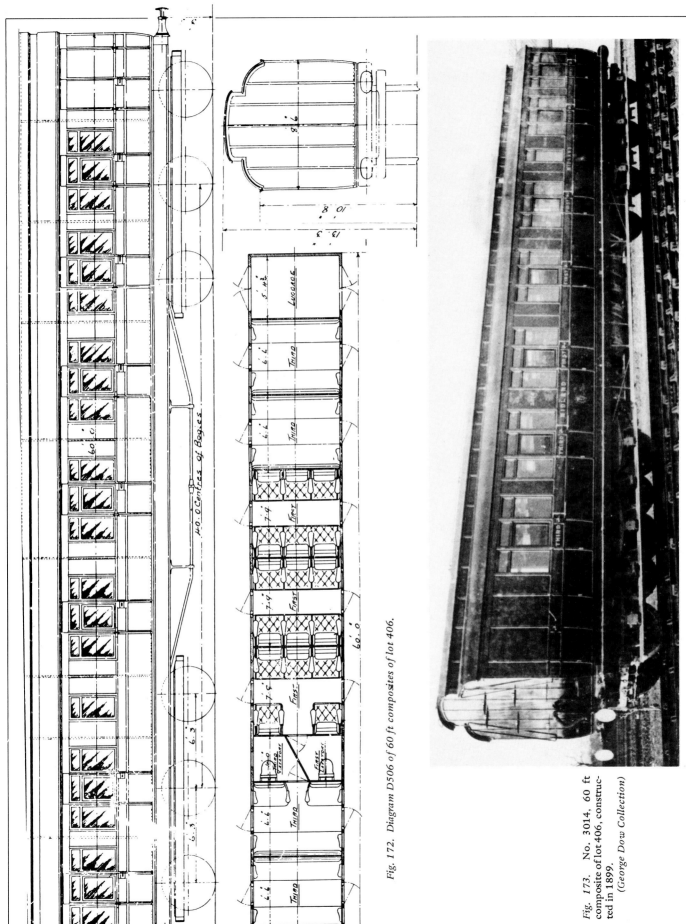

Fig. 172. Diagram D506 of 60 ft composites of lot 406.

Fig. 173. No. 3014, 60 ft composite of lot 406, constructed in 1899.

(George Dow Collection)

Fig. 174. 4–2–2 No. 127 heads a gleaming train of clerestory carriages, made up of 31 ft passenger brake van No. 593 (lot 400), 48 ft corridor thirds Nos. 3071 and 3067 (lot 439), 60 ft lavatory-third (lot 387), 60 ft dining carriage (lot 441), two 60 ft lavatory-composites (lot 406), two 48 ft lavatory-composites (lot 419) and a 31 ft passenger brake van. Photograph probably taken in 1899. (*DM 4139*)

pleted in 1899 and were similar to the carriages already built, with three first-class and four third-class compartments, a pair of lavatories (1 first, 1 third) and a luggage compartment. The height was 13 ft 3 in to the top of the roof and the lamps were in the clerestory top; later these lamps were replaced by new ones in the lower deck. Many of the carriages are believed to have remained gas-fitted to the end of their days. One of them, No. 3013, was burned out in the serious accident at Charfield on 13th October 1928, when the gas stored in its cylinders contributed to the fire. No. 3005 was withdrawn in November 1927 and No. 3003 was destroyed in another accident in October 1928. Nos. 3006-9/11/12/14 duly received the cypher prefix 0 and in 1933 were allotted Nos. 19808-14 by the LMS. All were withdrawn in the mid-1930s, No. 19810 (originally No. 3008) being the last in October 1936.

For convenience, the 48 ft and 50 ft express train non-corridor carriages ordered over the period 1897-1901 are summarised in lot order on page 159. Some of them, it will be seen, were ordered in batches at different times,

with three or even four batches to one lot. No photographs are known to exist of any of them as originally built, except for a few distant views in trains. The diagrams are, however, available in every case and these have all been reproduced.

Some comments are called for. The composites in lots 419 and 420 were built to the same drawing and diagram. Those in lot 419 had two first-class and three third-class compartments, two lavatories (1 first and 1 third) and a luggage compartment, as will be seen from D 508 in *Fig. 176*; 75 were built as renewals and 25 as additions to stock, the vehicles of lot 498, built for the Bradford-Bristol services, being altered to slip carriages in 1902-6. Those in lot 420 had the luggage compartment fitted with a handbrake, accommodation for the guard, droplight in one door on each side and, in the earliest examples, lookouts; 48 were built as renewals and 20 as additions to stock.

Lot 428 consisted of another design of composite, made up of three first-class and three third-class compartments and two first-class lavatories, illustrated in *Fig. 177*

Fig. 175. End of 60 ft lavatory-brake-third, photographed at St. Pancras in 1898. *(DM 10193)*

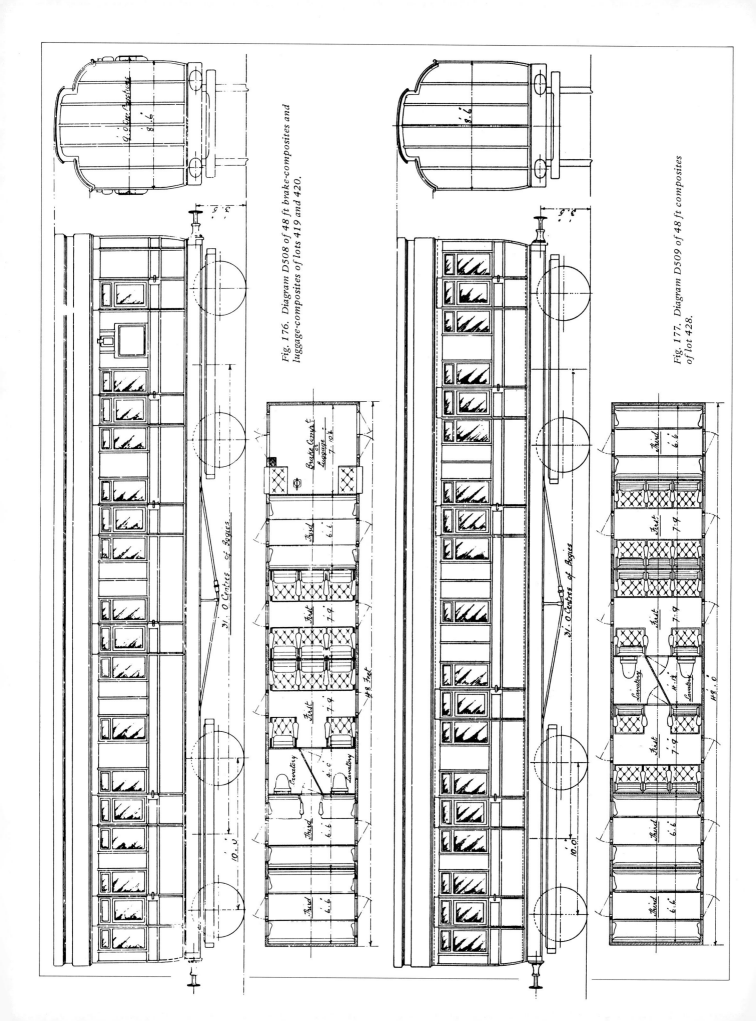

Fig. 176. Diagram D508 of 48 ft brake-composites and luggage-composites of lots 419 and 420.

Fig. 177. Diagram D509 of 48 ft composites of lot 428.

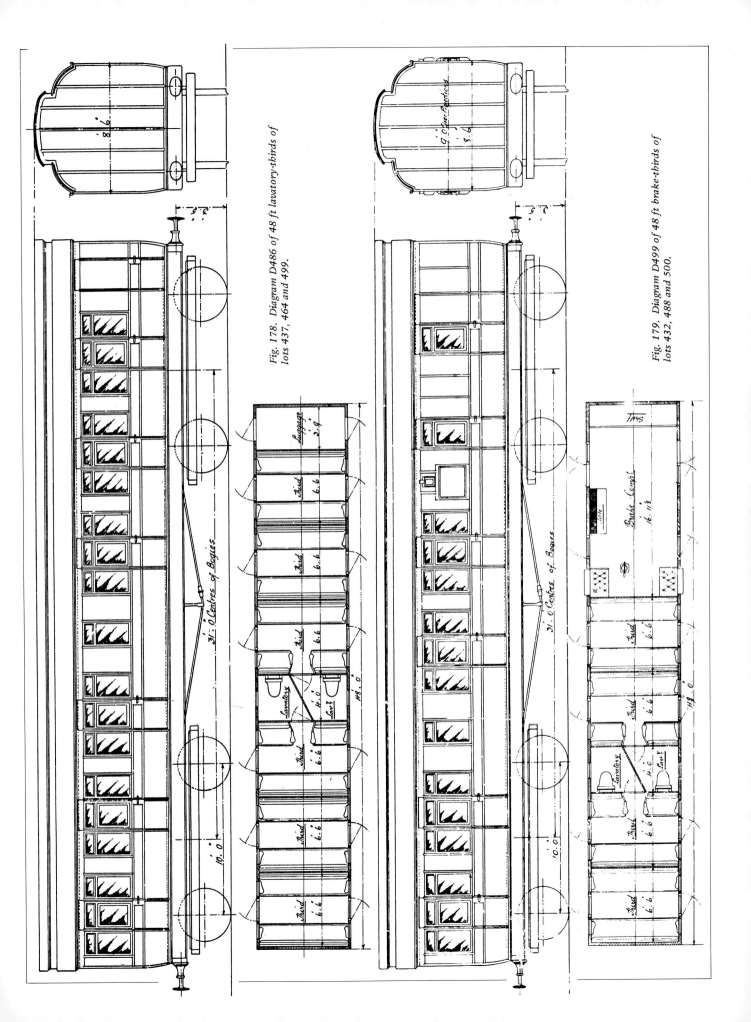

Fig. 178. Diagram D486 of 48 ft lavatory-thirds of lots 437, 464 and 499.

Fig. 179. Diagram D499 of 48 ft brake-thirds of lots 432, 488 and 500.

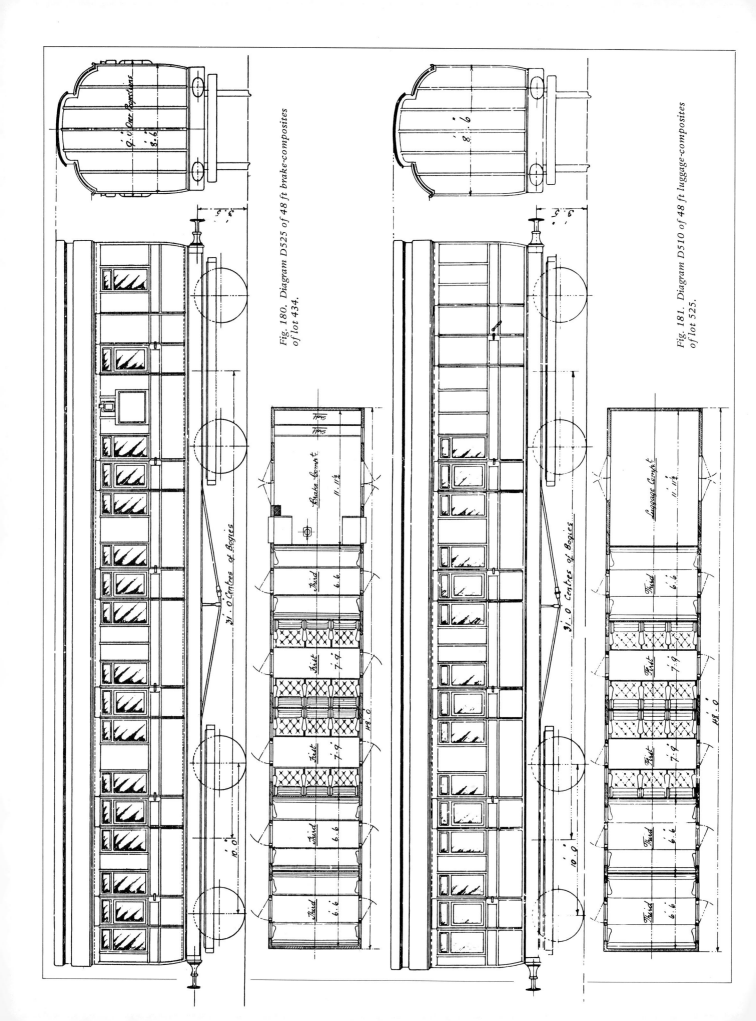

Fig. 180. Diagram D525 of 48 ft brake-composites of lot 434.

Fig. 181. Diagram D510 of 48 ft luggage-composites of lot 525.

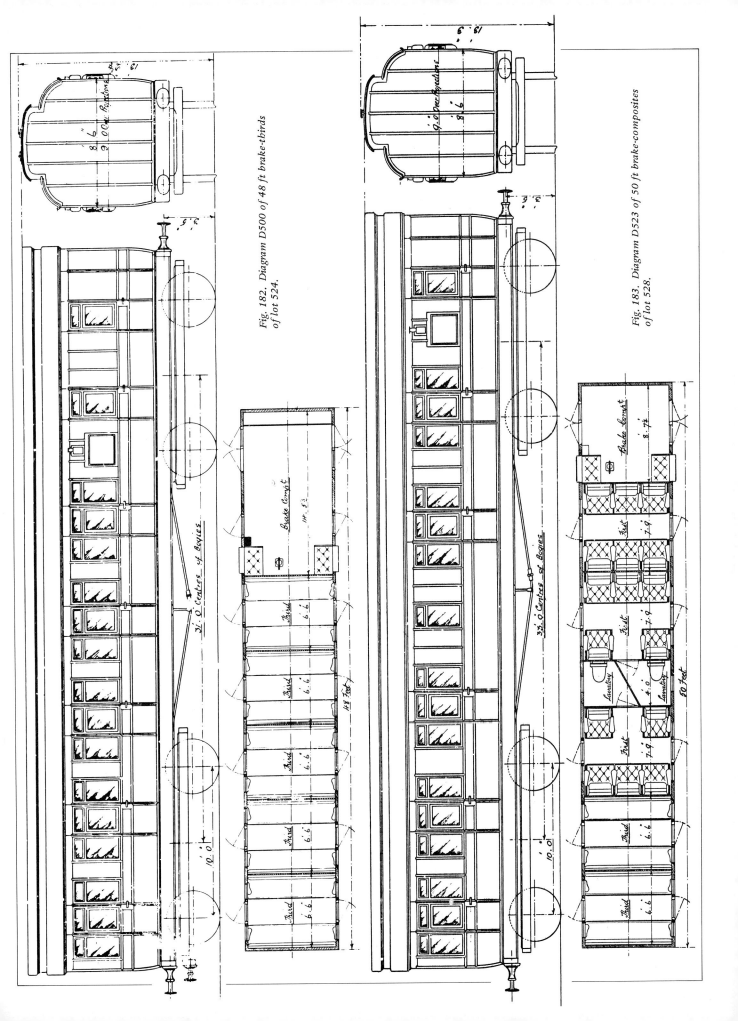

Fig. 182. Diagram D500 of 48 ft brake-thirds of lot 524.

Fig. 183. Diagram D523 of 50 ft brake-composites of lot 528.

Fig. 184. No. 35, one of four 60 ft sleeping cars built by the Pullman Company of the United States and introduced in 1900. (DY 6623)

of diagram D 509. It was the only type without a luggage compartment and all of the 49 constructed were regarded as renewals, the 16 of lot 496 being for the Bradford-Bristol services.

The most numerous class was the 48 ft lavatory-third to drawing 1243 and diagram D 486, shown in *Fig. 178*; this consisted of 122 vehicles (lots 437, 464 and 499), 52 built as renewals and 70 as additions to stock. They had six compartments, two lavatories and a luggage compartment. A 48 ft lavatory brake-third accounted for 61 carriages (lots 432, 488 and 500) 36 of which were renewals; it was made up of four third-class compartments, two lavatories and a long brake compartment and is illustrated in *Fig. 179* of diagram D 499. The final 48 ft vehicles were a brake-composite and a composite, sharing drawing 1238, but given separate diagrams D 525 and D 510 respectively, reproduced as *Figs. 180* and *181*. The former had a brake compartment, the latter a long luggage compartment without handbrake, but otherwise they were identical with two first-class and three third-class compartments. Only eleven of D 525 and five of D 510 were built, all as renewals.

Three other small lots were 525-527, all constructed as renewals and allocated to Sheffield-Manchester trains, the respective first cost per vehicle being recorded as £904, £1,060 and £994. Lavatory composite No. 3628 of lot 526 was destined to be lettered in the new style, with '1' or '3' on the doors instead of 'FIRST' and 'THIRD' to denote class designation, for the approval of the Board on 19th July 1906.

The 15 lavatory brake-composites of lot 528 were built for the London-Blackburn service. All were renewals, being of a new type to drawing 1543 and shown in *Fig. 183* of diagram D 523. They had, unusually for the period, three first-class, with two lavatories, and two third-class compartments. They were the only Clayton non-corridor 50 ft carriages and were his last design, all but one lasting until 1933, when they were given LMS Nos. 25192-25. Thereafter, No. 25916 was altered to brake-third and renumbered 25505. General withdrawal began in May 1936 with No. 25925 and ended with No. 25913 in December 1945.

CW 3668 of 2nd February 1900 notes in some detail an examination at Derby by the chairman and two members of the committee, accompanied by Clayton, of M & NB 50 ft bogie corridor lavatory composite No. 108 and Midland 48 ft lavatory composite No. 3145, gleaming in their new paint. Design aspects were thoroughly ventilated and some interesting decisions were made. For example, the M & NB vehicle had a door opposite each compartment on the corridor side and it was decided that in future such doors would be provided only opposite every other one; *Smoking* labels were to replace the frosted indication on the glass of smoking compartments; metal wash basins were to be standard equipment in lavatory compartments and catches to prevent WC seats from falling were to be fitted; and the lamps in all compartments of Anglo-Scottish joint stock and Midland main line carriages, including saloons, were to be fitted with movable coverings, to help those who wished to sleep on night journeys. A month later, when it was decided to fit 60 more carriages with oil-gas lighting, 22 of them being bogie vehicles, it was also agreed to label the dividing corridor door between first-class and third-class compartments 'To Third Class' and 'To First Class' respectively. In October 1900 it was decided to embody slate panels in the external waistline of guard's and luggage vans and, in the following month, to fit iron rails to the roofs of clerestory carriages. Later still, in June 1901, it was agreed that destination boards carried by Midland trains should in future consist of black lettering on a white background.

In September 1897 the Board resolved that 'the General Manager ask the Pullman and Wagner Companies to give descriptions, drawings, prices and dates of deliveries for 2 or 4 Sleeping Cars of their best patterns. Mr. Clayton to supply the outside dimensions necessary.' On 3rd February 1898 it was reported that four sleeping cars were to be ordered from the Pullman Company of America and early in April 1900 all four were ready for service, having been allotted Nos. 34-37 in the Pullman series. *Fig. 184* demonstrates how sumptuous-looking they were. Although they wore the Midland livery of crimson lake and carried two transfers of the company's coat of arms on each side, the character of the decorative gold lining, lettering and numerals, together with the domed ends of the clerestory roof, proclaimed their Pullman parentage. The ends were rounded, with side windows, but no inter-communication between cars was provided for, and the roof of the 60 ft body had a maximum height of 13 ft 1 in from rail level. The six-wheeled bogies were of Midland design and construction and all drawgear and running gear were provided by the Midland. Both vacuum automatic and Westinghouse brakes were fitted.

Internally, the layout was a modification of the usual Pullman standard. There were no upper berths and a plan given in the *Locomotive Magazine* of February 1901 showed that there was accommodation for eleven passengers, six in an open saloon convertible to three curtained-off longitudinal berths each side of a central gangway and five in four separate compartments (one double) served from a side corridor. At one end of the open saloon was a smoking room with two folding wash stands and, adjoining it, a gentlemen's W.C. and small buffet from which the attendant could supply light refreshments as desired. The separate compartments also had folding washstands and at the end of the corridor was a ladies W.C. and heater compartment, heating being provided by a Baker double coil heater with attachments for steam from the train pipe. Oil-gas gave illumination, with roof lamps of Midland pattern fixed each side of the clerestory roof. The interior woodwork was in mahogany with finely executed carved mouldings and decorations. The central and end partitions

carried elliptically shaped bevelled mirrors and the dividing doors had large upper panels of plate glass. The ceiling was decorated in gold and colour and the floor was covered with Wilton carpet in the saloon and compartments and with linoleum in the corridor. Brass grilles were fitted in front of heater pipes and gilded basket racks for passengers' light articles gave a final touch of luxury.

The cars were put immediately into service between London, Glasgow and Edinburgh, but after little more than four years in traffic it was agreed on 1st July 1904 (CW 4318) to carry out some major alterations to them. These involved the provision of a side corridor throughout and the conversion of the former saloon into four single berth compartments, so reducing the total accommodation to nine. New windows to suit the altered arrangement of compartments were fitted. A curious feature was that the doors in the new compartments opened inwards, whereas those in the four original compartments were left as built, opening outwards. The buffet, smoking compartment and two lavatories were retained, as will be seen from *Fig. 185* of diagram D 453, which gives the new layout. The changes were detailed in special works order No. 128 of 31st August 1906 and cost £300 per vehicle.

It is believed that electric lighting was installed in them in 1920. When taken over by the LMS Nos. 34, 36 and 37 were still in service and were given the Midland first-class series Nos. 2771-3, rendered vacant by a transfer of sleeping cars to M & NB stock; the fate of No. 35 is not known. The three cars were replaced in 1925 and ran as Nos. 02771-3 for a few years, but by 1933 they had all gone.

During the closing years of the century there was a considerable expansion of the dining car service of the Midland. In addition to the vehicles in the three Bradford-Bristol and two London-Manchester sets already described, 47 others were ordered in the years 1897-9. They included some corridor carriages fitted with dining tables and three composite dining carriages for M & NB joint stock, whilst a few were in replacement of old Pullman dining cars.

First to be ordered, on 6th February 1897, were the two 12-wheeled 60 ft third-class 39-seater dining carriages of lot 399. They were completed in 1898 to drawing 1154 and became Nos. 1866 and 1867. Allocated to the London-Leeds-Bradford service it is not clear how they were intended to be used, for as far as is known they only had a small pantry, which was extended in 1907 in accordance with diagram D 61, the final arrangement being shown in *Fig. 186* of diagram D 450. Possibly they were operated with Pullman first-class dining cars displaced from the Manchester service by the new trains built in 1898. Apart from the fact that No. 1866 was recorded as replaced in 1932, nothing is known of their history. According to the Weight Book, No. 1866 weighed 31 tons 18 cwts 2 qrs. when new, and No. 1867 weighed 32 tons 17 cwt 1 qr on 30th August 1905, the extra weight doubtless being that of the steam heating apparatus.

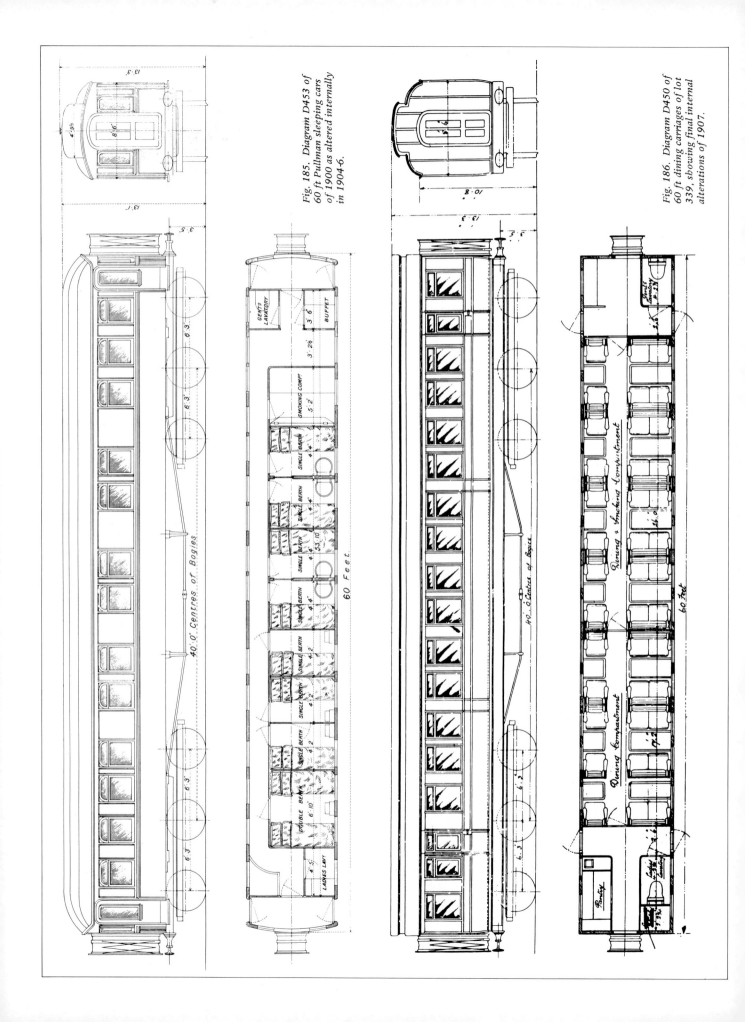

Fig. 185. Diagram D453 of 60 ft Pullman sleeping cars of 1900 as altered internally in 1904-6.

Fig. 186. Diagram D450 of 60 ft dining carriages of lot 339, showing final internal alterations of 1907.

13.3

8'.6"

4'.9½"

13'.1"

3'.5"

6'.3"

6'.3"

40'.0" Centres of Bogies

6'.3"

6'.3"

GENT'S LAVATORY

3'.6

BUFFET

3'.2½

SMOKING COMP'

5'.2"

SINGLE BERTH

4'.

SINGLE BERTH

4'.

53'.10'

SINGLE BERTH

4'.

SINGLE BERTH

4'.2

SINGLE BERTH

4'.2

SINGLE BERTH

4'.2

DOUBLE BERTH

6'.10'

4'.5

LADIES LAVY

60 Feet

9'.6"

8'.0"

13'.3

3'.5

40'.0' Centres of Bogies

6'.3

6'.3

Gent's Lavatory

Dining & Smoking Compartment

Dining Compartment

Pantry

60 Feet

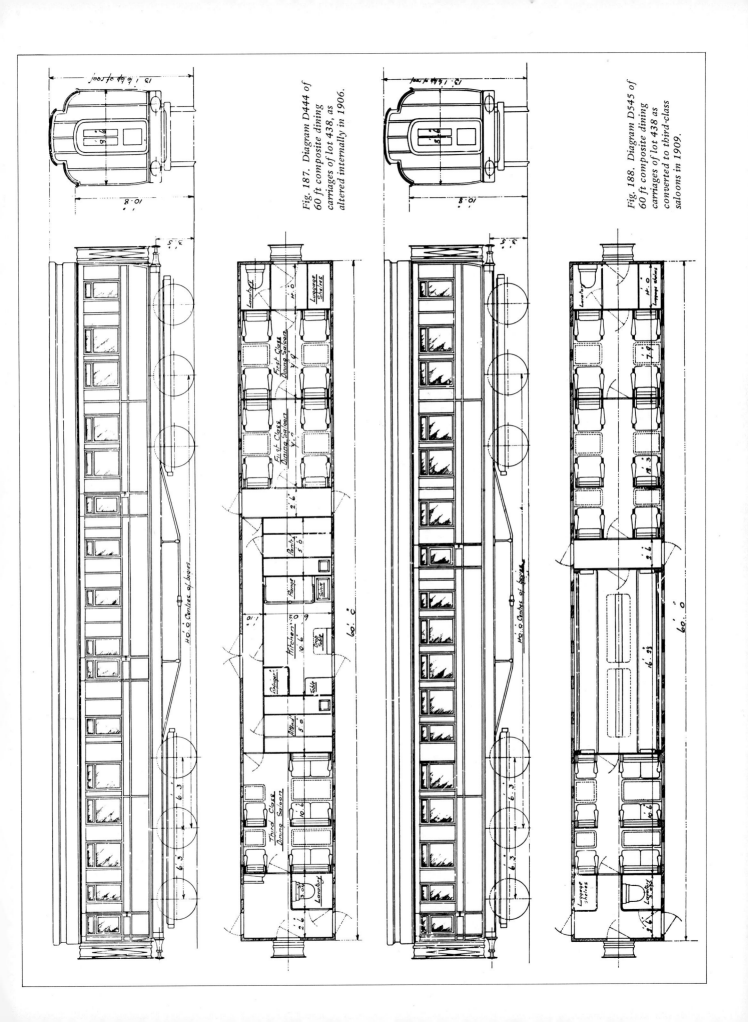

Fig. 187. Diagram D444 of 60 ft composite dining carriages of lot 438, as altered internally in 1906.

Fig. 188. Diagram D545 of 60 ft composite dining carriages of lot 438 as converted to third-class saloons in 1909.

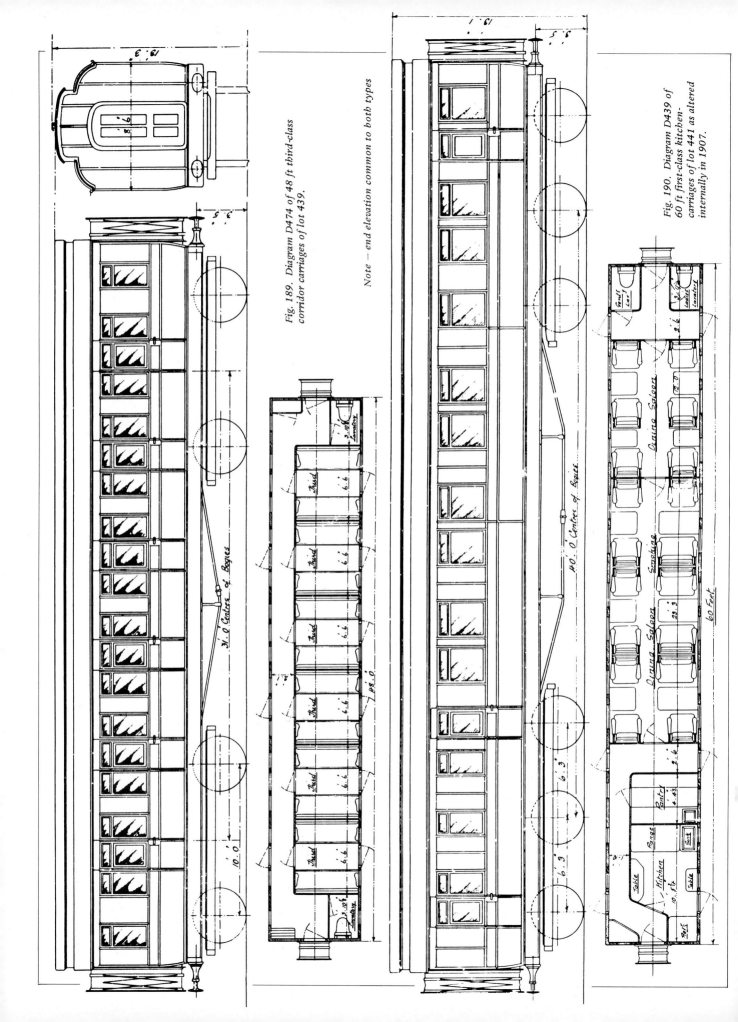

Fig. 189. Diagram D474 of 48 ft third-class corridor carriages of lot 439.

Note – end elevation common to both types

Fig. 190. Diagram D439 of 60 ft first-class kitchen-carriages of lot 441 as altered internally in 1907.

At the end of July 1897 Clayton reported that the Pullman dining cars Nos. 14-18 had reached the age of 22 years and would have to be rebuilt in the next two years. He produced three different designs, two of which embodied luggage compartments because it was intended that dining passengers should remain in their seats for the whole of their journeys. In considering the designs, the Traffic Commitee decided to explore alternatives and asked Clayton for details of the cost, weight and accommodation of vehicles fitted with side and middle passages. In consequence, the committee ruled that the dining carriages were to have a passage down the centre whilst the carriages to run with them were to be built on the corridor principle (CW 3301 of 16th September 1897). The outcome was the construction of the 18 vehicles of lots 438-441, all of which were ordered in June 1898.

The first of these was for five 12-wheeled 60 ft composite dining carriages to drawing 1248, seating ten first- and eight third-class passengers. All were completed before the end of 1898 and, numbered 3126-30, were placed in service in the Manchester expresses. As in all the early dining carriages, the kitchen occupied the full width of the vehicle, so there was no direct way through for passengers. This did not matter when the only corridor carriages were those attached to give extra third-class dining accommodation, but inevitably it became an inconvenience. By 1906, however, when the essential alterations to diagram D 11 were taken in hand, it had been decided to convert three to third-class saloons, so only Nos. 3128-9 were dealt with. Their improved internal arrangement, which cost £70 each, is shown in *Fig. 187* of diagram D 444. The third-class end was unchanged, save that one seat had to be removed to give access to the new 1 ft 10 in wide side corridor. But to make up for the space needed for the side corridor, the three compartments for attendants, kitchen and pantry had to be lengthened by 5 ft 6 in, as a result of which the first-class dining compartments had to be shortened by half a bay, losing two seats, and the entrance vestibule to the first-class end was moved accordingly. These alterations were carried out in 1907 and the carriages ran for a further 22 years or so, being replaced in 1929 and withdrawn before 1933.

Nos. 3126-7 and 3130, which were altered in 1909 to third-class saloons at a cost of £65 each, were renumbered 2253-5 at the same time. They are shown in their new guise in *Fig. 188* of D 545. The dining saloons at each end were unaltered, although the seats may have been retrimmed, but the kitchen quarters became a single saloon with longitudinal seats and tables, the usual Midland arrangement. The windows and doors in the sides of this saloon were replaced by larger windows matching those of the other compartments.

The second lot, 439, was for eight 48 ft third-class corridor carriages to drawing 1250. They embodied two lavatories and their six 6 ft 6 in long compartments provided a total of 36 seats. In April 1899, the year of their completion, it was ordered that the compartments were to be fitted with tables, together with bolts on the outer doors so that these could not be opened with the tables in position. These carriages, which replaced old brake-thirds of lot 3, bore Nos. 3064-71 and are illustrated in *Fig. 189* of diagram D 474. Their subsequent numbers and withdrawal dates were:

Original No.	1902 No.	1933 No.	Date withdrawn
3064	296	3053	11/43
3065	301	3054	11/42
3066	302	3055	10/42
3067	303	3056	1/37
3068	304	3057	10/36
3069	316	3058	11/38
3070	321	—	—
3071	323	3059	4/38

No. 321 having been withdrawn before 1933.

Lot 440 consisted of three 12-wheeled 60 ft composite dining carriages to drawing 1255, differing only in minor respects from those of lot 438. It is believed that they received Nos. 3131-33 on completion in 1899, but afterwards were transferred to the stock of M & NB vehicles and renumbered 119-121. They are therefore dealt with in Volume 2.

The last lot, 441, was a couple of 12-wheeled 60 ft first-class kitchen-carriages to drawing 1257. These were also constructed in 1899, each weighing 33 tons 9 cwt 1 qr and fitted with both vacuum and Westinghouse brakes. They were given Nos. 3007-8, which in 1902 were altered to Nos. 2557-8. They may not have been entirely suited to traffic demands because in 1904 an order was issued for their conversion to third-class. This was not carried out and in December 1906 was revised to cover retention as first-class but with the changed internal layout shown in D 439, which is reproduced as *Fig. 190*. The alterations included a passage past the kitchen and pantry, a new gangway, the transfer of the two lavatories to the other end of the vehicle and the removal of one compartment at that end. These changes increased the weight of each vehicle to 34 tons 12 cwt 3 qrs and reduced the size of the dining saloons, but the loss of seats was mitigated by widening four of those in the smoking saloons to make four more. This can hardly have been popular because on 1st April 1910, less then ten years later, they became common restaurant cars, namely for use by both classes of passenger. They did, however, retain their first-class numbers until replacement in 1929.

No. 2558 appears in a photograph taken of a Manchester express leaving St. Pancras in 1911 and shown as *Fig. 191*. The external changes visible include the removal of the gas lamps and the addition of battery boxes below the footboard and torpedo ventilators on the roof; there is still a gas cylinder for the cooker and most of the top lights are open (although it is believed that on ordinary carriages these had been screwed up before this time). The most unusual feature is the legend RESTAURANT

Fig. 191. The 12.15 p.m. Manchester express leaving St. Pancras on 9th January 1912. Nearest the camera is 60 ft restaurant carriage No. 2558 of diagram D439, originally No. 3008 when built in 1899 as part of lot 441. Ahead of No. 2558 is 48 ft first-class dining carriage No. 2762 of lot 478. *(DY 9734)*

CARRIAGE in the waist . . . hitherto DINING CARRIAGE had been *de rigueur*, as with SLEEPING CARRIAGE, *never* SLEEPING CAR! It was, however, only a short-lived departure from traditional practice.

The remaining extension of Midland dining car services called for the 28 additional vehicles of lots 477-80, all ordered on 24th October 1899.

Lot 477 consisted of ten 12-wheeled 60 ft kitchen-third-class dining carriages Nos. 2074-83, all built in 1900. They were constructed to drawing 1152, the same as that of Nos. 1864-5 of lot 398 for the Manchester sets of 1898, but were 13 ft 1 in high with gas lamps in the lower deck of the clerestory roof. The layout was generally similar to that of the first-class carriages of lot 441, and like them they were altered in 1907, with a passage past the kitchen and the lavatories moved as shown in *Fig. 192* of diagram D 449. In their altered form they seated 30 passengers. All but No. 2077 were assigned Nos. 148-156 in 1933, but it is unlikely that any carried these new numbers because all were withdrawn that year, mostly in December.

The three first-class dining carriages of lot 478 were completed in 1901 to drawing 1419 and were, it is believed, originally numbered 369-371 and renumbered 2762-4 in 1902. There is no record of their replacement or with-

drawal. As far as is known they were never altered, always being arranged as shown in *Fig. 193* of D 442, having two dining compartments and, at one end, a non-dining compartment with four seats. Although carried on the standard 48 ft underframe, they had 8 ft bogies at 31 ft centres and, along with the 48 ft vehicles of lot 479, were the only Clayton clerestory carriages to be so fitted. It is odd that the respective diagrams, D 442 and D 445, were both drawn incorrectly to indicate 8 ft bogies at 33 ft centres. There is no official photograph of the class but No. 2762, still gas-lit, is to be seen in *Fig. 191*.

Next came the nine 48 ft composite dining carriages of lot 479, just mentioned, all of which were built in 1901 to drawing 1416. Their original numbers are thought to be 939-947, altered to 3739-47 in 1902. Their diagram D 445, reproduced in *Fig. 194*, shows that they were 28-seaters and contained two third-class and two first-class compartments, one of each being for smokers, together with a lavatory and small compartment for an attendant. According to the Diagram Book, Nos. 3740-2 were altered to first-class in 1914 with 20 seats. Evidently the cramped pairs of seats in the third-class compartments were replaced by single first-class ones. In an official photograph of an express near Cotehill in August 1911, the leading vehicle

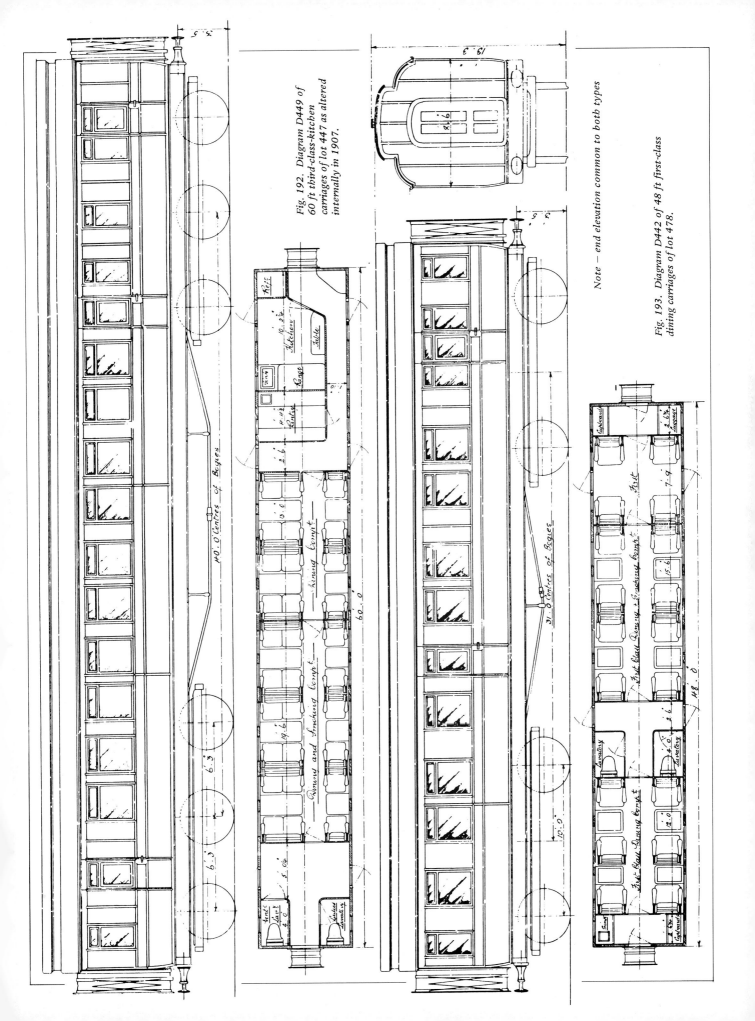

Fig. 192. Diagram D449 of 60 ft third-class-kitchen carriages of lot 447 as altered internally in 1907.

Note — end elevation common to both types

Fig. 193. Diagram D442 of 48 ft first-class dining carriages of lot 478.

was one of these composites. It is still gas-lit with long handrails on the clerestory and its waist carries no reference to dining carriage; however, a section of the gutter moulding has been cut away, presumably to give space for a long destination board of the kind fitted only to dining carriages. No record has been traced of the replacement of the vehicles of lot 479, which had all been withdrawn by 1933.

Finally, there was the batch of six 48 ft corridor thirds of lot 480, Nos. 2084-9. These were identical with the eight of lot 439 to drawing 1250 and diagram D 474 (*Fig. 189*), except that there were only three doors on the corridor side, in accordance with the decision of February 1900. They were renumbered 3060-65 in 1933 and two years later No. 3063 was observed with 8 ft wheelbase

bogies; it was evidently one of the 120 Clayton carriages which in 1907 had their 10 ft bogies removed for use on new Birmingham district suburban carriages and replaced by new 8 ft bogies of Bain design. The withdrawal dates of lot 480 were: No. 2084, 10/35; No. 2088, 9/36; No. 2087, 7/37; No. 2086, 7/40; No. 2085, 11/43; and No. 2089, 1/44.

An unexplained mystery relevant to the period reviewed by this chapter is general arrangement drawing 1403 of a 60 ft composite dining carriage, with saloons for 12 third-class and 8 first-class passengers, separated by a kitchen and pantry. It was never implemented and one can only assume that it may have been prepared for the discussions in June 1899 on new carriages as an alternative to the 48 ft composite diners which were actually built.

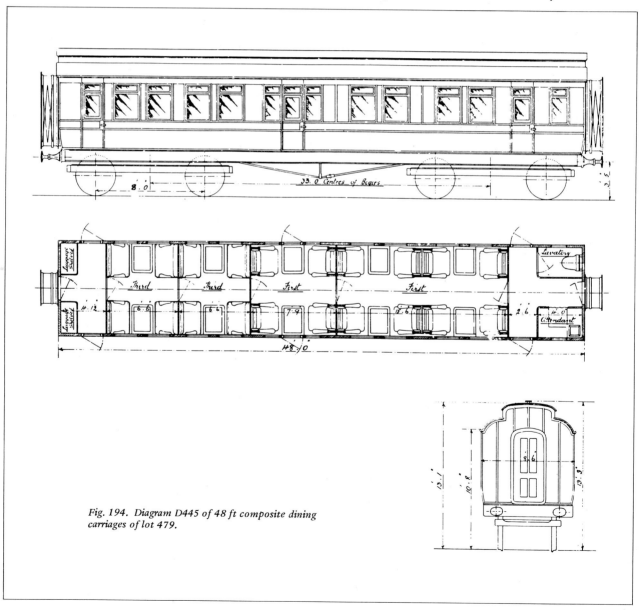

Fig. 194. Diagram D445 of 48 ft composite dining carriages of lot 479.

Summary of 48 ft and 50 ft express non-corridor carriages ordered 1897-1901

Lot No.	Date of order	Quantity ordered	Drawing number	Diagram number	Description	Date built	Original numbers
419	18/8/97	11	1171	D508	48 ft lavatory composite	1898-9	3015-25
419	not known	10	1171	D508	48 ft lavatory composite	1898-9	3098-107
419	16/11/98	21	1171	D508	48 ft lavatory composite	1898-9	3134-54
420	18/8/97	30	1171	D508	48 ft lavatory brake-composite	1898-9	3026-55
420	4/8/98	20	1171	D508	48 ft lavatory brake-composite	1898-9	believed to be 919-38
428	13/1/98	13	1219	D509	48 ft lavatory composite	1898-9	3074-86
428	not known	4	1219	D509	48 ft lavatory composite	1898-9	3117-20
428	not known	5	1219	D509	48 ft lavatory composite	1898-9	3121-25
428	16/11/98	5	1219	D509	48 ft lavatory composite	1898-9	3131-33, 3155-56
432	8/2/98	15	1232	D499	48 ft lavatory brake-third	1898-9	3041-55
432	13/5/98	4	1232	D499	48 ft lavatory brake-third	1898-9	3056-59
432	16/11/98	6	1232	D499	48 ft lavatory brake-third	1898-9	3086-91
434	15/2/98	11	1238	D525	48 ft brake-composite	1898-9	3087-97
437	13/5/98	4	1243	D486	48 ft lavatory third	1898	3060-63
437	16/11/98	14	1243	D486	48 ft lavatory third	1899	3072-85
464	6/4/99	50	1243	D486	48 ft lavatory third	1900	1994-2043
464	22/1/00	20	1243	D486	48 ft lavatory third	1900	2115-34
464	not known	3	1243	D486	48 ft lavatory third	1900	believed to be 3162-4
487	22/1/00	25	1171	D508	48 ft lavatory composite	1901	believed to be 948-72
488	22/1/00	25	1232	D499	48 ft lavatory brake-third	1900-1	2090-2114
496	15/10/00	16	1219	D509	48 ft lavatory composite	1901	3207-22
497	15/10/00	33	1171	D508	48 ft lavatory composite	1901	3223-55
498	15/10/00	9	1171	D508	48 ft lavatory brake-composite	1901	3256-64
499	15/10/00	31	1243	D486	48 ft lavatory third	1901	believed to be 3175-3205
500	15/10/00	11	1232	D499	48 ft lavatory brake-third	1901	believed to be 3206-16
524	1/11/01	10	1370	D500	48 ft brake-third	1902	Not known
525	1/11/01	5	1238	D510	48 ft composite	1902	3602/9/26/30/31
526	1/11/01	6	1219	D509	48 ft lavatory composite	1902	3603/6/17/19/28/35
527	1/11/01	9	1171	D508	48 ft lavatory brake-composite	1902	3597/8/3604/10/20/27/32/33
528	1/11/01	15	1543	D523	50 ft lavatory brake-composite	1902	3599, 3600/5/7/8/12/13/16/18/ 22-4/34/36

APPENDICES

APPENDIX 1 — First-class carriage stock changes 1844-1873

Date	Minute	Alteration	Total stock after alteration	Notes
2/9/44	B 159	−1	Not known	Altered to composite
9/10/44	B 176	−10	,,	Sold
/45	—	+	,,	From Birmingham & Gloucester and Bristol & Gloucester Railways
31/12/49	L 432		125	Stock list
14/5/50	L 396	−2		Altered to composite
		+2		Altered from second-class
30/6/50	L 432		123	Stock list
/52	—	+6	129	From North Western Railway
23/1/55	L 1914		130	Stock list
18/5/58	L 3087	+2	132	Altered from Post Office vans
/60	—	+16	148	Built at Derby
/61	—	+10	158	Built at Derby
17/5/64	L 4675	−50	108	Altered to third-class
5/6/66	L 5259	+20	128	Built by Metropolitan Co.
69-70	—	+4	132	Built at Derby
71-72	—	+15	147	Built at Derby
6/2/72	L 6956	+6	153	Saloons built by Metropolitan Co.
1/7/73			146	Believed to be total at this date

APPENDIX 2 — Second-class carriage stock changes 1844-1874

Date	Minute	Alteration	Total stock after alteration	Notes
10/9/44	B 159	−2	Not known	Altered to composite
9/10/44	B 176, 177, 219, 220	−28	,,	Sold
12/7/45	B 519	−4	,,	Altered to fourth-class
30/6/50	L 432		182	Stock list
14/5/50	L 396	−2	174	Altered to first-class
30/6/50	L 432		175	Stock list
/52	—	+13	188	From North Western Railway
12/60	—	+1	189	Built at Derby
1/61	—	+1	190	Built at Derby
3/7/72	—	+11	201	Built at Derby
1/75		−201	nil	All altered to third-class

APPENDIX 3 — Third-class carriage stock changes 1844-1873

Date	Minute	Alteration	Total stock after alteration	Estimated carriage numbers	Notes
8/10/44	B 219-20	−5	Not known	Not known	Sold
20/1/45	B 341	+6	,,	,,	Built by Smith & Dagley
/45	—	+	,,	,,	From Birmingham & Gloucester and Bristol & Gloucester Rlys.
31/12/49	L 432	−	187	1-187	Stock list. 130 closed, 57 open
14/5/50	L 396	+6	193	188-193	Altered from second-class
30/6/50	L 432	−	193	1-193	Stock list. 137 closed, 56 open
3/12/50	L 589	+100	293	194-293	Built by Brown, Marshalls
/52	—	+7	300	294-300	From North Western Railway
16/3/58	L 3060	+40	357	318-57	Built by Wright
3/12/60	—	+33	390	358-90	Built at Derby
1/6/61		+21	411	391-411	Built at Derby
17/5/64	L 4675	+50	461	412-61	Altered from first-class
15/2/65	L 4867	+50	511	462-511	Built by Gloucester Wagon Co.
		+50	561	512-61	Built by Oldbury Co.
5/6/66	L 5259	+100	661	562-661	Built by Gloucester Wagon Co.
4/9/66	L 5331	+4	665	662-65	From Spalding & Bourne Rly.
6/69-5/70	—	+33	698	666-98	Built at Derby
1/3/70	L 6172	+100			Built by Brown, Marshalls
		+100	918	699-918	Built by Railway Carriage Co.
		+20			Built at Derby
2-12/71	—	+5	923	919-23	Built at Derby
6/2/72	L 6956	+20			Built by Lancaster Co.
		+145	1131	932-1131	Built by Oldbury Co.
		+35			Built by Metropolitan Co.
1-5/72		+8	931	924-31	Built at Derby

APPENDIX 4 — Composite carriage stock changes 1844-1873

Date	Minute	Alteration	Total stock after alteration	Estimated carriage numbers	Notes
10/9/44	B 159	+3	Not known	Not known	1 altered from first-class 2 altered from second-class
9/10/44	B 176, 220	−10	,,	,,	Sold
/45	—	+	,,	,,	From Birmingham & Gloucester and Bristol & Gloucester Rlys.
31/12/49	L 432	−	55	1-55	Stock list
14/5/50	L 396	+2	57	56-7	Altered from first-class
28/5/50	L 407	+2	59	58-9	
30/6/50	L 432	−	58	1-58	Stock list
/52	—	+10	68	59-68	From North Western Rly.
5/11/61	L 4019	+20	102	83-102	Built by Brown, Marshalls
1/3/62	—	+4	106	103-106	Built Derby (2 family saloons)
12/62	L 4190	+1	107	107	Built Derby (family saloon)
5/5/63	L 4365	+60	167	108-167	Twin compos built by Metropolitan Co.
15/9/63	L 4474	+90	257	168-257	Twin compos built by Metropolitan Co.
8/9/65	—	+4	261	258-261	Family saloons built at Derby
5/6/66	L 5259	+50	311	262-311	24 ft twin compos built by Metropolitan Co.
4/9/66	L 5331	+6	317	312-7	From Spalding & Bourne Rly.
16/6/68	L 5738	+60	377	318-77	24 ft compos built by Metropolitan Co.
1/3/70	L 6172	+30		378-407	Twin compos built by Metropolitan Co.
		+20		408-27	1st, 2nd, 2nd, luggage
		+10	437	428-37	1st, 2nd 3rd, luggage
3/71	—	+1	438	438	Family saloon built at Derby
20/6/71	L 6726	+1	—	146	Built by Klett of Nuremberg
11/71	—	+1	439	439	Officer's inspection carriage built at Derby
6/2/72	L 6956	+15		510-24	Twin compos built by Oldbury Co.
		+6		440-5	Family saloons built by Metropolitan Co.
		+4		446-9	Invalid saloons
		+60	524	450-509	Twin compos

APPENDIX 5 — Passenger brake van stock changes 1844-1873

Date	Minute	Alteration	Total stock after alteration	Estimated van numbers	Notes
31/12/49	L 432	—	145	1-145	Stock list
30/6/50	L 432	−2	143	—	Stock list
/52	—	+5	Not known	—	From North Western Railway
17/3/63	L 4331	+20	159	140-159	Only 18 recorded built at Derby 5-9/63
16/2/64	L 4608	+40	199	160-199	Built by Oldbury Co.
5/6/66	L 5259	+30	229	200-229	Built by Oldbury Co.
4/9/66	L 5351	+2	231	230-1	Nos. 1 and 2 from Spalding & Bourne Rly.
2/3/69	L 5919	+20	251	232-51	Built by Railway Carriage Co.
1/3/70	L 6172	+30	281	252-81	Built by Railway Carriage Co.
6/2/72	L 6956	+50	331	282-331	Built by Oldbury Co.

APPENDIX 6 — Horsebox stock changes 1849-1873

Date	Minute	Alteration	Total stock after alteration	Estimated vehicle numbers	Notes
31/12/49	L 432	—	111	1-111	Stock list
30/6/50	L 432	—	111	1-111	Stock list
17/3/63	L 4331	+12	144	133-144	Built by Gloucester Wagon Co.
5/6/66	L 5259	+50	192	145-192	Built by Gloucester Wagon Co.
1/3/70	L 6172	+60	252	193-252	Built by Brown, Marshalls
6/2/72	L 6956	+50	302	253-302	Built by Claye

APPENDIX 7 — Carriage truck stock changes 1844-1873

Date	Minute	Alteration	Total stock after alteration	Estimated vehicle numbers	Notes
31/12/49	L 432	—	100	1-100	Stock list
30/6/50	L 432	—	100	1-100	Stock list
4/9/60	L 3736	+1	Not known	Not known	Built for Holmes & Co.
/61		+5	,,	,,	Built at Derby
18/2/62	L 4059	—	,,	,,	1 carriage truck replaced by corpse van
16/3/69	L 5930	+1	118	,,	Corpse van
1/2/70	L 6149	+21	139	119-139	Built at Derby (2 covered)
6/2/72	L 6956	+50	189	140-189	Built by Lancaster Co.
2/1/72	L 6938	+6	195	190-195	Milk vans built at Derby
2/1/72	L 6938	+10	205	196-205	Open poultry trucks built at Derby
2-4/73	—	+8	205	,,	Likely replacement of 8 carriage trucks by 8 milk vans

APPENDIX 8 — Post Office carriage stock changes 1844-1873

Date	Minute No.	Description
10/9/44	B 160	2 flying Post Offices from J. Wright
30/6/50	L 432	11 PO and mail carriages shown in stock list
28/8/50	L 481	2 PO carriages built for Tamworth-Gloucester
17/11/52	L 1284	2 PO carriages built for Rugby-Leeds
19/10/57	L 2978	PO carriages Nos. 1-3 renewed
18/5/58	L 3087	2 old PO carriages altered to 1st class and replaced by 2 six-wheel PO carriages
17/7/60	L 3709	3 additional PO carriages ordered
10/61	—	1 PO carriage renewed
4-8/64	—	4 PO carriages renewed
9/66	Post 30/179	2 PO carriages Nos. 13 and 17 in use on Lincoln-Tamworth service
6/11/66	L 5372	2 additional PO carriages ordered for Derby-Newcastle day mail
5/68	—	1 PO carriage renewed
10/70	—	1 PO carriage renewed

APPENDIX 9 — Midland Railway carriages ordered from private builders 1874-5 including those altered or cancelled

Date of order	Minute	Description of carriages	Drawing number	Number ordered	Carriage numbers	Builder	Notes
17/3/74	CW 91	29 ft slip composite	28	6	525-530	Metropolitan Co.	
17/3/74	CW 91	29 ft slip composite	29	14	531-544	Metropolitan Co.	
31/3/74	CW 97	28 ft composite	25	50	probably 272-321	Brown, Marshalls	Completed as first-class
30/6/74	CW 126	29 ft composite	27	20	569-588	Metropolitan Co.	
30/6/74	CW 126	29 ft composite	34	10	545-554	Midland Wagon Co.	
30/6/74	CW 127	29 ft third-class	35	50	probably 1132-1181	Ashbury Co.	Altered to first-class 1/12/74
30/6/74	CW 127	29 ft third-class	35	50	probably 1182-1231	Metropolitan Co.	Altered to first-class 1/12/74
6/10/74	CW 170	29 ft composite	34	14	555-568	Midland Wagon Co.	
6/10/74	CW 170	29 ft composite	27	36	589-624	Brown, Marshalls	
6/10/74	CW 171	29 ft third-class	35	75	probably 1232-1306	S. J. Claye	Cancelled 20/10/74
6/10/74	CW 171	29 ft third-class	35	75	probably 1307-1381	Swansea Wagon Co.	Cancelled 1/12/74
6/10/74	CW 172	29 ft brake-third	80	25 40 built	probably 1132-1171	Swansea Wagon Co.	Order amended to 50 20/10/74 and finally to 40 14/12/75
1/12/74	CW 201	29 ft first-class	86	50	probably 147-196	Ashbury Co.	Altered from third-class
1/12/74	CW 201	29 ft first-class	86	50	probably 197-246	Metropolitan Co.	Altered from third-class
2/3/75	CW 240	60 ft first-class	117	12	247-258	Metropolitan Co.	Cancelled 3/8/75 and 54 ft composites built instead
2/3/75	CW 240	60 ft third-class	118	12	1182-1193	Ashbury Co.	Cancelled 3/8/75 and 54 ft composites built instead
4/5/75	CW 278	27 ft first-class	131	25	probably 259-283	Gloucester Wagon Co.	For Moorgate Street services.
6/7/75	CW 298	28 ft family saloon	135	6	653-658	Metropolitan Co.	
6/7/75	CW 299	28 ft invalid saloon	136	4	649-652	Metropolitan Co.	
6/7/75	CW 300	30 ft composite	148	50	—	Brown, Marshalls	Replacements of old carriages
3/8/75	CW 327	54 ft composite	174	12	629-636	Ashbury Co.	In place of 60 ft third-class
3/8/75	CW 327	54 ft composite	174	12	637-648	Metropolitan Co.	In place of 60 ft third-class
17/8/75	CW 331	54 ft composite	174	20	659-678	Metropolitan Co.	For Settle-Carlisle line Scotch services
17/8/75	CW 332	30 ft composite	148	40	679-718	Gloucester Wagon Co.	For Settle-Carlisle line Scotch services

NOTE: All vehicles shown are additions to stock except the 50 composites ordered from Brown, Marshalls in 1875.

APPENDIX 10 — Pullman cars used on Midland Railway
(excluding those always owned by the Midland)

Name	Date entered service	Type	Year fitted with brakes Westinghouse	Vacuum	Date acquired by Midland	Number allotted by Midland	Weight and date weighed	Notes
Midland	3/74	Sleeping car	1877	—	3/88	21	23t 12cwt 1qr 4/9/90	Transferred to Continent 7/74, returning to Midland 20/6/77. Lent to Great Northern 26/4/79 to 10/7/79. Altered to picnic saloon 1895.
Excelsior	3/74	Sleeping car	1876	—	3/88	20	23t 6cwt 0qr 16/12/89	Altered to picnic saloon 1895.
Victoria	3/74	Parlour car	1877	—	—	—	—	To London & South Western in 1880, when name changed to *Alexandra* (III).
Enterprise	6/74	Sleeping car	1877	—	—	—	—	Burnt out 29/10/82. Replaced by *Missouri*.
Leo	6/74	Parlour car	1877	1878	12/83	14	27t 1cwt 3qrs 14/8/89	Altered to dining car 5/82 and renamed *Delmonico*.
Britannia	6/74	Parlour car	1876	—	12/83	15	27t 4cwt 1qr 6/89	Altered to dining car 7/82 and renamed *Windsor*.
St. George	28/6/75	Sleeping car	1877	—	3/88	22	22t 15cwt 1qr 6/89	Altered to picnic saloon 1895.
Princess	17/7/75	Sleeping car	1876	—	3/88	23	23t 5cwt 3qrs 13/6/90	
Jupiter	23/8/75	Parlour car	1877	1878	—	—	—	To London, Chatham & Dover in May 1882.
Saturn	9/75	Parlour car	1877	—	12/83	1	21t 18cwt 2qrs 25/9/89	Altered to picnic saloon 1894. Adapted for motor train working 1906.
Transit	13/10/75	Sleeping car	1877	—	3/88	24	22t 4cwt 1qr 6/89	
Saxon	2/76	Sleeping car	1877	—	3/88	25	23t 4cwt 1qr 23/8/89	Altered to picnic saloon 1895.
Juno	4/76	Parlour car	1876	—	12/83	2	22t 5cwt 3qrs 14/10/89	Altered to picnic saloon 1894. Adapted for motor train working 1906.
Mercury	4/76	Parlour car	1876	—	12/83	3	21t 13cwt 1qr 5/3/90	Altered to picnic saloon 1894.
Castalia	28/4/76	Sleeping car	1876	—	—	—	—	To Italy 1/83. Replaced by *St. Andrew*.
Scotia	28/4/76	Sleeping car	1876	—	3/88	26	22t 12cwt 1qr 20/6/90	
Venus	5/76	Parlour car	1876	—	12/83	4	22t 4cwt 1qr 2/4/90	Altered to picnic saloon 1894.
Norman	6/76	Sleeping car	1876	—	3/88	27	24t 1cwt 0qr 30/6/90	
Australia	20/6/76	Sleeping car	1876	—	—	—	—	To Italy 1/83. Replaced by *St. Mungo*.
Minerva	28/7/76	Parlour car	1876	—	12/83	5	22t 12cwt 1qr 25/8/89	Altered to picnic saloon 1894. Adapted for motor train working 1906.
Vesta	28/7/76	Parlour car	1876	—	12/83	6	21t 9cwt 0qr 12/2/90	Altered to picnic saloon 1894.
India	28/7/76	Sleeping car	—	—	—	—	—	To Great Northern 8/78.
Germania	28/7/76	Sleeping car	—	—	—	—	—	To Great Northern 8/78.
Planet	27/9/76	Parlour car	—	—	12/83	7	22t 3cwt 3qrs 7/11/89	Altered to picnic saloon 1894.
Albion	9/10/76	Parlour car	—	—	12/83	8	22t 5cwt 2qrs 20/12/89	Altered to picnic saloon 1894.
Comet	31/10/76	Parlour car	—	—	12/83	9	21t 19cwt 0qr 30/8/89	Altered to picnic saloon 1894.
Ariel	31/10/76	Parlour car	—	—	—	—	—	To London, Brighton & South Coast 10/81 when name was changed to *Louise*.
Apollo	19/1/77	Parlour car	1877	—	12/83	10	22t 3cwt 2qrs 17/8/89	Altered to picnic saloon 1894. Adapted for motor train working 1906.
Adonis	19/1/77	Parlour car	—	1878	—	—	—	To London, Brighton & South Coast 10/81 when name was changed to *Victoria*.
Aurora	1/5/77	Parlour car	1877	—	12/83	11	22t 0cwt 3qrs 14/5/90	Altered to picnic saloon 1894.
Ceres	1/5/77	Parlour car	—	1878	—	—	—	To London, Brighton & South Coast 10/81 when name was changed to *Maud*.
Alexandra (I)	10/7/77	Parlour car	—	—	12/83	12	22t 7cwt 1qr 4/4/94	Altered to picnic saloon 1894.
Eclipse	10/7/77	Parlour car	—	—	12/83	13	21t 19cwt 1qr 24/4/90	Altered to picnic saloon 1894.
St. Andrew	1/83	Sleeping car	—	—	3/88	28	22t 18cwt 1qr 3/8/89	
St. Mungo	1/83	Sleeping car	—	—	3/88	29	23t 9cwt 1qr 29/7/89	
St. Denis	1/7/83	Sleeping car	—	—	3/88	30	19t 3cwt 0qr 6/9/89	Six-wheeled vehicle rebuilt with bogies. Altered to picnic saloon 1894.
St. Louis	1/7/83	Sleeping car	—	—	3/88	31	19t 6cwt 2qrs 17/2/90	Six-wheeled vehicle rebuilt with bogies. Altered to picnic saloon 1894.
Michigan	9/83	Sleeping car	—	—	3/88	32	24t 1cwt 3qrs 30/10/89	
Missouri	9/83	Sleeping car	—	—	3/88	33	24t 8cwt 1qr 13/9/89	Replacement of *Enterprise*.

The vacant numbers 16-19 were allotted in 1884 to former Midland first-class day coaches Nos. 8-5 respectively. No. 5 was altered to a first-class parlour car in 1875, Nos. 6 and 7 to 12-wheeled dining cars in 1884 and No. 8 to 12-wheeled dining car *London* in the same year. All four had been withdrawn from traffic by the turn of the century.

APPENDIX 11

R. E. Lacy drawing 27 of Midland Railway
31ft carriage underframe of 1883-1895.

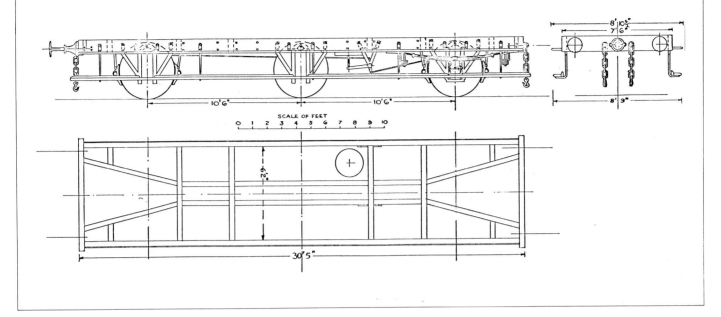

APPENDIX 12

R. E. Lacy drawing 33 of end and part side elevations
of typical Clayton arc roof carriage 7 ft 1 in high inside.

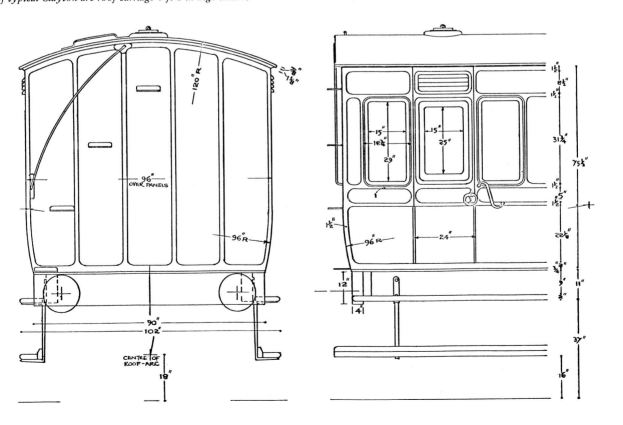

APPENDIX 13

Four styles of roof lamp, beginning with the oil lamp of 1875. The design of 1892 marked the introduction of gas lighting, and that of 1897 the type with which the new clerestory carriages of that year were fitted; it projected only 3 inches above the clerestory roof and had a deep pendant inside. After 345 carriages had been fitted the 1899 type appeared; this was located on the lower roof. (R. E. Lacy drawing 37)

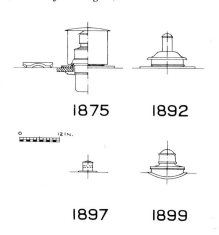

APPENDIX 14

Large ducket of 1897, removed in 1899 from the 129 vehicles then so fitted. From 1902 the shallow type shown was provided. (R. E. Lacy drawing 38)

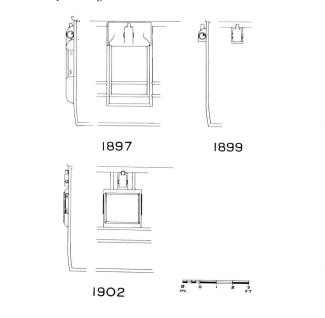

APPENDIX 15

R. E. Lacy drawings 26 and 25 of end and part side elevations of typical Clayton square light clerestory carriage, based on Midland Railway drawings 1848 and 1679 respectively. Vertical and bottom beading on doors is 2 in wide, the remainder 1¾ in wide; all beading is 3/8 in thick. Buffer beam and inner pair of longitudinal frames are 12 in deep, solebars 11 in. There is a 45° bevel round all windows; the dimensions are those of glass. Position of the end steps varied. When provided on both sides they were usually fitted at one end only. On other vehicles there was one set at each end.

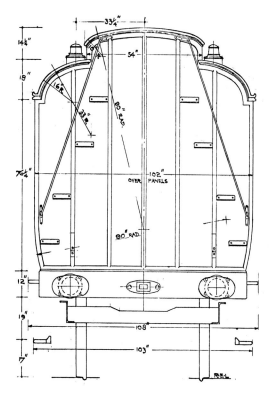

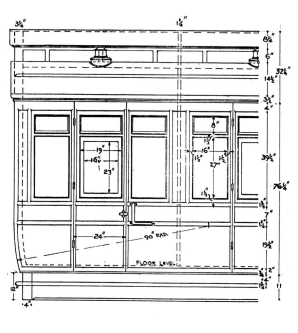

INDEX

Figures in bold type denote illustrations

CONTENTS OF VOLUME II

A train for Bristol stands ready to depart from No. 4 platform at Derby station, c.1902. *From a Valentine postcard in George Dow Collection.*